Over-Policing Black Bodies

The 2020 deaths of George Floyd and Breonna Taylor rekindled decades old concerns about the legitimacy of policing. They ignited the international recognition that Black people are subjected to forms of police violence that exceed the boundaries of formal law and human decency. This book confirms that the Floyd and Taylor cases are not isolated incidents and provides suggestions toward prevention.

The contributors to this book have served on both sides of the criminal legal system. They have been those who were tasked with enforcing the law and those who have been subject to law enforcement. Consequently, they are able to identify specific failures of a system that focuses on race, specifically Blackness, as a primary indicator of criminal propensity. Through these chapters, the authors suggest academically, morally, and practically sound corrective measures for moving toward a goal of equal, rather than discriminatory and excessively harmful, treatment under the law.

This book will be of interest to researchers and advanced students of Criminology, Race and Ethnic Studies, Politics, Human Rights, and Political Sociology. It was originally published as a special issue in the *Journal of Ethnicity in Criminal Justice*.

Delores D. Jones-Brown, J.D., Ph.D., has written extensively on the intersection of race and injustice, with a particular focus on policing. She is Professor Emerita at the CUNY Graduate Center and is retired from John Jay College of Criminal Justice. Her current affiliations include Howard University and Randolph-Macon College, USA.

Jason M. Williams, Ph.D., has written extensively on matters of race and gender. His work underscores racialized social control's role in society's institutions, especially the criminal justice system. He has published widely on policing, re-entry, and communities. He is Associate Professor of Justice Studies at Montclair State University, USA.

Over-Policing Black Bodies
The Need for Multidimensional and Transformative Reforms

Edited by
Delores D. Jones-Brown and Jason M. Williams

LONDON AND NEW YORK

First published 2023
by Routledge
4 Park Square, Milton Park, Abingdon, Oxon, OX14 4RN

and by Routledge
605 Third Avenue, New York, NY 10158

Routledge is an imprint of the Taylor & Francis Group, an informa business

Introduction, Chapters 1–7 © 2023 Taylor & Francis

All rights reserved. No part of this book may be reprinted or reproduced or utilised in any form or by any electronic, mechanical, or other means, now known or hereafter invented, including photocopying and recording, or in any information storage or retrieval system, without permission in writing from the publishers.

Trademark notice: Product or corporate names may be trademarks or registered trademarks, and are used only for identification and explanation without intent to infringe.

British Library Cataloguing in Publication Data
A catalogue record for this book is available from the British Library

ISBN13: 978-1-032-46003-1 (hbk)
ISBN13: 978-1-032-46004-8 (pbk)
ISBN13: 978-1-003-37965-2 (ebk)

DOI: 10.4324/9781003379652

Typeset in Minion Pro
by codeMantra

Publisher's Note
The publisher accepts responsibility for any inconsistencies that may have arisen during the conversion of this book from journal articles to book chapters, namely the inclusion of journal terminology.

Disclaimer
Every effort has been made to contact copyright holders for their permission to reprint material in this book. The publishers would be grateful to hear from any copyright holder who is not here acknowledged and will undertake to rectify any errors or omissions in future editions of this book.

Contents

Citation information vi
Notes on contributors viii

Introduction
Over-policing Black bodies: the need for multidimensional and
transformative reforms 1
Delores D. Jones-Brown and Jason M. Williams

Remember their names 8
Janice Joseph

1 From the field: Why I founded Black Cops Against Police Brutality 22
De Lacy Davis

2 Understanding the role of race, gender and age in request to consent search drivers 43
Anthony G. Vito and George E. Higgins

3 "I'm afraid of cops:" Black protesters' and residents' perceptions of policing in
the United States 64
Jennifer Cobbina-Dungy

4 U.S. policing as racialized violence and control: A qualitative assessment of
black narratives from Ferguson, Missouri 87
Jason M. Williams

5 *Is it a rally or a riot?* Racialized media framing of 2020 protests in the United States 111
Jonathan C. Reid and Miltonette O. Craig

6 Why we should stop using the term "Black-on-Black crime": An analysis
across disciplines 131
Delores D. Jones-Brown, Kenethia McIntosh Fuller, Paul Reck, and
Waverly Duck

7 Reform or revolution: 'Community Policing' is not a Quick-fix 159
Myrna Cintron

Index 167

Citation Information

The chapters in this book were originally published in the *Journal of Ethnicity in Criminal Justice*, volume 19, issue 3–4 (2021). When citing this material, please use the original page numbering for each article, as follows:

Introduction
Over-policing Black bodies: the need for multidimensional and transformative reforms
Delores D. Jones-Brown and Jason M. Williams
Journal of Ethnicity in Criminal Justice, volume 19, issue 3–4 (2021) pp. 181–187

Chapter 1
From the field: Why I founded Black Cops Against Police Brutality
De Lacy Davis
Journal of Ethnicity in Criminal Justice, volume 19, issue 3–4 (2021) pp. 202–222

Chapter 2
Understanding the role of race, gender and age in request to consent search drivers
Anthony G. Vito and George E. Higgins
Journal of Ethnicity in Criminal Justice, volume 19, issue 3–4 (2021) pp. 223–243

Chapter 3
"I'm afraid of cops:" black protesters' and residents' perceptions of policing in the United States
Jennifer Cobbina-Dungy
Journal of Ethnicity in Criminal Justice, volume 19, issue 3–4 (2021) pp. 244–266

Chapter 4
U.S. policing as racialized violence and control: a qualitative assessment of black narratives from Ferguson, Missouri
Jason M. Williams
Journal of Ethnicity in Criminal Justice, volume 19, issue 3–4 (2021) pp. 267–290

Chapter 5
Is it a rally or a riot? Racialized media framing of 2020 protests in the United States
Jonathan C. Reid and Miltonette O. Craig
Journal of Ethnicity in Criminal Justice, volume 19, issue 3–4 (2021) pp. 291–310

Chapter 6
Why we should stop using the term "Black-on-Black crime": an analysis across disciplines
Delores D. Jones-Brown, Kenethia McIntosh Fuller, Paul Reck, and Waverly Duck
Journal of Ethnicity in Criminal Justice, volume 19, issue 3–4 (2021) pp. 311–338

Chapter 7
Book Review Essay
Myrna Cintron
Journal of Ethnicity in Criminal Justice, volume 19, issue 3–4 (2021) pp. 339–346

For any permission-related enquiries please visit:
http://www.tandfonline.com/page/help/permissions

Notes on Contributors

Myrna Cintron is Department Head at the School of Juvenile Justice and Psychology at Prairie View A&M University, USA. She is Member of American Society of Criminology, Academy of Criminal Justice Sciences, and Southwestern Academy of Criminal Justice. Her areas of interests include criminal justice, delinquency theory and drugs, society, and policy.

Jennifer Cobbina-Dungy is Associate Professor in the School of Criminal Justice at Michigan State University, East Lansing, USA. She examines the intersection of race, gender, and crime as well as public response to police use of force. Her research interests also focus on gender and prisoner reentry, desistance, and recidivism.

Miltonette O. Craig is Assistant Professor in the Department of Criminal Justice and Criminology at Sam Houston State University, Huntsville, USA. Her research interests include police-community relations, race and crime, and prisoner re-entry.

De Lacy Davis is Executive Director at the Family Support Organization of Union County. He began his doctoral studies in the Ed.D. Program in Executive Leadership in 2017. He pursued his research in Police Use of Force: Examining the Factors Relating to Police Officers Shooting Unarmed Black Males under the direction of Sister Remigia Kushner and Dr. Kishon Hickman and received the Ed.D. degree in 2019.

Waverly Duck, Ph.D., is Urban Sociologist and Distinguished Scholar in Residence at the Center on Race and Social Problems at the University of Pittsburgh, USA. His current research investigates the challenges faced by socially marginal groups. However, his work is more directly concerned with how residents of marginalized communities identify problems and what they think are viable solutions to those problems.

Kenethia McIntosh Fuller, Ph.D., is Assistant Professor of Criminal Justice at North Carolina Central University, Durham, USA. Her research focuses on the influence of race and ethnicity in perspectives and treatment in the justice system, as well as criminal justice education, with an emphasis on Historically Black Colleges and Universities (HBCUs).

George E. Higgins is Professor in the Department of Justice Administration at the University of Louisville, USA. He received his Ph.D. in Criminology from Indiana University of Pennsylvania, USA, in 2001. He is the 2018 recipient of the ACJS Founder's award.

Delores D. Jones-Brown, J.D., Ph.D., has written extensively on the intersection of race and injustice, with a particular focus on policing. She is Professor Emerita at the CUNY Graduate Center and is retired from John Jay College of Criminal Justice. Her current affiliations include Howard University and Randolph-Macon College, USA.

Janice Joseph is a Distinguished Professor of Criminal Justice at Stockton University. She is the Editor of the Journal of Ethnicity in Criminal Justice. Her broad research interests include victimology, violence against women, women and criminal justice, juvenile delinquency, and minorities in the criminal justice system.

Paul Reck, J.D., Ph.D., is Assistant Professor of Sociology at Ramapo College, USA, where he supervises the Criminology Concentration of the Sociology major and the Crime and Justice Studies minor. His research interests focus on the social construction of race, class, and gender and how such constructions contribute to structural inequality, particularly within the context of the criminal justice system.

Jonathan C. Reid is Assistant Professor in the Department of Criminal Justice and Criminology at Sam Houston State University, Huntsville, USA. His research interests investigate the overarching issues of race, socio-political inequalities, and crime.

Anthony G. Vito is Assistant Professor at Ball State University in the Department of Criminal Justice and Criminology, USA. His areas of research include capital punishment, policing, drug use, criminological theory, and issues surrounding race/gender in the criminal justice system

Jason M. Williams, Ph.D., has written extensively on matters of race and gender. His work underscores racialized social control's role in society's institutions, especially the criminal justice system. He has published widely on policing, re-entry, and communities. He is Associate Professor of Justice Studies at Montclair State University, USA.

INTRODUCTION

Over-policing Black bodies: the need for multidimensional and transformative reforms

Delores Jones-Brown and Jason M. Williams

ABSTRACT
This special issue of JECJ presents empirical evidence, both qualitative and quantitative, that despite several decades of attempted police reform, Blacks continue to experience policing as a repressive social institution, whether they are engaged in crime or not. The research reveals continued patterns of racially disparate treatment during traffic stops, in police response to protestors, and in mainstream media representations of protest events. Consistent with this special issue's theme, the over-policing of Black bodies is shown to extend beyond mere "perception" to a lived experience that is documented via social media and the narratives of individuals, including former police officers, directly affected by repeat and aggressive police encounters. The researchers make several recommendations to change the current empirical reality. Their reform recommendations include: altering current police training to center the needs of the community as identified by a broad spectrum of residents, especially those who have experienced multiple forms of trauma; the reallocation of police funding to community-based crime prevention efforts; banning officers from requesting consent to search during vehicle stops;encouraging greater participation of highly policed populations in local governance and political processes; and, eliminating racial categories in government-sponsored crime statistic reports. By recognizing existing racialized patterns and working to deliberately uncouple Black racial identity from criminal identity, the U.S. can begin to reverse a long-standing culture of violence within policing that disproportionately targets Blacks.

With the advent of social media, a single incident of police brutality can be made available to millions of viewers around the world. Accordingly, the officer-involved killing of George Floyd on May 25, 2020 drew severe criticism from inside and outside of the United States and from both civilians and law enforcement personnel (Jones-Brown, 2020). Months-long protests were reported across, multiple countries (Black Lives Matter, 2020), evidence that the incident (again) raised serious questions about the role

---

The Minorities and Women Section of the Academy of Criminal Justice Sciences dedicates this Special Issue to Black families who have lost their loved ones to police violence.
This article has been republished with minor changes. These changes do not impact the academic content of the article.

of police in civil society and especially societies under democratic governance.

Though not filmed, the fatal police attack against Breonna Taylor, in her home, that same year, intensified feelings within the Black community that policing is not a uniform institutional source of care and safety (Brunson, 2007; Kendi, 2021); but is, instead, a substantial source of fear and danger (Cobbina, Forthcoming; Reid & Craig, 2021, in this volume; Williams, 2021). This reality stands in strong contrast to the image of policing promulgated by contemporary police unions, political slogans, and academic research that extolls the benefits of various police-led crime control strategies (see, for example, NASEM, 2018). This phenomenon is not new. It is a pattern and practice that was documented in one of the first investigative reports on policing and criminal justice commissioned by a U.S. president and published more than four decades ago (Katzenbach, 1967).

The 207 names compiled by Joseph, that begin this volume, are evidence that fatal police violence continues to disproportionately claim Black lives regardless of age, gender, sexual orientation or gender identity. Though the majority of the victims were shot, others died under circumstances that suggest that they suffered before dying and that officers had considerable time to reconsider their fatal actions. Perhaps not surprisingly, most of the reported incidents occurred in the South. Disturbingly, despite public protests, the list of names increased rather than decreased between 2011 and 2020. The scholars who have contributed to this volume recognize the urgent need to transform the social institution called policing and the racialized structure in which it is embedded.

This special issue presents empirical evidence, both qualitative and quantitative, that the perceptions and lived experience of policing, for Blacks in the United States, remains both repressive and racially disparate and presents distinct social consequences. The contributions include empirical analyses of narratives provided by citizens most affected by police contact, misconduct and violence, but begins with a candid deconstruction of American policing from the lived experiences of a Black former officer. In an autoethnographic account of the time he served as a police officer in the Northeast, Davis presents an insider's perspective on the impact of race on police behavior in the community and within police organizations. He chronicles the challenges that he faced as a Black police officer; why he was motivated to found a police officers association against police brutality; the broad spectrum of advocacy work in which the group engaged; and his personal commitment to helping youth who are at risk of dangerous police encounters. Based on his experience, Davis suggests that transformative police reform requires policing that is community-centered; utilizes appreciative inquiry (a focus on the positive); incorporates "true" community policing; and, that is trauma-informed.

Next, Vito and Higgins use police data, propensity score matching, and social conditioning theory to test for the presence of racial profiling within traffic stops in the state of Illinois. Their findings build on the existing racial profiling literature, concluding that in comparison to White drivers, Black male drivers whether young or older, when stopped for a moving violation, are more often asked to consent to a search of their vehicles. The authors present evidence that this discriminatory treatment of Black male drivers can be reduced by the mandatory use of written consent forms or a uniform ban of consent searches by police.

In "I'm Afraid of Cops:" Black Protesters' and Residents' Perceptions of Policing in the United States," Cobbina reports the findings from interviews she conducted with Black protesters and residents of Ferguson, Missouri and Baltimore, Maryland after the officer-involved deaths of Michael Brown and Freddie Gray. She found that one-quarter of the participants expressly stated that they are afraid of the police, citing police intimidation, previous negative experiences with police, and fear of police mistreatment as the source of their fear. Even among respondents who reported they did not fear the police, their narratives reflected feelings of distrust and anxiety about what officers might do during a direct encounter. Acknowledging that feelings of fear, distrust and anxiety make it difficult to expect that community members and law enforcement officers will work together to solve crimes or prevent violence, Cobbina provides existing examples of how reallocating (some) funding away from coercive law enforcement to human centered services (such as education, employment, housing, and healthcare) may lead to reduced crime and an improved quality of life for individuals who live in marginalized communities. In addition, she encourages more recognition of and funding for innovative approaches that communities currently use to promote safety and wellbeing outside of formal policing.

The fourth article "U.S. policing as racialized violence and control: A qualitative assessment of black narratives from Ferguson Missouri" by Williams, also draws from narratives collected in Ferguson, Missouri. The analysis is grounded in the colonial model, arguing that policing in Ferguson played a distinct role in racialized social control that undermined the freedom and liberty of its Black residents. The all-Black sample of participants exhibited strong distrust in policing, including Black officers. Participants' sense of freedom was severely hindered by their perception of abandonment by political officials, which they believed, laid the groundwork for the racialized policing under which they lived. Drawing on the narratives, he concludes that true democratic governance can only be achieved when the voices like those in his study are included rather than excluded from decision-making about policy and governance.

In their article, "Is It a Rally or a Riot? Racialized Media Framing of 2020 Protests in the United States," Reid and Craig use protest policing literature, theories of race relations and news reports from major U.S. media outlets to address the question of whether the objective of social movements influence how they are policed and how they are framed in media coverage. By comparing media coverage of Black Lives Matter (BLM) protests and protests opposing COVID-19 restrictions, they found that media coverage most often presented BLM protests as threatening the public's interests in safety and property. In addition, they found that coverage often inaccurately reported BLM protests as violent and minimized the extent of police violence used against protestors. Though the BLM protestors were racially mixed and, in many places mostly White, the racial justice focus of the protests correlated with media presentations of the movement as violent and dangerous. Despite the substantial public health threat and the fact that some protestors visibly carried firearms, Reid and Craig found that media coverage of COVID-19 protests was not similarly framed. The study adds to an existing body of literature that is critical of mainstream media and how it reflects and perpetuates the American racial stratification system. In their view, media coverage of BLM, hindered the movement's ability to effect racial justice change, promoted racial stereotyping, and contributed to an aggressive law enforcement response toward BLM supporters. They call for more diversity and minority representation in media leadership and the recognition and elimination of racially biased reporting. They also call for law enforcement's unequivocal public acknowledgement that many of its policing strategies are racially biased and that they have been the source of substantial trauma within Black communities. They believe that this acknowledgement paves the way for better screening and recruitment of potential officers, improved evidence-based training; and, the potential for stronger more inclusive community-based partnerships.

The substantive articles in this special issue end with a call from Jones-Brown, et al to end the racialization of crime and crime statistics. They call for the abandonment of racial disproportionality analysis (RDA) and terminology such as "Black on Black" crime because such terminology and analyses contribute to police and public belief that Blacks are violent, dangerous, and commit more crime than other racial or ethnic groups (Robinson, 2000). They point out that decades of raw arrest data reveal that this widely held belief is not empirically true. Drawing on four decades of national homicide data, they demonstrate that the percentage of intra-racial victimization among Blacks and Whites is almost equal. And, through another analysis that examined media coverage between 2012 and 2020, they found that conservative media commentators, politicians, and law enforcement officials repeatedly used the term "Black on Black" crime to refocus concerns about police victimization of Blacks to Blacks' victimization of each other. Consequently, these researchers call for a complete uncoupling of racial identity from criminal identity. This would include: eliminating racialized terms like "Black-on-Black crime" from social science research, public policy, and public discourse; the complete elimination of race as a variable in criminological research; and, most importantly the elimination of racial categories from officially reported crime statistics, in favor of other variables that reflect the structural correlates of crime that can be changed by non-punitive government intervention if there is political will to do so.

Academic disciplines such as criminology and criminal justice have not always partnered with those who are engaged in social movements to produce knowledge that enhances the understanding of the reasons for and expected outcomes from those movements. Instead, academic disciplines have shown a preference for promoting knowledge purported to be objective. The need to examine race, racism and policing through an interdisciplinary lens, in order to fully understand the intersecting and ripple effects, is a common theme among the current papers, as is recognition that those effects are embedded in a powerful and longstanding structural context that is dependent upon and extends beyond the criminal legal system. Social psychologists, historians, critical sociologists, criminologists and political scientists, media studies scholars and others have exposed the fallacy of objectivity inherent to social science, recognizing that researchers and the general public operate within social environments that impact how they "see" and interpret the world and social behavior within it (Eberhardt et al., 2004; Pryor et al., 2020). The contributions to this special issue affirm that, if we ever hope to achieve sustained change that reduces the over-policing of Black bodies, it is essential to analyze and elevate the voices and lived experiences of citizens most affected by police behavior, including those who experience that behavior *inside* law enforcement agencies. Another recurrent theme is that sustained change is not possible unless there is transference or sharing of power between those who are policed and those who make policy about and/or engage in policing. The papers also make clear that re-imagining and transforming policing from a source of oppression to a social institution that supports the safety and positive development of all citizens, regardless of race, requires a multidimensional approach that extends far beyond claims of devotion to community policing or commitment to hiring Black officers.

The three books that are reviewed by Cintron serve three important purposes in this scholarship and conversation. Richie's *Invisible no More*, raises awareness that like their male counterparts, Black women and other women of color, including Indigenous women and transgender women, are disproportionately the victims of police violence. Gascon's, *The Limits of Community Policing*, debunks the idea that the term "community policing" encompasses a single agreed upon approach to policing that resolves the conflicts and cures the imbalance of power between police and the Black public. Finally, *You Can't Stop the Revolution* by Boyles provides an additional ethnographic analysis of the complexities associated with the quest for Black empowerment in Ferguson, Missouri. Those seeking to understand the prevalence, sources and possible solutions to police violence in Black neighborhoods are encouraged to read each.

Disclosure statement

No potential conflict of interest was reported by the author(s).

ORCID

Jason Williams http://orcid.org/0000-0003-4663-8993

References

Black Lives Matter Protests. (2020). https://www.creosotemaps.com/blm2020s.

Brunson, R. (2007). 'Police don't like Black people': African-American young men's accumulated police experiences. *Criminology & Public Policy*, 6(1), 71–101. https://doi.org/10.1111/j.1745-9133.2007.00423.x

Cobbina, J. (Forthcoming). "I'm Afraid of Cops:" Black protesters' and residents' perceptions of policing in the United States. *Journal of Ethnicity in Criminal Justice*.

Eberhardt, J. L., Goff, P. A., Purdie, V. J., & Davies, P. G. (2004). Seeing Black: Race, crime, and visual processing. *Journal of Personality and Social Psychology*, 87(6), 876–893.

Jones-Brown, D. (2020, June 3). Is the blue wall of silence crumbling. *The Crime Report*. https://thecrimereport.org/2020/06/03/is-the-blue-wall-of-silence-crumbling/.

Katzenbach, N. (February, 1967). *The Challenge of Crime in a Free Society*: A Report by the President's Commission on Law Enforcement and the Administration of Justice. Washington, DC: Government Printing Office. https://www.ojp.gov/sites/g/files/xyckuh241/files/archives/ncjrs/42.pdf.

Kendi, I. (2021, April 19). Compliance will not save me. *The Atlantic*. https://www.theatlantic.com/ideas/archive/2021/04/compliance-will-not-save-my-body/618637/.

National Academy of Sciences, Engineering, and Medicine (NASEM). (2018). *Proactive policing: effects on crime and communities*. The National Academies Press.

Pryor, M., Buchanan, K., & Goff, P. (2020). Risky situations: sources of racial disparity in police behavior. *Annual Review of Law and Social Science*, 16(1), 343–360. https://doi.org/10.1146/annurev-lawsocsci-101518-042633

Reid, J. C., & Craig, M. O. (2021). Is it a rally or a riot? Racialized media framing of 2020 protests in the United States. *Journal of Ethnicity in Criminal Justice*, 1–20. https://doi.org/10.1080/15377938.2021.1973639

Robinson, M. (2000). The construction and reinforcement of myths of race and crime. *Journal of Contemporary Criminal Justice*, *16*(2), 133–156. https://doi.org/10.1177/1043986200016002002

Williams, J. M. (2021). U.S. policing as racialized violence and control: A qualitative assessment of black narratives from Ferguson, Missouri. *Journal of Ethnicity in Criminal Justice*, 1–24. https://doi.org/10.1080/15377938.2021.1972890

Remember their names

Janice Joseph

Blacks killed by police between 2020–2011 (most recent incidents listed first)

Males

2020

- Andre Hill killed at age 47 years on December 22 in Columbus, Ohio (Shot).
- Bennie Edwards killed at age 60 years on December 11 in Oklahoma City, Oklahoma (Shot).
- Joshua Feast killed at age 22 years on December 11 in La Marque, Texas (Shot).
- Casey Goodson Jr. killed at age 23 years on December 4 in Columbus, Ohio (Shot in the back five times).
- Rodney Applewhite killed at age 25 years on November 19 in Albuquerque, New Mexico (Shot).
- Sincere Pierce killed at age 18 years on November 13 in Cocoa, Florida (Shot).
- Walter Wallace Jr., having a mental crisis, killed at age 27 years on October 26 in Philadelphia, Pennsylvania (Shot).
- Jonathan Price killed at age 31 years on October 3 in Wolf City, Texas (Shot).
- Kurt Reinhold killed at age 42 years on September 23 in San Clemente, California (Shot).
- Dijon Kizzee, mentally ill, killed at age 29 years on August 31 in Los Angeles, California (Shot).
- Damian Daniels, mentally suffering veteran, killed at age 30 years on August 22 in San Antonio, Texas (Shot).

Below is a list of names of members from the Blacks community killed by police and whose deaths were unnecessary and unavoidable. This list is not complete because there are no comprehensive government data in the United States on this topic.

- Anthony McClain killed at age 32 years on August 15 in Pasadena, California (Shot).
- Julian Lewis killed at age 60 years on August 7 in Sylvania, California (Shot).
- Gulia Dale, suffering from a PTSD episode, killed at age 61 years on July 4 in Newton, New Jersey (Shot).
- Rayshard Brooks killed at 27 years on June 12 in Atlanta, Georgia (Shot).
- Carlos Carson, suffering from mental health, killed at age 36 years on June 6 in Tulsa, Oklahoma (Pepper Sprayed/Shot in Head).
- David McAtee killed at age 53 years on June 1 in Louisville, Kentucky (Shot).
- George Floyd killed at age 46 years on May 25 in Minneapolis, Minnesota (Knee on Neck/Asphyxiated).
- Maurice Gordon killed at age 28 years on May 23 in Bass River, New Jersey (Shot).
- Finan H. Berhe killed at age 30 years on May 7 in Silver Springs, Maryland (Shot).
- Dreasjon "Sean" Reed killed at age 21 years on May 6 in Indianapolis, Indiana (Shot).
- Steven Taylor killed at age 33 years on April 18 in San Leandro, California (Shot).
- Daniel Prude, with mental issues, killed at age 41years on March 23 in Rochester, New York (Asphyxiation).
- Barry Gedeus killed at age 27 years on March 8 in Fort Lauderdale, Florida (Shot).
- Manuel Ellis killed at age 34 years on March 3 in Tacoma, Washington (Physical Restraint/Hypoxia).
- Ahmaud Arbery killed at age of 25 years on February 23 in Satilla Shores, Georgia (Shot).
- Jaquyn Oneill Light killed at age 20 years on January 29 in Graham, North Carolina (Shot).
- William Green killed at age 43 years on January 27 in Prince George's County, Maryland (Shot while handcuffed).
- Darius Tarver, mentally suffering, killed at age 23 years on January 21 in Denton, Texas (Shot while handcuffed).

2019

- Jamee Johnson killed at age 22 years on December 14 in Jacksonville, Florida (Shot).

- John Elliot Neville killed at age 56 years on December 4 in Winston-Salem, North Carolina (Asphyxiated, hog-tied in prone position/Heart Attack/Brain Injury).
- Michael Dean killed at age 28 years on December 2 in Temple, Texas (Shot).
- Christopher Whitfield killed at age 31 years on October 14 in Ethel, Louisiana (Shot).
- Elijah McClain killed at age 23 years on August 30 in Aurora, Colorado (Chokehold/Ketamine/Heart Attack).
- De'Von Bailey killed at age 19 years on August 3 in Colorado Springs, Colorado (Shot).
- Eric Logan killed at age 54 years on June 16 in South Bend, Indiana (Shot).
- Brandon Webber killed at age 20 years on June 12 in Memphis, Tennessee (Shot).
- Ryan Twyman killed at age 24 years on June 6 in Los Angeles, California (Shot 34 times).
- Miles Hall, with mental illness, killed at age 23 years on June 2 in Walnut Creek, California (Shot).
- Javier Ambler killed at age 41 years on March 28 in Austin, Texas (Tasered/Electrocuted).
- Sterling Lapree Higgins, mentally suffering, killed at age 37 years on March 25 in Union City, Tennessee (Choke hold/Asphyxiation).
- Osaze Osagie, in the midst of a mental health crisis, killed at age 29 years on March 20 in State College, Pennsylvania (Shot).
- Bradley Blackshire killed at age 30 years on February 22 in Little Rock, Arkansas (Shot; at least 15 shots through the windshield of the car).
- Willie McCoy killed at age 20 years on February 9 in Vallejo, California (Shot by six police officers).
- Jimmy Atchison killed at age 21years on January 22 in Atlanta, Georgia (Shot).
- Dettrick Griffin killed at age 18 years on January 15 in Atlanta, Georgia (Shot).

2018

- Jonathan Hart killed at age 21 years on December 4 in Hollywood, California (Shot).
- Emantic "EJ" Bradford Jr. killed at age 21 years on November 22 in Hoover, Alabama (Shot).

- Jemel Roberson killed at age 26 years on November 11 in Midlothian, Illinois (Shot).
- Charles "Chop" Roundtree Jr. killed at age 18 years on October 17 in San Antonio, Texas (Shot).
- Chinedu Okobi killed at age 36 years on October 3 in Millbrae, California (Tasered/Electrocuted).
- Botham Shem Jean killed at age 26 years on September 6 in Dallas, Texas (Shot).
- Antwon Rose Jr. killed at age 17 years on June 19 in Pittsburgh, Pennsylvania (Shot).
- Robert Lawrence White killed at age 41 years on June 11 in Silver Spring, Maryland (Shot).
- Maurice Granton killed at the age 24 years on June 6 in Chicago, Illinois (Shot).
- Saheed Vassell, suffering from mental illness, killed at age 34 years on April 4 in Brooklyn, New York (Shot).
- Danny Ray Thomas killed at age 34 years on March 22 in Houston, Texas (Shot).
- Stephon Clark killed at age 22 years on March 18 in Sacramento, California (Shot).

2017

- Dominique Tyrell White killed at age 30 years on September 28 in Topeka, Kansas (Shot).
- Patrick Harmon killed at age 50 years on August 13 in Salt Lake City, Utah (Shot).
- DeJuan Guillory killed at age 27 years on July 6 in Mamou, Louisiana (Shot).
- Joshua Barre, suffering from depression, anxiety and paranoia, killed at age 29 years on June 9 in Tulsa, Oklahoma (Shot).
- Jordan Edwards killed at age 15 years on April 29 in Balch Springs, Texas (Shot).
- Desmond Phillips killed at age 25 years on March 17 in Chico, California (Shot).
- Chad Robertson killed at age of 25 years on February 15 in Chicago, Illinois (Shot).

2016

- Alfred Olango, experiencing a mental health crisis, killed at age 38 years on September 27 in El Cajon, California (Shot).

- Keith Lamont Scott killed at age 43 years on September 20 in Charlotte, North Carolina (Shot).
- Terence Crutcher killed at age 40 years on September 16 in Tulsa, Oklahoma (Shot).
- Terrence Sterling killed at age 31 years on September 11 Washington, DC (Shot).
- Jamarion Robinson, diagnosed with paranoid schizophrenia, killed at age 26 years on August 5 in East Point, Georgia (Shot 50 times).
- Korryn Gaines killed at the age of 23 years on August 1 in Randallstown, Maryland (Shot).
- Paul O'Neal killed at age 18 years on July 28 in Chicago, Illinois (Shot).
- Joseph Curtis Mann, mentally ill, killed at age of 51 years on July 11 in Sacramento, California (Shot).
- Philando Castile killed at age 32 years on July 6 in Falcon Heights, Minnesota (Shot).
- Alton Sterling killed at age of 37 years on July 5 in Baton Rouge, Louisiana (Shot).
- Jay Anderson Jr. killed at age 25 years on June 23 in Wauwatosa, Wisconsin (Shot).
- Akiel Denkins killed at age 24 years on February 29 in Raleigh, North Carolina (Shot).
- David Joseph killed at age 17 years on February 8 in Austin, Texas (Shot).
- Gregory Gunn killed at age 58 years on February 5 in Montgomery, Alabama (Shot).
- Antronie Scott killed at age 36 years on February 4 in San Antonio, Texas (Shot).

2015

- Quintonio Legrier killed at age 19 years on December 26 in Chicago, Illinois (Shot).
- Mario Woods killed at age 26 years on December 2 in San Francisco, California (Shot).
- Jamar Clark killed at age 24 years on November 15 in Minneapolis, Minnesota (Shot).
- Corey Lamar Jones killed at age of 31 years on October 18 in Palm Beach Gardens, Florida (Shot).
- Jeremy "Bam Bam" McDole killed at age 28 years on September 23 in Wilmington, Delaware (Shot).
- Christian Taylor killed at age 19 years on August 7 in Arlington, Texas (Shot).

- Samuel DuBose killed at age 43 years on July 19 in Cincinnati, Ohio (Shot).
- Darrius Stewart killed at age 19 years on July 17 in Memphis, Tennessee (Shot).
- Jonathan Sanders killed at age 39 years on July 8 in Stonewall, Mississippi (report that his breathing had been obstructed by officer Kevin Herrington for as much as 30 minutes).
- Brendon Glenn killed at age 29 years on May 5 in Venice, California (Shot).
- William Chapman killed at age 18 years on April 22 in Portsmouth, Virginia (Shot).
- Freddie Gray killed at age 25 years on April 19 in Baltimore, Maryland (Brute Force/Spinal Injuries).
- Walter Scott killed at age 50 years on April 4 in North Charleston, South Carolina (Shot).
- Eric Harris killed at age 44 years on April 2 in Tulsa, Oklahoma (Shot).
- Phillip White killed at the age of 32 years on March 31 in Vineland, New Jersey (K-9 Mauling/Respiratory distress).
- Anthony Hill, suffering from mental illness, killed at age 26 years on March 9 in Chamblee, Georgia (Shot).
- Tony Robinson Jr. killed at age 19 years on March 6 in Madison, Wisconsin (Shot).
- Charly Keunang killed at age 43 years on March 1 in Los Angeles, California (Shot).

2014

- Jerame Reid killed at age 36 years on December 30 in Bridgeton, New Jersey (Shot).
- Rumanin Brisbon killed at age 34 years on December 2 Phoenix, Arizona (Shot).
- Tamir Rice killed at age 12 years on November 22 in Cleveland, Ohio (Shot).
- Akai Gurley killed at age 28 years on November 20 in Brooklyn, New York (Shot).
- Laquan McDonald killed at age 17 years on October 20 in Chicago, Illinois (Shot).
- Darrien Hunt killed at age 22 years on September 10 in Saratoga Springs, Utah (Shot).
- Kajieme Powell, mentally disturbed man, killed at age 25 years on August 19 in St. Louis, Missouri (Shot).

- Donte Parker killed at age 36 years on August 12 in Victorville, California (Tasered/Excessive Force).
- Ezell Ford killed at age 24 years on August 11 in Los Angeles, California (Shot).
- Michael Brown killed at age 18 years on August 9 in Ferguson, Missouri (Shot).
- John Crawford III killed at age 22 years on August 5 in Beavercreek, Ohio (Shot).
- Tyree Woodson killed at 38 years on August 5 in Baltimore, Maryland (Shot).
- Eric Garner killed at age 43 years on July 17 in Staten Island, New York (Choke hold/Suffocated).
- Jerry Dwight Brown killed at age 41 years on July 1 in Zephyrhills, Florida (Shot).
- Dontre Hamilton killed at age 31 years on April 30, (Milwaukee, Wisconsin (Shot).
- Victor White III killed at age 22 years on March 3 in New Iberia, Louisiana (Shot).
- McKenzie J. Cochran killed at age 25 years on January 29 in Southfield, Michigan (Pepper Sprayed/Compression Asphyxiation).
- Jordan Baker killed at age 26 years on January 16 in Houston, Texas (Shot).
- Gregory Hill Jr. was killed at age 30 years on January 14 in Fort Pierce, Florida (Shot).

2013

- Andy Lopez killed at age 13 years on October 22 in Santa Rosa, California (Shot).
- Jonathan Ferrell killed at age 24 years on September 14 in Charlotte, North Carolina (Shot).
- Larry Jackson killed at age 32 years on July 26 in Austin, Texas (Shot).
- Terrance Franklin killed at age 22 years on May 10 in Minneapolis, Minnesota (Shot).
- Wayne Jones, who was diagnosed with schizophrenia, killed at age 50 years on March 13 in Martinsburg, West Virginia (Shot 23 Times).
- Kimani "KiKi" Gray killed at age 16 years on March 9 in Brooklyn, New York (Shot).

2012

- Jamaal Moore Sr. killed at age 23 years on December 15 in Chicago, Illinois (Shot).

- Timothy Russell killed at age 43 years on November 29 in Cleveland, Ohio (137 Rounds/Shot 23 times).
- Noel Palanco killed at age 22 years on October 4 in Queens, New York (Shot).
- Mohamed Bah, mentally suffering, killed at age 28 years on September 25 in New York City, New York (Shot).
- Reynaldo Cuevas killed at age 20 years on September 7 in Bronx, New York (Shot).
- Chavis Carte killed at the age of 21 years on July 28 in Jonesboro, Arkansas (Shot).
- Tamon Robinson killed at age 27 years on April 18 in Brooklyn, New York (Run over by police car).
- Kendrec McDade killed at age 19 years on March 24 in Pasadena, California (Shot).
- Ervin Lee Jefferson III, killed at age of 27 years on March 24 in Atlanta, Georgia (Shot).
- Jersey K. Green killed at age 38 years on March 12 in Aurora, Illinois (Tasered/Electrocuted).
- Wendell Allen killed at age 20 years on March 7 in New Orleans, Louisiana (Shot).
- Nehemiah Lazar Dillard killed at age 30 years on March 5 in Gainesville, Florida (Tasered/Electrocuted).
- Dante Lamar Price killed at age 25 years on March 1 in Dayton, Ohio (Shot).
- Raymond Luther Allen Jr. killed at age 34 years on February 29 in Galveston, Texas (Tasered/Electrocuted).
- Johnnie Kamahi killed at age 44 years on February 13 in Dothan, Alabama (Tasered/Electrocuted).
- Manuel Loggins Jr. killed at age 31 years on February 7 in San Clemente, Orange County, California (Shot).
- Trayvon Benjamin Martin killed at age 17 years on February 5 in Miami, Florida (Shot).
- Ramarley Graham killed at age 18 years on February 2 in Bronx, New York City, New York (Shot).

2011

- Anthony Lamar Smith killed at age 24 years on December 20 in St. Louis, Missouri (Shot).
- Kenneth Chamberlain Sr. killed at age 68 years on November 19 in White Plains, New York (Tasered/Electrocuted/Shot).
- Cletis Williams killed at age 57 years on October 31 in Jonesboro, Arkansas (Tasered and Shot).

- Alonzo Ashley Jr. killed at age 29 years on July 18 in Denver, Colorado (Tasered/Electrocuted).
- Kenneth Harding Jr. killed at age 20 years on July 16 in San Francisco, California (Shot).
- Derek Williams killed at age 22 years on July 6 in Milwaukee, Wisconsin (Blunt Force/Respiratory distress).
- Robert Ricks, mentally suffering, killed at age 23 years on February 6 in Alexandria, Louisiana (Tasered by police).
- Raheim Brown Jr. killed at age 21 years on January 22 in Oakland, California (Shot).
- Reginald Doucet killed at age 26 years on January 14 in Los Angeles, California (Shot).

Females

2020

- Helen Jones killed at age 47 years on December 28 in Phoenix, Arizona (Shot).
- Breonna Taylor killed at age 26 years on March 13 in Louisville, Kentucky (Shot).

2019

- Atatiana Koquice Jefferson killed at age 28 years on October 12 in Fort Worth, Texas (Shot).
- Dominique Clayton killed at age 32 years on May 19 in Oxford, Mississippi (Shot).
- Pamela Shantay Turner, mentally suffering, killed at age 45 years on May 13 in Baytown, Texas (Shot).
- Latasha Nicole Walton killed at age 32 years on March 12 in Miami, Florida (Shot).
- Nina Adams killed at age 47 years on March 13 in Greensburg, Pennsylvania (Shot).

2018

- April Webster, suffering from bi-polar disorder and schizophrenia, killed at age 47 years on December 16 in Darlington County, South Carolina (Shot).
- Lajuana Phillips killed at age of 36 years on October 2 in Victorville, California (Shot).

- Dereshia Blackwell killed at age 39 years on September 9 in Missouri City, Texas (Shot).
- LaShanda Anderson killed at age 36 years on June 9 in Deptford, New Jersey (Shot).
- Crystal Danielle Ragland, suffering from mental illness, killed at age 32 years on May 30 in Huntsville, Alabama (Shot).
- Shukri Ali Said, suffering from bipolar disorder, killed at age 36 years on April 28 in Johns Creek, Georgia (Shot).
- Decynthia Clements killed at age 34 years on March 12 in Elgin, Illinois (Shot).
- Crystalline Barnes killed at age 21 years on January 27 in Jackson, Mississippi (Shot).
- Geraldine Townsend killed at age 72 years on January 17 in Bartlesville, Oklahoma (Shot).

2017

- Cariann Denise Hithon killed at age 22 years on October 8 in Miami Beach, Florida (Shot).
- India Nelson killed at age 25 years on July 17 in Norfolk, Virginia (Shot).
- Charleena Chavon Lyles killed at age 33 years on June 18 in Seattle, Washington (Shot).
- Jonie Block killed at age 27 years on May 15 in Phoenix, Arizona (Shot).
- Alteria Woods killed at age 21 years on March 19 in Gifford, Florida (Shot).
- Morgan London Rankins killed at age 30 years on February 22 in Austin, Texas (Shot).

2016

- Michelle Lee Shirley killed at age 39 years on October 31 in Torrance, California.
- Deborah Danner killed at age 66 years on October 18 in Bronx, New York (Shot).
- Korryn Gaines killed at age 23 years on August 1 in Randallstown, Maryland (Shot).
- Deresha Armstrong killed at age 26 years on May 5 in Orlando, Florida (Shot).
- Kisha Arrone killed at age 35 years on April 17 in Dayton, Ohio (Shot).

- India Beaty killed at age 25 years on March 19 in Norfolk, Virginia (Shot).
- Jessica Nelson-Williams killed at age 29 years on March 19 in San Francisco, California (Shot).
- Kisha Shelly Michael killed at age 31 years on February 21 in Inglewood, California. (Shot).
- Janet Wilson, with mental illness, killed at age 31 years on January 27 in Dearborn, Michigan (Shot).

2015

- Bettie "Betty Boo" Jones killed at age 55 years on December 26 in Chicago, Illinois (Shot).
- Marquesha McMillan killed at age 21 years on October 25 in Washington, DC (Shot).
- India Kager killed at age 27 years on September 5 in Virginia Beach, Virginia (Shot).
- Redel Jones killed at age 30 years on August 12 in Los Angeles, California (Shot).
- Sandra Bland killed at age 28 years on July 13, Waller County, Texas (Excessive Force/Wrongful Death/Suicide).
- Alexia Christian killed at age 25 years on April 30 in Atlanta, Georgia (Shot).
- Meagan Hockaday killed at age 26 years on March 28 in Oxnard, California (Shot).
- Janisha Fonville killed at age 20 years on February 18 in Charlotte, North Carolina (Shot).
- Natasha McKenna killed at age 58 years on February 8 in Fairfax County, Virginia (Tasered/Cardiac Arrest).
- Yuvette Henderson killed at age 38 years on February 3 in Emeryville, California (Shot).

2014

- Tanisha Anderson killed at age 27 years on November 13 in Cleveland, Ohio (Physically Restrained/Brute Force).
- Michelle Cusseaux, mentally ill, killed at age 50 years on August 14 in Phoenix, Arizona (Shot).
- Gabriella Monique Nevarez killed at age 23 years on March 2 in Citrus Heights, California (Shot).
- Yvette Smith killed at age 48 years on February 16 in Bastrop County, Texas (Shot).

2013

- Miriam Iris Carey killed at age 34 years on October 3 in Washington, DC (Shot 26 times).

2012

- Shelly Marie Frey killed at age 27 years on December 6 in Houston, Texas (Shot).
- Malissa Williams killed at age 30 years on November 29 in Cleveland, Ohio (137 Rounds/Shot 24 times).
- Alesia Thomas killed at age 35 years on July 22 in Los Angeles, California (Brutal Force/Beaten).
- Shantel Davis killed at age 23 years on June 14 in New York City, New York (Shot).
- Sharmel T. Edwards killed at age 50 years on April 21 in Las Vegas, Nevada (Shot).
- Shereese Francis killed at age 26 years on March 15 in Queens, New York City, New York (Suffocated to death).
- Rekia Boyd killed at age 22 years on March 12 in Chicago, Illinois (Shot).

2011

- Brenda Mae Williams killed at age 57 years on April 27 in Los Angeles, California (Shot).

Members of the black LGBTQ community

2020

- Roxanne Moore, transgender woman with a history of mental health issues, killed at age 29 years on September 13 in Reading, Pennsylvania (Shot 16 times).
- Tony McDade, transgender man, killed at age 38 years on May 27 in Tallahassee, Florida (Shot).

2017

- Kiwi Herring, a transgender woman, killed at age 30 years on August 22 in St. Louis, Missouri (Shot).

2015

- Mya Shawatza Hall, transgender woman, killed at age 27 years on March 30 in Fort Meade, Maryland (Shot).

2013

- Kayla Moore, transgender woman, and in the middle of health crisis, killed at age 42 years on February 13 in Berkeley, California (Restrained face-down prone).

Chart 1: Descriptive data of males (listed above).

Age	
18–24	24%
25–34	39%
35–44	19%
45–54	10%
55 and over	8%
How Killed	
Shot	91%
Other	9%
Victim with mental illness	
Yes	10%
Region where Killed	
Northeast	11%
Midwest	19%
West	7%
South	63%

Chart 2: Descriptive data of females (listed above).

Age	
18–24	40%
25–34	26%
35–44	14%
45–54	20%
How Killed	
Shot	94%
Other	6%
Victim with mental illness	
Yes	9%
Region where Killed	
Northeast	9%
Midwest	17%
West	7%
South	67%

Sources: Avanzar, 2019; Chughtai/AlJareeza, 2020; CBC News, 2017; Dzhanova, Ardrey, Cranley, Beckler, & Grant 2021; Gonzaga University, 2020.

Notes

1 In the United States, there is systematic collection of data to identify the race or ethnicity of individuals killed or injured by law enforcement officers. As a result, the Report of the United Nations High Commissioner for Human Rights (2021) title *Promotion and protection of the human rights and fundamental freedoms of Africans*

and of people of African descent against excessive use of force and other human rights violations by law enforcement officers, recommends that "regularly publish data, disaggregated by victims' race or ethnic origin, on deaths and serious injury by law enforcement officials and related prosecutions and convictions, as well as any disciplinary actions" (p. 22) is necessary to end impunity and pursue justice. For additional information in this report see https://undocs.org/A/HRC/47/53.

References

Avanzar. (2019). *Safety, justice, empowerment*. https://avanzarnow.org/did-you-know/.

Chughtai, A./AlJareeza (2020). *Know their names: Black people killed by the police in the US*. https://interactive.aljazeera.com/aje/2020/know-their-names/index.html.

CBC News. (2017, December 07). *14 High-profile police-related deaths of U.S. blacks*. https://www.cbc.ca/news/world/list-police-related-deaths-usa-1.4438618.

Dzhanova, Y., Ardrey, T., Cranley, E., Beckler, H., & Grant, B. (2021). *50 Black women have been killed by the police since 2015. Most of the officers who shot them didn't face consequences*. Insider Inc. https://www.insider.com/black-women-killed-by-police-database-2021-6.

Gonzaga University. (2020). *Say their name*. https://www.gonzaga.edu/about/offices-services/diversity-inclusion-community-equity/say-their-name.

United Nations High Commission. (2021). *Promotion and protection of the human rights and fundamental freedoms of Africans and of people of African descent against excessive use of force and other human rights violations by law enforcement officers*. https://undocs.org/A/HRC/47/53.

From the field: Why I founded Black Cops Against Police Brutality

De Lacy Davis

ABSTRACT
Controlling police use of unwarranted force is a recurring problem within police agencies, especially those that operate in urban spaces. Black people are disproportionately the recipients of such force. Using my experiences as a Black police officer as the backdrop, I describe my journey from rookie officer to community activist and founder of Black Cops Against Police Brutality (B-CAP). Readers will come to understand the complex world of policing and the difficult road to police reform, from the inside out. Four recommendations are made for police reform: 1) that it be community-centered; 2) that it utilize appreciative inquiry; 3) that it incorporate "true" community policing; and, 4) that trauma-informed policing be supported for all levels of law enforcement.

Introduction

Acts of protest like those that followed the officer-involved death of George Floyd in Minneapolis, Minnesota, on May 25, 2020, have led to nine large scale government-sponsored investigations dating back nearly a century– The Wickersham Commission Report, *Lawlessness in Law Enforcement* (1929), President's Commission on Law Enforcement and Administration of Justice (1967), Kerner Commission Report (1968), Knapp Commission Report (1972), Christopher Commission Report (1991), Mollen Commission Report (1994), Task Force on Twenty-first Century Policing (2015); and, most recently, the President's Commission on Law Enforcement and the Administration of Justice (2020). The recruitment and hiring of Black police officers is a recurring recommendation among these reports, with the expectation that hiring more Black officers will reduce the likelihood that police violence and misconduct will spark such uprisings again. While the number of Black officers in policing has grown over time, especially in large urban departments, for example from 6 percent in 1997 to 28 percent in 2016 (Leatherby & Oppel, 2020), the evidence of whether this increase has led to more positive outcomes during police-civilian encounters is mixed.

The result of studies that examine the impact of Black officers generally have findings that tend to fall within one of three groupings. Some sources suggest that Black officers become socialized into a police culture that is brutal and racist, especially against Blacks (Nicholson-Crotty, Nicholson-Crotty, & Fernandez, 2017; Weitzer, 2000). Consequently, their hiring produces no change in the quality of the contact that Blacks have with police agents. The results of a recent study show that racially and ethnically diverse departments report having fewer civilian complaints and fewer serious use of force incidents than departments that lack diversity (see for example Ba, Knox, Mummolo, & Rivera, 2021). However, in a few studies, Black officers were found to be more aggressive and brutal than White officers and especially toward civilians who were also Black (Dunham & Alpert, 2004; Forman, 2017). Explanations that have been offered to address this latter finding is that Black officers may feel the need to prove that they are loyal to police culture (Kleinig, 2016) and deserve to be a part of the department. Or, that they feel under pressure to avoid being seen as showing leniency, loyalty, or favoritism toward Black suspects and consequently overcompensate by being more aggressive during encounters with Black people (Forman, 2017).

These mixed findings about the impact of Black officers on the quality and outcome of police and civilian encounters suggest that recommendations to "hire more Black cops", as *the* primary strategy for reducing police violence, misconduct; and future protests, are both overly simplistic and naïve. As a Black officer within an urban police department in the Northeast, I came to know internal police racism firsthand (see Kelling & Moore, 1988; Williams & Murphy, 1990). However, I experienced some forms of maltreatment at the hands of both Black and White officers. I also witnessed external racism—unwarranted violence, misconduct and discourtesy by police against Black civilians of varying ages. Consistent with the research that found no improvement in the quality of police and civilian encounters when more Blacks were hired, this violence, misconduct and discourtesy were perpetrated by both Black and White officers. These lived experiences pushed me to become an advocate for the community rather than an adversary. Having responded to the call for more Blacks to join police departments, for 20 years I witnessed the over-policing of Black bodies in "high need" neighborhoods (Haldipur, 2019); and, was transformed into a community activist aimed at assisting those most in need of being protected and served.

Black Cops Against Police Brutality (B-CAP) was founded in 1991 while I was a rookie officer—a time when I was most vulnerable to negative consequences for failing to comply with formal and informal policing practices in place to protect the image of policing at all costs. I founded the organization with another Black male officer after he was illegally arrested by a police agency to which he had applied but was not hired. While walking down the street in that jurisdiction, after he was hired in my department, two officers stopped him saying that they saw a gun in his waistband. He produced appropriate police identification and a badge but was arrested and taken into custody nonetheless. He was placed in a holding cell with other arrested individuals, instead of a separate cell for his protection. Eventually the arresting agency reached out to his department. A police supervisor verified the officer's right to carry a gun and he was released. The charges against him were dropped.

On the heels of that experience, B-CAP was formed to assist and protect vulnerable individuals, hold police accountable and restore and preserve the legitimacy of the profession. In the following pages, I share my experiences as a Black police officer including both my treatment within the profession and my interactions with the community. Based on those experiences and more than a decade of delivering education and training aimed at transforming the experiences that were negative, I make four primary recommendations for 21st century police reform: 1) that it be community-centered; 2) that it utilize appreciative inquiry; 3) that it incorporate "true" community policing; and, 4) that trauma-informed policing be supported for all levels of law enforcement—federal, state, and local. In addition, communities are encouraged to develop a "crisis action plan" on how to effectively organize against and respond to incidents of police violence, misconduct and abuse. The implementation of these reforms, which are discussed in detail later, requires a radical shift in the current balance of power between police and community, and specifically in how power has been structured between police and members of the public who are Black.

Policing while Black

Sir Robert Peel is often credited with being the founder of modern policing. Among the nine principles of law enforcement that he developed to guide the London Metropolitan Police Department in 1829, the seventh states that, "the police are the public and the public are the police" (Gov. UK, 2020). In the United States the roots of policing have been traced back to the slave patrols of the 1700s, posses of White men who kidnapped and tortured Blacks who they suspected or accused of being runaway slave. Slave patrollers also lynched free Blacks as a means of punishing them for behavior the posse saw as being insubordinate (Reichel, 1988;

Williams & Murphy, 1990). In the aftermath of African enslavement, police agencies in the U.S. were still charged with controlling, containing and discriminating against Blacks as they enforced so-called Jim Crow laws. These laws were passed by states and municipalities to denigrate and restrict the liberty of Blacks, as a means of restricting competition for work and social status; and, as a mechanism for maintaining White supremacy (Alexander, 2010; Ward, 2017). The internal racism and maltreatment that I witnessed or experienced, during my time as a police officer, reflected Peel's seventh principle in a way that he might not have anticipated. That is, although I and other Blacks had made the decision to join the police department, too often we were treated with as much indignity and disrespect as Black civilians. Consequently, B-CAP was formed to address these slights and acts of violence against Black civilians and Black police officers.

By way of example, in October 1994, just three years after B-CAP was formed, the new president of the New Jersey Council of Black Police Associations invited me to his office. He informed me that a young city police officer in northern New Jersey was being threatened with the loss of his job over a dispute with a White male, county police officer. The Black officer had refused to shake hands with the county officer after a professional dispute. According to the officer under attack, his refusal to shake hands led to the local prosecutor demanding that he agree to apologize to the White officer in a room full of people. He refused. It was understood that the NJ Council of Black Police Associations, Black Cops Against Police Brutality (B-CAP) and other Black police officer organizations would have to organize with a sense of urgency to protect this fellow officer.

According to the young Black officer, because of the dispute with the White officer, he had been ordered to the county prosecutor's office along with his police director and police chief. His account of what transpired during the meeting is as follows:

> The prosecutor walked in the room and said, 'Good you're here, because I wanted to see exactly who you are!" "Everyone seems impressed with your work and (city of employment) thinks you're a bi[g] deal and a good street cop. But I'm telling you THAT YOU AIN'T S—T! I heard about your altercation with my guy and how you disrespected him and this office, and I really wish that it had gone to fisticuffs because he would have KICKED YOU'RE A-. Whether you know it or not, he's an ex-state champion wrestler—and if you don't think he could've, I'm an old man and I COULD KICK YOU'RE A-!" "Let me tell you something…YOU BETTER WATCH YOURSELF FOR THE REST OF YOUR F—KING CAREER!"

After using multiple profanities while screaming at me his next statement was: "You are going to make a public apology in front of all of the men and in front of [the officer involved] and you will shake his hand in front of all of the men, and if you don't I'll have you taken out of the [assigned unit] – and I will convene a GRAND JURY and have you're A—in front of them 9:00 a.m. tomorrow morning and you can explain it to them. And, if you don't think I'll do it you better get your F—KING attorney ready because I will" (Personal interview, Davis, September 10, 1994).

The city where the embattled officer was employed had a Black mayor and a Black police director. As B-CAP members, we were alarmed by their failure to defend this young Black officer against the actions of the White county prosecutor—actions which appeared to us to be racially motivated bullying. The Black officer was being threatened with criminal charges if he failed to publicly apologize to the White officer with whom he had had a disagreement. In a later conversation with others, the prosecutor characterized his own behavior during the meeting as simply having "a stern" conversation with the Black officer. However, the Black police director, who was present at the meeting, confirmed the accuracy of the profanity-laced account as reported by the Black officer. (Personal interviews, September 10, 1994 and August 22, 2020).

In a move that is contrary to the findings of most policing literature, fifty members of B-CAP advocated for the Black officer at a city council meeting, standing for six hours before the mayor would allow "visitors" to speak on his behalf. Our advocacy was successful and the officer remained on the force until he retired, as a lieutenant, 25 years later. This victory led to increased visibility and credibility for B-CAP nationally. As the organization grew in its influence, we would have occasion to assist other Black officers experiencing internal racism while also supporting community members in their quest to achieve justice through protest.

Defying police culture

I began a career in law enforcement that was filled with contradictions. I was Black and the majority of law enforcement officers across the country were White, even in areas where the residential population was majority minority. Additionally, police leaders would tell me one thing, then do something else based on political expediency, inconvenient truths or structural racism. The contradictions in policing ideology and practice fueled my activism and laid the foundation for the community crisis action plan that I would develop twenty years later. The mission of B-CAP is to be the conscience of the criminal justice system, to improve community – police relationships, and to enhance the quality of life for African people. The mission is driven by the second principle of Kwanzaa,

Kujichagulia, a Kiswahili word for self-determination (National Museum of African American History, 2021). It means that, in contrast to historic and contemporary policing policy and practices, Black communities (including its police officers) are entitled to create, name, define and speak for ourselves rather than to allow other people to do these things for us. This framing runs counter to the historical structural arrangement between the community and the police, particularly the arrangements between police departments and Black people. For Black police, this orientation conflicts with the paramilitary style of policing organizations which is driven by and emphasizes following orders.[1] To address the goal of improving community-police relations, membership in B-CAP is open to active duty and retired police officers and an intentionally broad spectrum of community stakeholders who are not police. The activities of the organization take a holistic approach to achieving its mission, and function in ways that are often outside the scope of traditional policing.

Early in my career I learned that there is danger in Black police officers standing up for Black people (Nicholson-Crotty et al., 2017); and, that there are entrenched values and customs that encourage and pressure all officers to support a racially-biased status quo. In other words, I learned that police culture and support of community activism are largely incongruent, particularly within departments that promote and support a warrior mentality (Stoughton, 2015),–a policing mindset found to be prevalent among officers who work in low-income urban neighborhoods inhabited by people of color (POC) (Balko, 2014; Lum & Nagin, 2017; Stoughton, 2015). I have found that the warrior mentality is coupled with an insistence on blind loyalty within the ranks (Kleinig, 2016). When these two features of policing are enforced, it creates a perfect environment for police misconduct, including racially-biased violence, as revealed by the incident below:

> In 1986 with less than a year on the job, I remember the dispatcher reporting a burglary in progress—a man climbing on the fire escape of an apartment building and breaking into an apartment. Uniformed and plainclothes police officers in marked and unmarked police cars rushed to the scene which was a few blocks from the police department. A terrified Black man was pulled from a fire escape at gunpoint, as he tearfully tried to explain that he had locked himself out. Both Black and White police officers were present on the scene. Before his wallet was checked for identification, he was cursed at, choked, tugged on, handcuffed, and placed in a patrol car in preparation for transport to the police station. When he was finally checked, his identification confirmed that he was indeed the tenant of the apartment. Rather than offering the man a sincere apology, the officers involved in the incident called for a supervisor. They then coordinated their stories to avoid being held accountable for violating the innocent man's rights.

I walked away from that incident in dismay. I had just been introduced to the code of silence, and the police culture of *groupthink*—the practice of supporting a narrative crafted by line officers and their supervisors, in violation of notions of right or wrong. This practice in police culture indoctrinates officers to embrace the mindset of remaining silent and turning a blind eye to unconstitutional, criminal and brutal police behavior – behavior that statistics, and my lived experience, confirm are disproportionately engaged in against Black Indigenous people of color (BIPOC). Officers who break the silence or alter the rehearsed narrative run the risk of being labeled a "rat" who must then "walk the beat alone" (see Campbell, 2001). I also came to learn that the role of racial antipathy or disrespect among police can be compartmentalized as was evident in the incident below:

During my first year on the job, I recall leaving the police roll call (start of the tour of duty) and being assigned to ride with a White officer to drive other officers to their walking posts. As we approached an intersection in a predominantly Black community, a Black mother and her daughter stepped off the curb in front of the police van, forcing the driver to apply the brakes hard. After slamming on the brakes, the officer rolled down the window and said, "Get out of the street, you f—king N's." He then turned toward me and apologized. I remained calm because I already knew that many people in his race felt this way about me and my community.

Through these rookie experiences, I quickly learned that the environment in which I had become immersed was complex – it was rough, rugged, compassionate, sometimes considerate, raw and racist.

The collateral consequences of integrity and activism

Personal experiences as a Black police officer led me on a journey from rookie officer to community activist. The road was not easy. I was faced with ethical dilemmas that threatened to derail my efforts. To combat the often-raised critique that Black people only care about police violence against them to the exclusion of adequately denouncing community crime, B-CAP has worked to reduce, eliminate, and prevent police abuse/misconduct *and* community violence. Innovative techniques and programs, including community forums and partnerships; public protests and demonstrations; and, educational workshops are used to achieve these goals. Community-based activities have been the mainstay of my work against the abuse of Black residents by the police who are paid to protect and serve them; and, by civilians who struggle to conform to pro-social community standards when they are faced with overwhelming levels of need (see Haldipur, 2019). Their need is recognizable through the absence of adequate food, housing, employment, recreation, and healthcare in the spaces where they live.

Speaking out against police brutality and misconduct as an active-duty police officer is challenging on many levels. It runs counter to traditional police culture and its "Blue wall of silence." It is also dangerous and potentially life and career ending. Sometimes it requires speaking out against the "Black wall of unity," when the abusive officers are Black. W.E.B Du Bois (1903) viewed the struggle with Black identity in White spaces as "double consciousness"—the condition of the Black experience that may force Black police officers to view themselves through the lens of a dominate White American society. Viewing oneself through the eyes of a White society that historically has been oppressive to the collective Black community contributes to an identity crisis for Black police officers caught within a profession that requires them to hold dual beliefs—beliefs about how they see themselves and how both Black and White America sees them (Lyubansky & Eidelson, 2005). In a recent study, Kochel (2020) examines this status via the construct "double marginality". The researcher explored the experiences of Black police officers during the Ferguson protests. The officers expressed a challenge in trying to balance their racial identity and experiences with the identity imposed by their employment as police officers.

Pittman (2016) maintains that, even among civilians, Black people are (often) caught between their blackness and a White world that oppresses and devalues them. DuBois describes this struggle as an internal "twoness." This concept exposes the duplicitous existence of a Black police officer that may, but need not be, debilitating. Kochel (2020) maintains that such "twoness" represents a double marginality in which Black police officers are isolated from and ostracized by their racial group within the community and by their occupational peers. A highly publicized case, discussed below, involving my police department and an adjacent one illustrates the difficulty of being a Black cop with integrity:

> On April 8, 1999, four months after my promotion to sergeant, a Black female police officer, from a neighboring police department was investigating an armed robbery. She confronted a Black male who shot her in the head and abdomen. The officer died from those injuries (Newman 1999). Later that evening, while watching television coverage of the shooting, I saw that the police had released images of a license plate on a vehicle believed to have been driven by the suspect.
>
> After midnight, I received a telephone call from an unknown black male. He told me that the police were searching for him. He was afraid that the police would kill him. He informed me that he did not shoot the officer and wanted me to turn him in. I was faced with an internal challenge as a police sergeant who was also known as the B-CAP activist in the Black community.
>
> I called my police chief and explained the situation and asked him how he felt about me going to pick up the alleged suspect who by now was on the state's most

wanted list. There was also a countywide multi-agency police task force searching the streets for him. My chief said, "Well..., go pick him up." I asked "Am I picking him up as the founder of Black Cops Against Police Brutality or..." He interrupted me and said, "Pick him up as the police sergeant of our Community Services Unit. Tell us, what do you need to bring him in safely?" I advised the chief that I needed permission to drive a personal vehicle; have one of our police officers as my back up; and, I needed the chief to notify the desk commander that I was coming in.

Upon arrival at the police headquarters with the suspect, I followed all of the legal procedures such as handcuffing him and videotaping his physical condition in front of the commanding officer when dealing with the suspect. However, a White male captain later called me into the detective bureau and proceeded to question me as if I were the suspect. I had brought in the suspect unharmed and provided him with the opportunity to secure an attorney. However, it appeared that I had violated an unwritten practice in law enforcement which is to pressure the suspect into a confession or to falsely claim that he gave one. I didn't comply with *groupthink*. Frustrated, the captain ordered me to submit a report immediately. My exercise of tactical restraint (see Stoughton, 2015) in this highly volatile situation became a point of consternation rather than applause; and, members of the taskforce were attempting to convince another captain at the county prosecutor's office to have me prosecuted for interfering with their case. Fortunately, she refused to allow any charges to go forward against me. It was later determined that the Black male suspect who surrendered to me was not involved in the murder of the police officer. He was eventually released.

B-CAP's community activism

Several days later, officers searching for the person who killed Officer Joyce Carnegie encountered Earl Faison, a Black male who was an up and coming rap music producer. He was approached by at least five police officers, one of whom was Black. Earl Faison fled after existing a taxicab. He was caught, handcuffed, beaten, maced in the mouth and nose and robbed (Gold, 2006; Newman, 1999).[2] It was later determined that Earl Faison had nothing to do with the death of the officer. Twenty-seven-year-old Earl Faison died from his encounter with these police officers.

Consistent with B-CAP's mission, I put the Faison family in touch with a community activist. I was unable to attend the Faison protest because I was participating in another protest out of town. I was later ostracized at the funeral for Officer Carnegie. Specifically, as I approached the church, I extended my hand to a Black police officer to offer condolences. The officer attempted to punch me in the face and had to be restrained by other officers. He shouted and yelled that I was not welcome at the funeral because I had organized the protest at their police department. He demanded that I leave, so I returned to my vehicle and directed the officers under my command to attend the services without me. As a policeman, I understood why the officer was angry. But, from the perspective of Kochel's (2020) double marginality, this officer was over-identifying with his occupation and failed to identify with me as a Black man who happened to be in his profession. He lashed out at me and condemned my membership and advocacy through B-CAP, a group in which he was not a member.

Five police officers faced trial and were convicted for violating Earl Faison's civil rights (Gold, 2006). I can recall being confronted by a family member of the only Black officer convicted for his role in the death. She said she did not understand why I would not support a Black man and a fellow officer whom I had known for several years. The answer was simple. "I believe that he is guilty." It is this dichotomy of being a Black man in a blue uniform that many Black police officers struggle with. Generally, it is easier to side with the police against Black and Brown communities because there is less pressure to do otherwise. There is more peer support for taking the side of the police; and, there is a built-in economic reward—a continuous paycheck. As advocates for change and social justice, I believe we must take principled positions when it comes to police terror in our communities. I take the unpopular but principled position that if we can step up and voice outrage when White police officers kill Black men, we must be equally vocal and outraged when a Black police officer illegally kills a Black person.

It has consistently been the hope of civil rights leaders that the addition of Black police officers to police departments would result in less police violence. Since the research on this point is inconsistent and Black officers have been implicated in high profile cases like the death of Sean Bell in New York in 2006 and Freddie Gray in Baltimore in 2015, it is important for advocates for police reform to recognize that Black police officers who kill Black people under circumstances that are unequivocally illegal must be held accountable too. This is true despite the many mechanisms that exist to disproportionately absolve White police officers in such cases. (See for example, the New York state prosecution of Francis Livoti for the death of Anthony Baez in 1994).

With each protest and demonstration that B-CAP helped organize; and, in which I participated, I came to understand that I was crushed between my oath and obligation to protect and serve the community as a Black police officer and my desire for Black people to enjoy the same freedoms afforded other Americans. As a Black man, I knew that I could be one traffic accident, one motor vehicle stop, or one rogue police officer away from a life-ending encounter. I recognized that my badge and gun might not protect me from a rogue police officer; and, that being an armed

Black man might, in fact, ensure that such an encounter would result in my death (See for example the deaths of Officers Christopher Ridley (Mount Vernon, New York in 2008) and Cornel Young Jr. (Providence, Rhode Island in 2000)).

The literature on the reinforcing self-protective and self-perpetuating nature of traditional White male dominated police culture is vast. The biggest challenge in creating and sustaining B-CAP was developing a support system that would preserve my life and my career as I stood against brutal and disrespectful policing. I refer to that scaffolding as my "safety net"— a system of affiliations with Black policing organizations and community alliances. On the policing side, the affiliations were not easy to foster or maintain. I was elected president of the National Black Police Association's (NBPA) Northeast Region from 1996 to 2000. Many of my colleagues outside of the northeast found B-CAP's brand of community advocacy radical and extreme. We believed in a direct, often confrontational, approach to addressing incidents of police brutality. This assertive posture that prioritized community well-being above face-saving for individual officers or departments was not embraced by all members of the organization.[3]

In 2002, the groups that seceded from the NBPA formed the National Association of Black Law Enforcement Officers (NABLEO). Unlike traditional policing organizations where membership is only open to active or retired sworn law enforcement, NABLEO's website includes an invitation to membership for community partners and "a real opportunity to work on and enhance issues that have a direct impact on how law enforcement interacts with the community they are sworn to serve." The site notes that participation from community partners is welcome at the organizations training conferences, community service programs and other activities. Like B-CAP, the NABLEO's mission statement includes a commitment to "protect our communities from those **BOTH WITHIN AND WITHOUT** our profession who would prey on them" [emphasis in original]; and, a commitment to "community-based solutions to policing issues which have a direct impact on communities of color." This approach is radically different from the popular one-size-fits-all approaches developed and implemented by White male academics and police practitioners over the last three decades. These so-called 'proactive' policing strategies such as hot spots policing, broken windows policing (Kelling & Wilson, 1982) and the aggressive use of stop-question-and-frisk (NASEM, 2018), have increased the amount of police contact experienced by Blacks, especially those who reside in high need communities. The simultaneous adoption and acceptance of a warrior style policing model in these communities, and beyond, precipitated, fuels and sustains the need for B-CAP, NABLEO, and other organizations where police stand up to police ourselves in partnership with members of the public.

Expanding the parameters of community policing – reaching the youth

While B-CAP was founded in the Northeast, our activism took us across the U.S. and to other countries. Outside the Northeast region we organized and participated in protests and other forms of education and activism in the South, Midwest and West. As part of holistic approach to protecting children who are at risk for brutal police contact, we organized trips to Ghana, South Korea and Las Vegas where they met world leaders, participated in the world peace games and interacted with police officers during a Thanksgiving weekend football tournament, respectively. We developed a curriculum for "What to Do When Stopped by the Police" and see it as a precursor to "The Talk" that parents give to Black youth, especially males, regarding how to handle police encounters.

While many police agencies have established mentoring programs for youth at risk of brutal police contact, with the assistance of my mother, I chose to take four children into our home—children who I met through my work as a police officer. The ages at which I met them ranged from 11 to 14. One was formally adopted. Three were taken in by my mother and I at the request of their parent or guardian. They had come in contact with the police for a range of activities including being a chronic runaway, drug and alcohol abuse, sexual acting out, theft and gang involvement. They had spent time in the juvenile justice and child welfare systems and two had official diagnoses for mental health and learning disabilities. Today, each is an adult who is gainfully employed. One is in a police academy. Only one of them had an additional contact with the criminal legal system, for theft, after they came to live with my family.

I have no doubt that two of my "adopted" daughters were at high risk for brutal contact from the police because one suffered from oppositional defiance disorder and the other was diagnosed as bipolar and schizo-effective. We have seen time and time again how police are inadequately prepared to interact with children and adults who are experiencing an emotional or mental health crisis. My son was also statistically at risk for harmful police contact because he was a young Black male in an urban setting. During police encounters, too often, community members like my son and daughters are seriously injured or killed. As a Black police officer, I felt socially close to the son and daughters I "adopted." Though we were not related by blood, they were members of my community who I felt compelled to assist and serve rather than control and brutalize.

Successfully supporting high-need youth like those whom I "adopted" helped grow my police department's Community Services Unit's youth programs from serving 150 children to 2,600 children during a three-year period. It also changed the trajectory of these individual youth's lives. Reducing the emotional distance between police and the community, is a vision that I have for all police contact—regardless of the officers' or civilians' race. Increasing officers' capacity for care and empathy for those they serve is essential. Though this may be more challenging in high need communities, my experience shows that the investment is worth the return.

Recommendations for police reform

Fatal and nonfatal brutal behavior, by police, against George Floyd, Breonna Taylor, Jacob Blake and other Black people have heightened and renewed long-standing calls for police reform. Large systemic changes such as defunding or abolishing police agencies, greater accountability and oversight, and greater civil and criminal liability for police have been proposed (again). The following recommendations are intended to affect policing at a more granular level and in a more immediately practical way to bring about change.

The recent reliance on the use of "big data" as the gold-standard of performance in policing and the academic study of policing has masked the profoundly interpersonal nature of police service. The prolonged protests in the aftermath of the deaths of George Floyd, Breonna Taylor and others, before and during 2020, have exposed flaws in police science; particularly, how policing and research focused primarily on crime reduction and control produce outcomes that are avoidable and unjust. That, after nearly a century of investigation and academic study, these avoidable and unjust outcomes are still disproportionately experienced by Black people, is troubling. As is the fact that hiring Black police officers has not consistently provided measurable evidence that policing has improved.

Community-centered policing

With few exceptions, the introduction of police unions has made it nearly impossible for residents of high need communities to control, effectively criticize, oversee or partner with police in their neighborhoods, on the residents' own terms. Policing strategies that purport to be community-oriented often exclude large segments of residents from decision-making, if the input of residents is solicited at all. In my experience, walking the beat and wanting to *help* solve everyday problems *with* the community is the beginning of police reform. During the three years that my police department committed to focusing on the needs of neighborhood children and adolescents, juvenile crime was reduced by 33 percent. Community-centered policing requires that police agencies share power with a broad cross-section of residents, especially those who have been policed the most. Community and police must be allowed and encouraged to work together to identify problems; and, police must allow the community to take the lead in proposing solutions. This means that policing agencies must be open to community generated ideas and be non-defensive in their feasibility assessments. Police leaders cannot reject community solutions simply because they have not been tried before or because they "didn't work" once. They cannot support solutions that prioritize the rights of some community members over others. They must not push popular "one-size-fits-all" strategies onto residents simply because some residents accept them when others do not. Most importantly, departments must listen to public complaints and make adjustments that reflect consensus among a broad spectrum of the community, not just those who "support" the police.

Community-centered policing means that police agencies and agents must also stand with the community against police misconduct. B-CAP and its progeny, NABLEO, provide models for how Black police officers can use their position to demand a reimagining of policing that is facilitative rather than excessive, coercive and punitive (see note 2). For more than two decades, B-CAP has successfully intervened to create change for Blacks who have had police encounters. Our advocacy was not limited to police accountability for brutality in its narrow sense. B-CAP advocacy has extended to cases involving the violent application of criminal procedures in other parts of the legal system as well. Results from the activism of B-CAP were often not immediate and occasionally did not produce long term change. But, it was always cathartic for families, communities or survivors. (See note 4). Models for police reform should follow the community-centered example set by B-CAP.

Policing and appreciative inquiry

Community-centered policing is supported by appreciative inquiry – a strengths-based approach to organizational change. Through the process of appreciative inquiry, stakeholders define, discover, dream, design, and deliver the change that all stakeholders can accept and value as achieving a common goal (Cooperrider, Whitney, Stavros, & Fry, 2008). B-CAP fulfilled its mission through community education using the "What to Do When Stopped by the Police" curriculum as an introduction to help save the lives of Black and Brown people. The program which was featured on national television shows like Nightline with Ted Koeppel, MTV and Court TV, involves role playing scenarios with police officers and audience participants on a motor vehicle stop, a street corner stop and a knock at someone's front door.[5] As developed by Cooperrider and his colleagues (2008), an appreciative inquiry approach calls for focus on those things that work right in situations rather than those that go wrong, with the idea that the positive/successful actions should be replicated and elevated as central to the functioning of the organization. B-CAP facilitated candid community-police discussions about the local, regional and national policing protests using the appreciative inquiry approach. To secure the participation of a broad spectrum of the local community, broaden the cultural awareness of the police, and reduce the potential for counterproductive tension, community conversations were held as part of an annual Pre-Kwanzaa Festival. The appreciative inquiry approach was successful in helping to bring the community into the room to engage with the police. This often is not easy in so many jurisdictions where the community-police relationship is tremendously strained, often because of police violence, misconduct or disrespect.

"True" community policing

"True" community policing must be care-based, non-coercive and non-patriarchal. It must give the collective community, not just those who volunteer or who are hand-picked by the police department, a role in public safety decision-making. It must be supportive not adversarial to the idea of sharing decision-making power and to the possibility of the police department having to defer to community decisions. This happens in affluent communities as a matter of norm. Residents of high need communities are all too familiar with coercive and punitive treatment. They do not need it from those who have sworn to protect them. Policing strategies that indiscriminately cast a net of suspicion over specific types of individuals, identities or groups have been shown to have the potential to increase rather than decrease crime in those neighborhoods (Wiley, Slocum, & Esbensen, 2013); and, to decrease the community cooperation needed to solve serious crimes (Fratello, Rengifo, Trone, & Velazquez, 2013).

Though few police officers may feel comfortable taking troubled youth into their homes like I did, visionary police leaders have instituted or sponsored mentoring and "adopt a family" programs as means to support and connect with high need families under non-enforcement supportive circumstances. "True" community policing involves guardian-style policing (see Stoughton, 2015), even in high need communities, because those who are not engaged in serious crime unequivocally deserve it. In addition, guardian style policing increases the likelihood that community partnerships can successfully be formed. Such partnerships may assist in the identification of individuals who require more coercive police tactics (Lum & Nagin, 2017).

The need for trauma-informed policing

The federal government has the ability to recommend that police agencies use trauma-informed policing (Vera Institute, 2021) as foundational to reducing conflicts between police officers and high need communities—neighborhoods with high concentrations of residents who struggle financially and have limited upward social mobility. For example, an officer who responds to a crime scene where there is a victim who is visibly agitated can be trained to ask, "What happened to you?" instead of "What's wrong with you?"—a question that might further irritate the victim. A trauma-informed police officer develops the skills to provide a victim with safety and security; the opportunity to vent about her concerns; and prepares her for the next steps in the public safety process (Vera Institute, 2021). Trauma-informed policing can save both lives and money. Before getting involved with my family, my third "adopted" daughter would run away, each time, it cost the city $127.66 in manpower hours. She was a chronic runaway and would run away 30 times within a year. Trauma-informed training helped officers come to understand why she was running away. Her involvement in a female mentoring program implemented by my department helped reduce her running away to only one time a year—a savings of $4,400 of the police department's budget.

Community crisis action plans

In 2006, just before my retirement, I released the book, "Black Cops Against Police Brutality: A Crisis Action Plan," a how-to book on dealing with police violence, misconduct and abuse. Twenty years of police work and 10 years as an educator and police trainer allowed me to document the tactics and strategies that were effective in my community and policing activism.

The crisis action plan is a tool that the Black community and other fragile communities need in order to effectively stand up against excessive police behavior. Frequently, victims of police misconduct find themselves traumatized, distraught and feeling helpless (Vera Institute, 2021). The crisis action plan helps communities find their voice by guiding the reader through steps that help identify community stakeholders who develop a council of elders to design and implement a process for engaging in action that will promote police reform, police accountability and community safety. The criminal justice program at Kingsborough Community College in New York has used the crisis action plan as required reading. The plan was implemented in New Haven, Connecticut by Emma Jones, during her demands for a civilian review board, after the death of her son Malik. In 2015, Marq Lewis, from "We the People Oklahoma" implemented the plan to demand changes to the Tulsa County Sheriff's department. Black residents of the county used the plan to demand changes in five areas: hiring and training, personnel policy, civilian oversight and transparency, body-worn cameras, and to ban chokeholds and other life-threatening police restraint techniques.

Conclusion

Academics, policy makers, advocates, police practitioners and the public have debated whether the disproportionate harm caused by police behavior in communities of color, is due to systemic racism, bad policy, bad police actors or some combination of these. This harm is experienced by people who are Black, regardless of their ethnic identity, and must be diminished. America's police must learn to provide service without harm to those who need policing services most. A community crisis action plan helps communities make that demand in an organized, intelligence-led, politically powerful and impactful way. Though much of B-CAP's early work was reactive; that is, protests that occurred in the aftermath of an incident involving police violence–our current advocacy, education, training and political action are heavily focused on holistic harm reduction and care. In my view, B-CAP has delivered on the hope that hiring (some) Black police officers would produce better outcomes for Blacks who have police contact. B-CAP's work has required that Black officers have courage, integrity, support, commitment, and ethics. Above all else, it has required that we care deeply about the communities where we work. Trauma-informed policing is also a necessary component of self-care for police whistleblowers and others who are willing to engage in acts of self-sacrifice and stand up for the community and themselves when faced with daunting opposition.

Hopefully, the reader can now better understand the complex world of policing and the difficult road to police reform from the inside out. My experience as a retired police officer affirms the Black community's long-standing complaints that there is over-policing of Black bodies. My police experiences have led to these recommendations for police reform: (a) that it be community-centered, (b) that it utilize appreciative inquiry, (c) that it incorporates true community policing, and (d) that trauma-informed policing be supported for all levels of law enforcement. The involvement of Black Cops Against Police Brutality has had a positive effect on the outcomes of several cases that the organization has taken on. These accomplishments are bold steps that can be taken to improve the relationship between the Black community, the police and other components of the criminal justice system. Future research should examine the impact of militarized policing on the capacity of police officers to use discretion, empathy, and compassion toward Black people and other marginalized groups. Once the recommendations that are suggested here are implemented, the effects of these shifts away from traditional policing will need to be evaluated. Academic researchers must be as committed to studying the impact of these "softer" approaches to policing as they have been to studying those that are more aggressive, punitive and surveillance driven.

Acknowledgments

I honor the editorial work, support, and contributions of Dr. Delores Jones-Brown. This work could not have been accomplished without Dr. Jones-Brown's genuine belief in and commitment to the success of this project. For this, I am thankful and grateful.

Notes

1 This is true despite the considerable literature on police discretion.
2 In *United States v. Smith*, it was revealed that one of the officers involved in the death of Mr. Earl Faison removed money from his pocket and suggested that it be given to the family of the slain police officer, Joyce Carnegie. Retrieved from https://caselaw.findlaw.com/us-3rd-circuit/1362689.html.
3 A clash of perspectives led to the NBPA's National Office making decisions that caused 44 Black police chapters from New Jersey, New York, Connecticut, Rhode Island, New Hampshire, and Vermont to withdraw their membership. The seceding chapters refuse to accept an increase in national dues without an increase in services to the chapters.
4 In addition to the information already provided throughout this paper, here are other examples of the successful work of B-CAP. These measures are qualitative, not quantitative. The mission of the organization is to be the conscience of the criminal justice system, to improve community-police relationships, and to enhance the quality of life for African people. Police officers from B-CAP actively protesting in the streets with the community is consistent with the organization's mission to improve community-police relationships. These protest marches and demonstrations on behalf of victims of police violence included protesting against two NJ State Troopers who shot three unarmed men of color in a van on the NJ Turnpike. The victims were Daniel Reyes, Jarmaine Grant and Rayshawn Brown. In 1999, following a protest partially organized by B-CAP and which shut down the highway for 11 hours, the officers entered guilty pleas and were dismissed from the State Police with an agreement that they could no longer work in law enforcement, https://www.nytimes.com/1998/06/04/nyregion/metro-news-briefs-new-jersey-no-race-profiling-found-in-stops-on-turnpike.html. The Lionel

Tate Case is another example, https://www.sun-sentinel.com/news/fl-xpm-2004-10-30-0410300189-story.html. He was a 12-year-old Black male and the youngest person in the history of the United States to be sentenced to life without parole. B-CAP members advocated for his release, wrote his reentry plan and secured his release after a successful appeal of his sentence. Lionel Tate's release from incarceration enhanced the quality of his life. In 2009, B-CAP filed an Amicus Brief, US Supreme Court, 08-1065/ on behalf of Terry J. Harrington & Curtis W. McGhee Jr. They had served approximately 25 years for allegedly killing a White police captain. Based in part on the efforts of B-CAP, both men were exonerated and won jury awards totaling $12 million based on prosecutorial misconduct, https://congressionaldigest.com/issue/prosecutorial-immunity/black-cops-against-police-brutality-amicus-curiae/. These activities reflect B-CAP's commitment to holding the Criminal Justice System accountable on behalf of Black people.
5 B-CAP workshops were featured on Nightline with Ted Koepel, https://www.worldcat.org/title/nightline-the-life-of-a-black-cop/oclc/262479385.

Disclosure statement

No potential conflict of interest was reported by the author.

References

Alexander, M. (2010). *The new Jim Crow: Mass incarceration in the age of colorblindness.* New York: The New Press.

Ba, B. D., Knox, D., Mummolo, J., & Rivera, R. (2021). The role of officer race and gender in police-civilian interactions in Chicago. *Science (New York, N.Y.), 371* (6530), 696–702.

Balko, R. (2014). *Rise of the warrior cop: The militarization of America's Police Forces.* New York: Public Affairs.

Campbell, J. (2001). Walking the beat alone: An African American Police Officer's Perspective on Petit Apartheid. In D. Milovanovic & K. Russell (Eds.), *Petit apartheid in the U.S. criminal justice system: The dark figure of racism,* Carolina Academic Press, Durham, North Carolina, (pp. 15–20).

Cooperrider, D. L., Whitney, D., Stavros, J. M., & Fry, R. (2008). The appreciative inquiry process: How it works. In D. Cooperrider, D. D. Whitney, & J. Stavro (Eds.),

Appreciative inquiry handbook for leaders of change (pp. 38–48). Oakland, CA: Berrett-Koehler Publishers.

Du Bois, W. E. B. (1903). *The souls of Black folks: Essays and sketches*. Chicago: A.G. McClurg.

Dunham, R., & Alpert, G. (2004). The effects of officer and suspect ethnicity in use-of-force incidents: Miami-Dade County, Florida. In D. Jones-Brown & K. Terry (Eds.), *Policing and minority communities: Bridging gap*. Upper Saddle River, NJ: Prentice Hall.

Edward, T. (1994, September 10). Personal interview.

Edward, T. (2020, August 22). Personal interview.

Forman, J. (2017). *Locking up our own: Crime and punishment in Black America*. New York: Farrar, Straus and Giroux.

Fratello, J., Rengifo, A. F., Trone, J., & Velazquez, B. (2013). *Coming of age with stop and frisk: Experiences, perceptions, and public safety implications*. New York: Vera Institute of Justice.

Gold, J. (2006, January 7). *N.J. police convicted in beating*. Retrieved from ABC News: https://abcnews.go.com/US/story?id=94660&page=1

Gov.UK. (2020, September 25). *History: Past prime ministers*. Retrieved from UK.Gov: https://www.gov.uk/government/history/past-prime-ministers/robert-peel-2nd-baronet

Haldipur, J. (2019). *No place on the corner: The costs of aggressive policing*. New York: New York University Press.

Kelling, G. L., & Moore, M. H. (1988). *The evolving strategy of policing*. Washington, DC: Emerson Collective.

Kelling, G. L., & Wilson, J. Q. (1982, March). Broken windows: The police and neighborhood safety. *The Atlantic*. Retrieved from https://www.theatlantic.com/magazine/archive/1982/03/broken-windows/304465/. Accessed June 15, 2021.

Kleinig, J. (2016, May 24). To protect & serve. *The Critique*, 1–168.

Kochel, T. R. (2020). Protest policing by black police officers: Double marginality and collateral consequences. *Policing: An International Journal*, 43(4), 659–673. https://doi.org/10.1108/PIJPSM-02-2020-0031

Leatherby, L., & Oppel, R. A. (2020). Which police departments are as diverse as their communities? *New York Times*. Retrieved from http://www.nytimes.com/interactive/2020/09/23/us/bureau-justice-statistics-race.html

Lum, C., & Nagin, D. S. (2017). Reinventing American policing. *Crime and Justice*, 46(1), 339–393. https://doi.org/10.1086/688462

Lyubansky, M., & Eidelson, R. J. (2005). Revisiting Du Bois: The relationship between African American double consciousness and beliefs about racial and national group experiences. *Journal of Black Psychology*, 31(1), 3–26. https://doi.org/10.1177/0095798404268289

National Academy of Sciences, Engineering, and Medicine. (2018). *Proactive policing: Effects on crime and communities*. Washington, DC: The National Academies Press.

National Museum of African American History & Culture. (2021, March 10). *The seven principles of Kwanzaa*. Retrieved from National Museum of African American History & Culture: https://nmaahc.si.edu/blog-post/seven-principles-kwanzaa

Newman, A. (1999, April 9). Police officer in Orange, N.J., Is shot to death as she confronts robbery suspect. *New York Times* (Section B, p. 5). Retrieved from https://www.nytimes.com/1999/04/09/nyregion/police-officer-in-orange-nj-is-shot-to-death-as-she-confronts-robbery-suspect.html

Nicholson-Crotty, S. N., Nicholson-Crotty, J., & Fernandez, S. (2017). April: Will more Black cops matter? Officer race and police-involved homicides of Black citizens. *Public Administration Review, 77*(2), 206–216. https://doi.org/10.1111/puar.12734

Pittman, J. P. (2016, March 21). Double consciousness. In E. N. Zalta (Ed.), *Stanford encyclopedia of philosophy*. California: Stanford University. Retrieved from https://plato.stanford.edu/entries/double-consciousness/

Stoughton, S. (2015). Law enforcement's "warrior" problem. *Harvard Law Review Forum, 128*, 225–234.

Vera Institute of Justice. 2021. *Trauma-informed policing*. Retrieved on August 23, 2020. https://www.vera.org/research/trauma-informed-policing

Ward, E. (2017, June 29). *Skin in the game: How antisemitism animates White nationalism*. Retrieved from Political Research Associates: https://www.politicalresearch.org/2017/07/29/skin-in-the-game-how-antisemitism-animateswhite-nationalism

Weitzer, R. (2000). White, black, or blue cops? Race and citizen assessments of police officers. *Journal of Criminal Justice, 28*(4), 313–324. https://doi.org/10.1016/S0047-2352(00)00043-X

Wiley, S., Slocum, L., & Esbensen, F. (2013). The unintended consequences of being stopped or arrested: An exploration of the labeling mechanisms through which police contact leads to subsequent delinquency. *Criminology, 51*(4), 927–966. https://doi.org/10.1111/1745-9125.12024

Williams, H., & Murphy, P.V. (1990). *The evolving strategy of police: A minority view*. Washington, DC: U.S. Department of Justice.

Understanding the role of race, gender and age in request to consent search drivers

Anthony G. Vito and George E. Higgins

ABSTRACT
This study sought to understand the issue of racial profiling in police requests to consent search the driver. The social conditioning model was applied as a theoretical explanation of the officer based on the citizen's race, gender, and age. The propensity score matching (PSM) results show that Black drivers (vs. White drivers), Black male drivers (vs. White Male drivers), and young Black male drivers (vs. young white Male drivers) are all more likely to have the officer request to consent search the driver. Similar results were found when considering the reason for the stop is a moving violation. Overall, the results show evidence of racial profiling for Black drivers, Black male drivers, and young Black male drivers.

Introduction

Problems related to the treatment of minority citizens by police are not a new issue. Prior studies have shown the use or citizen perception of racial targeting by law enforcement in the U.S. through the enforcement of drug laws (Covington, 2001; Harris, 2002; Heumann & Cassak, 2003), the perception that stopping Black citizens is because of "driving while Black" (DWB) (Harris, 1999; Lundman & Kaufman, 2003), and profiling related to the war on terror (Bah, 2006). Racial profiling and law enforcement are most concerning when it comes to traffic stops because this is the most common type of police-citizen interaction (Harrell & Davis, 2020). The current study uses the ACLU's (2009) definition of racial profiling that views discriminatory police behavior as targeting citizens for suspicion of criminal involvement because of the citizen's race, ethnicity, religion, or national origin.

Request to consent search and consent searches

An understudied issue regarding racial profiling in the field of criminal justice/criminology is that of consent search requests. Gau (2013) examined consent requests using the 2008 Police-Public Contact Survey (PPCS). If a driver had a consent request, they were less likely to view the officer as procedurally just and less likely to view the stop as legitimate. The use of consent requests "cause people to question the motives and intentions of officers" (Gau, 2013, p. 771). Nowacki and Spencer (2019) consider the issue of consent search requests using four different datasets, all for the year 2013, including the Law Enforcement Management and Administrative Statistics (LEMAS) survey, the Illinois Traffic Stop Study, the American Community Survey, and the Uniform Crime Reports (UCR). The analysis for that study included information for 96 police departments in Illinois. Departments with specialized units were more likely to have larger amounts of consent search requests. Racial issues in consent search requests found that officers making stops in predominately nonwhite areas were less likely to request a consent search of the Driver. The reason for this could be that due to a higher number of nonwhite residents, this group can build or strengthen public support with the police and reduce the chances that officers use discriminatory practices.

In criminal justice/criminology, there are a far greater number of studies on consent searches. The importance of a consent search is that the officer uses their discretion to see if the civilian will allow them to conduct a search absent the need for probable cause. Law enforcement favors the use of consent searches for several reasons, including the ease of use in comparison to getting a warrant (Van Duizend et al., 1985), a consent search minimizes the risk of the evidence being excluded at trial (LaFave, 2004a), and a consent search limits the possibility that the citizen would say "no" to the search (McGlinchy, 2018). One thing that can better determine the issue of consent searches is to capture the initial request to conduct a consent search.

Prior research on consent searches shows that certain factors influenced the likelihood of a consent search. First, stops for moving violations are more likely to result in a consent search (Fallik & Novak, 2012; Smith & Petrocelli, 2001). Second, not only are male drivers more likely to be involved in a consent search, but that the odds are even greater for Black male drivers (Briggs & Keimig, 2017; Close & Mason, 2007; Fallik & Novak, 2012; Pickerill et al., 2009; Schafer et al., 2006). The final factor is both the age and gender of the driver because prior research shows that younger male drivers have a greater chance of being involved in a consent search (Briggs & Keimig, 2017; Fallik & Novak, 2012: Pickerill et al., 2009; Rosenfeld et al., 2012; Schafer et al., 2006; Tillyer et al., 2012).

Swencionis and Goff (2017) identify five risk factors related to bias that may impact an officer's daily activities, and two of these could apply to the use of consent searches. First is an officer's discretion and that officers are allowed to use throughout their job but may more greatly influence patrol or traffic stop enforcement. The problem is that when people, including police officers, have broad discretion, this increases the chances of bias impacting their work, and this would relate to the use of consent searches which is primarily done at the discretion of the officer (Bloche, 2001; Pryor et al., 2020; Smith & Levinson, 2011). The second risk factor related to consent searches is the emphasis that law enforcement places on their officers fighting crime or being crime fighters. If an officer views their job from this perspective, there could be an issue of stereotyping people of color with crime (Eberhardt et al., 2004; Goff et al., 2008; Pryor et al., 2020). This could lead to the officer using or requesting a consent search as a crime-fighting strategy and not being aware of using this in a racially disparate way. An issue related to searches during traffic stops is the justification given by the officer as to why the citizen was stopped and will be discussed in the following section.

Pretextual stops

Police officers can provide multiple reasons for stopping and searching a vehicle. What separates an officer's decision to search a vehicle is that it raises the traffic stop's intrusiveness and potential seriousness (e.g., potential arrest or potential driver and officer conflict). When officers request permission to search a stopped vehicle, the stop changes from a routine traffic stop where the result might be a warning or a citation to a stop where the officer is looking for a more serious criminal offense (Higgins et al., 2012; LaFave, 2004b; Steinbock, 2001; Whorf, 1997). When it comes to conducting a search, there are certain legal requirements the officer must follow with most searches following under either probable cause (i.e., the officer observes some type of criminal activity displayed by the driver or passenger) (*Brinegar v. United States*, 1949) or a voluntary consent search where the citizen gives the officer voluntary consent to search the vehicle thus avoiding the need for probable cause (*Schneckcloth v. Bustamonte*, 1972).[1] Investigatory vehicle stops warrant more study because they have been upheld by the Supreme Court (*Whren et al., v. United States, 1996*). The Whren decision has been criticized as a potential mechanism for allowing officers to engage in "fishing" expeditions—evidence of other crimes—during traffic stops (Jones-Brown & Maule, 2010, p. 156).

When discussing racial profiling from traffic stops, it is important to consider multiple types of traffic stops classified as traffic safety stops or investigatory stops. Traffic safety stops occur because the driver demonstrates unsafe driving behavior, and police conduct the stop to protect the driver or the public (Baumgartner et al., 2018; Epp et al., 2014). Following the *Whren* decision, it has become increasingly difficult to differentiate a vehicle stop based on probable cause of a traffic violation from an investigatory stop that occurs because the officer has reasonable suspicion that the driver or passenger is engaged in more serious criminal activity. Previous research shows that officers use traffic stops that are done for minor violations or equipment violations as a tactic to conduct investigatory stops even when the officer does not have legally sufficient reasons to suspect greater criminal activity (Baumgartner et al., 2018; Epp et al., 2014; Gizzi, 2011; Novak, 2004; Withrow, 2007). If the officer is basing suspicion according to a person's racial identity for either the driver or passenger, this would be an example of legally insufficient and prohibited reasoning.

Prior research has considered how either the racial identity of the driver or passenger(s) impacts the officers' decisions to make investigatory stops. There is conflicting evidence in terms of showing racial bias (Armenta, 2017; Baumgartner et al., 2017; Lundman & Kaufman, 2003; Novak, 2004; Roh & Robinson, 2009), no evidence of racial bias for Black and White drivers (Kamalu, 2016; Miller, 2008; Smith & Petrocelli, 2001; Withrow, 2007) or mixed results meaning that depending on the results the authors found both evidence of racial bias and no evidence of racial bias (Schafer et al., 2006; Miller, 2009). Two large-scale studies have considered the issue of traffic safety and investigatory stops. Epp and colleagues (2014) used a stratified random sample of the Kansas City metropolitan area driving population in 2003 and 2004. The survey results showed that investigatory stops were more likely to involve Black drivers, young Black male drivers, or stops involving Black drivers in predominately White areas. Baumgartner and researchers (2018) studied 20 million traffic stops in North Carolina between 2000 and 2016. The traffic stop data findings show that minority drivers were more likely to be involved in an investigatory stop. Even considering the research to date, it is also important to provide a theoretical explanation for the officer's decision-making. In the next section, social conditioning model will be explained and is the theory used in the current study.

Social conditioning model

Smith and Alpert (2007) developed the concept of the social conditioning model from psychology. Social conditioning model is a theory to explain the decision-making of a police officer. The viewpoint of a police officer within this theory is that the officer identifies as a "crime fighter" or that there is some particular type of crime there trying to combat from a "war on crime" perspective (Kraska, 2001; Kraska & Kappeler, 1997; Smith & Alpert, 2007). Using this viewpoint may cause the officer to develop a shorthand way to identify citizens because of the citizen's potential involvement in some form of criminal behavior.

Based on the social conditioning model, an officer may become jaded or suspicious of certain citizens because of certain perspectives or stereotypes based on racial identity. It could be that when interacting with the public, an officer does not have regular contact with certain racial groups. This could result in the officer having cognitive overload, resulting in stereotypes of the citizen based on their race, which influences the officers' thoughts and actions. Such situations may also cause the officer to develop a script when interacting with certain citizens based on individual factors, citizen behavior, or suspicious cues but may also be influenced by the citizen's race, gender, or age. Previous research shows that a person's race is linked with criminal behavior or that such a view is reinforced through the media or vicarious experiences (Costelloe et al., 2009; Ghandnoosh, 2014; Gilliam et al., 2002; Hurwitz & Peffley, 1997; Lever, 2007).

The social conditioning model has been applied as a theoretical explanation for police officer decision-making, including post-stop outcomes such as citations, warnings, or arrests. This literature review will focus on articles that applied the social conditioning model to frisks or searches. Tillyer and Colleagues (2012) found that Black drivers are less likely to face a discretionary search but that young Black male drivers are more likely to face a discretionary search. This shows that it is not race alone that explains discretionary searches but is the interaction effect of race, gender, and age that explains officer decision making. Carroll and Gonzalez (2014) found that Black drivers were more likely to be frisked or searched in comparison to White drivers and that using an interaction variable for stops occurring in predominately White areas found that Black drivers were more likely to be frisked in predominately White areas. Based on the results from Carroll and Gonzalez (2014), the findings show that when an officer's safety is a concern, they may use implicit stereotypes that result in an association with Black citizens and danger that impacts the officer's decision to conduct a frisk or search. However, when an officer has more time to process information and determine probable cause for a search, the citizen's race does not impact officer decision-making. Klahm and Tillyer (2015) research showed that for discretionary searches, Black drivers, Hispanic drivers, male drivers, and younger drivers were all at an increased odds of having a discretionary search occur. This finding shows that it could be due to repeated interaction or long-term exposure to these certain driver demographics that may result in a stereotype which could cause the officer to use some type of shorthand that motivates their actions akin to the social conditioning model.

Even with these studies, using propensity score matching (PSM) to analyze and match individuals based on social conditioning modeling has not been considered. By using both PSM and social conditioning modeling, the researchers hope to add to the existing literature while also expanding the racial profiling literature by examining the officer's decision to request a consent search of the driver. The following section will cover PSM.

Current study

Prior researchers have been critical of certain methodologies or data collection practices used in the racial profiling literature. First is concern about law enforcement falsifying the data when conducting a traffic stop (Lundman, 2010; Meehan & Ponder, 2002; Skolnick & Caplovitz, 2004). Second are questions regarding the quality of the data and the citizen's demeanor during the stop and whether the citizen viewed the stop as legitimate (Lundman & Kaufman, 2003; Reisig et al., 2004). Lastly, the issue with using statistical techniques such as the hit-rate or benchmark test is that there is no appropriate benchmark to determine a comparison group of non-stopped drivers to stopped drivers (Engel & Calnon, 2004; Neil & Winship, 2019; Ridgeway & MacDonald, 2010).

Two different articles recommended using PSM as a better way to examine racial profiling while also considering the previous methodological or data collection issues (Fallik, 2019; Neil & Winship, 2019). Utilizing PSM allows the researcher to better understand if the driver's race "matters," thus allowing for a better understanding of how race may influence the result of a traffic stop and determine the extent that racial profiling may or may not exist. Prior studies have shown the utility of using PSM with traffic stop data (Ridgeway, 2006; Vito et al., 2018, 2020). Using PSM in the current study will allow the researchers to determine whether the driver's race influences the police officer's request for a consent search of the driver.

Using PSM allows the researchers to create a quasi-experimental design that will allow for matched stops based on the driver's race. This is important because it shows whether racial profiling may occur based on race and from whom officers are requesting a consent search. This study adds to the racial profiling literature regarding requesting a consent search and shows how this type of decision-making can be an investigatory stop technique. This study seeks to answer four research questions:

Research Question 1: What effect does a driver's race have on the odds that the officer will request consent to search the driver?

Using PSM, the researchers can better examine the observable racial differences among similarly situated drivers (i.e., Black drivers vs. White drivers)

Research Question 2: Using an interaction effect based on the drivers' race and being a male driver. How will this interaction impact the likelihood that an officer requests a consent search of the driver?

Through PSM, the researchers will examine the observable racial differences along with the driver being male (i.e., Black male drivers Vs. White male drivers).

Research Question 3: Is there an interactive effect regarding the Driver's race, being a male driver, and a younger driver (ages 15 to 29), and the chances that the officer will request consent to search the driver?

In order to answer the third research question, an interaction effect measure was created that allows for the researchers to consider the observable racial differences for male drivers who are between the ages of 15 to 29 (i.e., Black male drivers aged 15 to 29 vs. White male drivers aged 15 to 29).

Research Question 4: How does the reason for the stop being a moving violation influence the chances that the officer will request consent to search the driver?

A keep if analysis was performed for moving violations along with PSM analysis to address the previous three research questions, but the analysis was done for moving violation stops.

Data

The state of Illinois passed The Illinois Traffic and Pedestrian Stop Statistical Study act in 2004. The act requires that law enforcement document and report their traffic stop data to the Illinois Department of Transportation. This study's data is a sample (n = 1,167,408) of all traffic stop data for 2012–2018. The reason for this time period is because it had complete information for all variables used in this study. For the manageability of the data analysis—there are more than 14 million traffic stops during our study period—the analysis here uses a random sample of 10% of all traffic stops.[2]

Dependent measure

A dichotomous dependent measure was a request to consent search the driver[3] (0 = No, the officer did not request to consent search the driver, 1 = Yes, the officer requested to consent search the driver).

Independent measures

Social conditioning model

Three measures were developed to measure the social conditioning model, including the driver's race, gender, and age. Driver race was operationalized as Black driver (reference category White driver). Driver gender was dummy coded (0 = female, 1 = male). A dichotomous measure was used to measure drivers between the ages of 15 to 29 (0 = 30 years of age or older, 1 = 15 to 29 years of age) (Tillyer et al., 2012; Tillyer & Engel, 2013). Interaction effect variables were also created based on these three driver demographics: Black driver*Male Driver and Black driver*Male driver*Drivers' between the ages of 15–29.

Traffic stop characteristics

The reason for the stop includes moving violation (0 = no, 1 = yes), equipment violation (0 = no, 1 = yes), and license plate/registration (0 = no, 1 = yes). If the stop was for a moving violation, there were five types of reasons given, with the reference category for each type being all other reasons: speeding violation, lane violation, seat belt violation, traffic sign or signal violation, and follow to close violation. The year of the vehicle is a continuous measure.

Analysis plan

The current study's statistical analysis method is propensity score matching (PSM) because it allows the researchers to better examine racial differences amongst matched White and Black drivers. Using PSM will enable the researchers to better assess the role that the driver's race has at influencing the officer's decision-making (Bai & Clark, 2018; Guo & Fraser, 2014). The PSM analysis was done using Stata 15. PSM is a four-step analysis, with the first step being the calculation of the descriptive statistics for all measures with the mean value interpreted for each measure.

The second step is to match the drivers according to their race. For this study, the matching uses the nearest neighbor technique (1-to-1 matching without replacement), thus allowing the researchers to put one driver in the treatment group for every one driver placed in the control group. This study uses a caliper (i.e., standard deviation) of 0.20, and the caliper will match drivers according to driver race (Rosenbaum & Rubin, 1985).

Step three is to assess the quality of the matching using two pieces of information. The first piece is that the mean value for the matched groups should be identical or almost identical. The second piece is that the standardized bias after matching or the mean standardized bias after matching must be ≤5 percent for the PSM to be acceptable (Caliendo & Kopeinig, 2008). Within this step, researchers can acquire the descriptive statistics for the treatment group (i.e., Black drivers) and the comparison group (i.e., White drivers). Without performing PSM, statistical results would be biased because the sample of White and Black drivers are different on the measures of interest. Our use of PSM removes the bias among these measures resulting in a group of matched White and Black drivers. The remaining differences should be attributed largely to race, and our weighted logistic regression analysis will be used for this examination.

The fourth step is to conduct a logistic regression based on the weighted matches from the PSM. In order to interpret the findings, the odds ratios are used and will show the likelihood that the officer requests to consent search the driver according to race. In this study, since the treatment variable is the driver's race, the cases are matched on all other variables in the model to better show the potential impact of the driver's race and request to consent search the driver.

Results

The descriptive statistics for all measures can be found in Table 1. Crosstabs were also performed to show the percentage of traffic stops based on the

Table 1. Descriptive statistics.

Measures	Minimum	Maximum	Mean/Percentage	SD
Dependent variable				
Consent search requested of the driver	0	1	1.00	0.10
Independent variables				
Social conditioning model				
Black driver	0	1	26.30	0.44
Driver gender	0	1	62.62	0.48
Drivers' aged 15 to 29	0	1	39.75	0.49
Black driver*Male	0	1	17.94	0.38
Black driver*Male*Young	0	1	8.73	0.28
Traffic stop characteristics				
Moving violation	0	1	66.83	0.47
Equipment violation	0	1	20.79	0.41
License plate/registration violation	0	1	11.41	0.32
Speeding violation (reason for the moving violation)	0	1	54.12	0.50
Lane violation (reason for the moving violation)	0	1	9.31	0.29
Seat belt violation (reason for the moving violation)	0	1	3.88	0.19
Traffic sign or signal violation (reason for the moving violation)	0	1	17.02	0.38
Follow to close violation (reason for the moving violation)	0	1	0.67	0.08
Vehicle year	0	2022	2005.98	7.77

officer requesting to consent search the driver. The crosstabs show, based on race, that more White drivers (59.06%) did have a consent search request occur in comparison to Black drivers (40.94%). When considering the gender of the driver, it was male drivers (81.76%) who had a much higher number of traffic stops where the officer asked to consent to search the driver versus that of female drivers (18.24%). In terms of the driver's age, drivers between the ages of 15 to 29 (61.26%) have a higher percentage of stops where the officer requests to consent search the driver compared to drivers who are 30 years of age or older (38.74%).

Before explaining the results of all six models, the standardized bias percentage for each measure or the mean standardized bias percentage after using PSM was ≤5 percent showing that the PSM was acceptable in all models.[4] For purposes of explaining the results, the findings presented here will focus solely on explaining the social conditioning model measures through the use of PSM. Readers who would like to see the significance of other variables can be found in the tables.

Table 2 presents the weighted logistic regression results for the first three models. In model one, the results show that matched Black drivers in comparison to White drivers are 1.74 times more likely ($b = 0.55$, S.E. = 0.042, $Exp(b) = 1.74$) to have the officer request to consent to search the driver. For model two, the findings show that matched Black male drivers are 127 percent more likely to have the officer request to consent search them versus White male drivers. The results for the third model show that matched young Black male drivers versus that of young White male drivers are 3.00 times more likely to have an officer request to consent search them ($b = 1.10$, S.E. = 0.124, $Exp(b) = 3.00$).

Table 2. Weighted logistic regressions for Models 1 to 3: request to consent search the driver.

Measure	Model 1: Black driver vs. White driver			Model 2: Black male driver vs. White male driver			Model 3: Young Black male driver vs. Young white male driver		
	b	S.E.	Exp(b)	b	S.E.	Exp(b)	B	S.E.	Exp(b)
Black Driver	0.55***	0.042	1.74	–	–	–	–	–	–
Black Driver*Male	–	–	–	0.82***	0.065	2.27	–	–	–
Black Driver*Male*Young	–	–	–	–	–	–	1.10***	0.124	3.00
Vehicle Year	−0.03***	0.001	0.97	−0.03***	0.001	0.97	−0.03***	0.001	0.97
Drivers' aged 15 to 29	0.70***	0.048	2.01	0.66***	0.053	1.94	–	–	–
Driver Gender	0.98***	0.08	2.67	–	–	–	–	–	–
Moving Violation	2.22***	4.601	9.19	2.19***	4.471	8.93	1.84	6.325	6.31
Equipment Violation	2.32***	5.192	10.36	2.25***	4.755	9.49	1.90	6.767	6.75
License Plate/Reg. Violation	2.32***	5.097	10.17	2.22***	4.621	9.21	1.84	6.298	6.28
2 Log-likelihood =	−38154.12			−28364.48			−14949.99		
Chi-Square =	3635.37***			2086.10***			1217.29***		
Pseudo R-Squared =	0.05			0.04			0.03		
n =	613,910			376,160			165,632		

***$p < 0.001$.

In addition to the findings discussed in models one through three, a significant and positive link with the reason for the stop being a moving violation was found, and so models four through six examine those stops where the reason for the stop was a moving violation. Also, before presenting the PSM findings, crosstabs results were performed again to show the percentage of traffic stops based on the officer requesting to consent search the driver when the stop was for a moving violation. Similar to the prior crosstabs results regarding race and the reason for the stop is a moving violation, White drivers (60.25%) were more involved in requests to consent search the driver verses that of Black drivers (39.75%). Based on the gender of the driver and the reason being a moving violation, it was male drivers (82.14%) who had a much higher number of requests to consent search the driver than female drivers (17.86%). For the driver's age and the reason being a moving violation, drivers between the ages of 15 to 29 (60.16%) also account for more requests to search the driver than drivers who are 30 or older (39.84%).

Table 3 presents the weighted logistic regression results based on the stop being a moving violation for models four through six. The results for model four show that stops for a moving violation that matched Black drivers versus that of White drivers are 70 percent more likely to have officers request to consent search the driver. In the fifth model, when the stop is for a moving violation its matched Black male drivers in comparison to White male drivers who are 2.24 times more likely ($b = 0.81$, S.E. $= 0.084$, $Exp(b) = 2.24$) to have an officer request to consent search them. In the final model, where the stop is a moving violation, it is matched

Table 3. Weighted logistic regressions for Models 4 to 6: moving violation stops and request to consent search the driver.

Measure	Model 4: Black driver vs. White driver			Model 5: Black male driver vs. White male driver			Model 6 Young Black male driver vs. young White male driver		
	b	S.E.	Exp(b)	b	S.E.	Exp(b)	b	S.E.	Exp(b)
Black driver	0.53***	0.054	1.70	–	–	–	–	–	–
Black driver*Male	–	–	–	0.81***	0.084	2.24	–	–	–
Black driver*Male*Young	–	–	–	–	–	–	1.14***	0.17	3.13
Vehicle year	−0.03***	0.001	0.97	−0.03***	0.001	0.97	−0.03***	0.002	0.97
Drivers' aged 15 to 29	0.73***	0.065	2.08	0.70***	0.072	2.02	–	–	–
Driver gender	1.06***	0.116	2.88	–	–	–	–	–	–
Speeding violation	−1.03***	0.015	0.36	−1.00***	0.018	0.37	−0.94***	0.026	0.39
Lane violation	0.16**	0.054	1.17	0.14**	0.06	1.14	0.21**	0.089	1.23
Seat belt violation	−0.49***	0.045	0.61	−0.46***	0.051	0.63	−0.40***	0.07	0.67
Traffic sign/Signal violation	−0.24***	0.034	0.79	−0.22***	0.039	0.80	−0.22**	0.054	0.80
Follow to close violation	−0.16	0.159	0.85	−0.28	0.168	0.75	−0.59	0.20	0.56
2 Log-likelihood =	−21858.73			−16501.72			−8544.83		
Chi-square =	3141.12***			1876.96***			984.71***		
Pseudo R-squared =	0.07			0.05			0.05		
n =	364,970			221,172			97,328		

**$p < 0.01$, ***$p < 0.001$.

young Black male drivers compared to young White male drivers who are 213 percent more likely to have an officer ask to request search them.

Discussion

The purpose of the present study was to examine a relatively understudied area of racial profiling. Rather than focus on consent searches, the present study focused on the officer's request to consent search the driver. We derived four research questions, and our results behaved as expected.

The first research question concerns the effect a driver's race has on the officer's chances to request to search the driver. Two prior studies have considered consent search requests and found issues with citizens' perceptions (Gau, 2013) and that consent search requests are less likely with a greater percentage of nonwhite residents (Nowacki & Spencer, 2019). The current study's findings show that amongst matched White and Black drivers, officers would be more likely to request to consent search Black drivers.

The second research question concerned whether race and gender change the officer's chances to request a consent search. Our results indicate this does have an effect. Black male drivers are more likely than White male drivers to receive a request for a consent search. The current findings are consistent with the research on consent searches involving male drivers (Briggs & Keimig, 2017; Close & Mason, 2007; Fallik & Novak, 2012; Pickerill et al., 2009; Schafer et al., 2006).

The third research question focused on the impact that a driver's race, age, and gender influence the likelihood that an officer would request to consent search the driver. Similar to the previous results, findings show that there is a statistically significant effect. Amongst matched young Black male drivers (i.e., ages 15 to 29) and young White male drivers, there is a greater chance that an officer will request to consent search a young Black male driver. This finding is consistent with prior research concerning an interaction effect between race, gender, and age and searches (Klahm & Tillyer, 2015; Tillyer et al., 2012).

The fourth research question was concerned with whether the reason for the traffic stop was for a moving violation and if that impacts the officers' decision to request a consent search of the driver based on their race, gender, and age. Our results were similar to the prior three research questions and that a traffic stop for a moving violation impacts the officers' decision to request a consent search of the driver for three different matched groups with increased odds for Black drivers vs. White drivers, Black male drivers vs. White male drivers, and young Black male drivers vs. young White male drivers. These results are consistent with prior research on consent searches and moving violations (Fallik & Novak, 2012; Smith & Petrocelli, 2001).

While this study provides important insights into the request for a consent search, the study is not without its limitations. We recognize the study does not provide information about the race and experience level of the officer. It is important to keep in mind; this is one of the first studies that examined an officer's request to consent search the Driver as part of the consent search process. The hope is that it will encourage future scholars to determine what officers need additional education and training.

The study is limited to one geographical area (Illinois); however, future studies of this part of the process need to be administered in other sections of the country for comparison. Although the sample in the present study is large, it is cross-sectional, and the changes in this behavior over time are not captured. Longitudinal research, specifically monitoring the officers who tend to ask for consent searches, would help understand officers' decision-making who request a consent search. The use of investigatory stops is also a limitation because of how police are legally able to conduct investigatory stops. Levit (1996) provides the legal criticism of this practice, "We sanction investigatory auto stops on a standard less stringent than reasonable suspicion-in fact on the basis of a standard that we all meet almost every time we enter a car-a minor traffic offense" (p. 187). Similar to other studies the argument here is that officers may conduct traffic stops for "investigatory" reasons but that there is a greater chance of the officer using minor offenses as it relates to the stop and could be a pretext for pulling the Driver over (Baumgartner et al., 2018; Epp et al., 2014). However, even with this limitation, the measurement of what would be considered factors of an investigatory stop are consistent with prior research using similar measures (Baumgartner et al., 2017, 2018; Epp et al., 2014; Miller, 2009; Warren et al., 2006).

The policy implications of this study are notable as they emphasize the need for training and education. In our view, we are likely dealing with two classes of law enforcement. First is the class of law enforcement officer that does not realize they are behaving in the manner that our results indicate. Second, a class of officers exists that realizes they are behaving in the manner our results indicate. To assist in reducing disparities found in the present study, we recommend that implicit (i.e., the first class of law enforcement described) and explicit (i.e., the second class of law enforcement described) bias training be mandatory for all law enforcement at all levels.

When it comes to implicit or explicit bias, there are certain recommendations that may help reduce issues of racial bias as it relates to policing. First is intergroup contact, which follows the premise that racial bias can be reduced when people interact with those outside their social groups in non-negative interactions (Spencer et al., 2016). Police departments could achieve this type of contact through the use of community-oriented policing with the goal of creating pro-social interactions with communities where issues of racial bias may be evident. The second is reducing an officer's discretion because it reduces the chances of an officer acting in a biased manner (Spencer et al., 2016).

Studies analyzing the impact of implicit bias training have not found promising results in terms of the types of interventions being shown to be ineffective, whether after several hours or several days or that such interventions would result in long term changes (Forscher et al., 2019; Lai et al., 2016). The NYPD implemented implicit bias training for 36,000 sworn personnel between May 2018 and April 2019. Officer's attitudes initially showed that they felt that the training was beneficial. Still, in follow-up interviews, most officers reported they had not used the training in their duties as an officer. Overall, the results of the study found "insufficient evidence to conclude that racial and ethnic disparities in police enforcement actions were reduced as a result of the training" (Worden et al., 2020, p. vi).

Given the discretionary manner of police decision-making in traffic stops, it is vital to make officers aware of how their decision-making impacts citizens. By considering the officer's discretionary behavior, it allows officers to make use of their knowledge and experiences as a practitioner. As police departments continue to use technology to try and deal with crime issues and interact and treat citizens, Drenth and van Steden (2020) provide five recommendations that would also apply to U.S. police departments. First is searching for relevant clues that allow officers to use their legal knowledge and legal powers through direct contact with citizens or what occurs in specific locations (such as hot spots) and considers what type of behavior is tolerated in that specific area. Second, the officer will define the situation by observing or collecting information to determine if there is criminal activity or if citizens are in danger. The third recommendation is that when officers arrive at a scene or deal with hostile or disrespectful citizens, the officer anticipates the situation. This includes talking with other officers about what has occurred and taking appropriate action based on trust and communication. Fourth is the consideration of how to deal with citizens and the need to be transparent with their decision-making and that officers understand and legitimize the citizen's feelings. This also relates to the request to consent search and ensuring the citizen understands what the request implies. Another recommendation is that officers end the situation but do so in a firm but gentle manner.

Two strategies related to consent searches and the police to deal with potential racial disparities are the mandatory use of written consent forms or the banning of consent searches. Three cities in North Carolina (Fayetteville, Durham, and Chapel Hill) all had their police departments implement the mandatory use of written consent forms for consent searches that make citizens aware of their rights. After each city implemented the use of written consent forms, there was a drastic reduction in the number of consent searches, but this reduced racial disparities in consent searches and also helped serve as a way to rebuild trust with minority communities (Baumgartner et al., 2018). The second strategy would be recommending the banning of consent searches. Removing this type of search would also help reduce the chances of racial bias and coincide with Swencionis and Goff (2017) recommendations, where greater discretion increases the likelihood of bias impacting officer decision-making.

Due to racial bias in policing, especially when it comes to traffic stops, another recommendation is to change the enforcement patterns away from traditional traffic stop enforcement. Considering recent national events and growing concerns of wanting to "defund the police," it would be necessary to consider the use of "self-enforcing" streets. The solutions recommended by using what is called "self-enforcing" streets include "narrowing roadways, protected bike lanes, and pedestrian plazas with the goal of reducing speeding, traffic crashes and injuries" (Transportation Alternatives, 2020, p. 9). Recent findings from New York City show that using red-light cameras, speed enforcement cameras, and automated enforcement cameras resulted in safer driving behavior (Fried, 2014; NYC DOT, 2018a, 2018b). Using such strategies is better at changing driver behavior than traditional traffic stop enforcement practices (Conner, 2017).

Citizens should also be aware of new or emerging technologies that would benefit their protection when interacting with law enforcement or making sure they document their side of the story. Various apps are now available to help citizens know their rights when interacting with police or record the interaction (Please see Ram, 2015 webpage article for a review of some of the available apps). The authors wish to highlight two technologies available for both citizens and citizen and police interaction during a traffic stop. The Ring Car Cam allows drivers to have a dashcam in their car, which among other things, can record a traffic stop by saying, "Alexa, I'm being pulled over" (Hawkins, 2020). Thus, allowing for the Driver to record the traffic stop from their perspective. The other is The Check App, which allows for video calling technology to replace the traditional traffic stop interaction. Hopefully, this app will allow for better communication and keep both the driver and officer safe (Check, 2021). Even though these recommendations might help keep the driver safe, these recommendations cannot determine if the officer decided to stop the driver or if the officer made a request to consent search the driver based on the driver's race.

One of the main issues that arises from these types of searches is trust between the community and law enforcement. Law enforcement agencies should reinstitute police-citizen academies. This will allow for a better understanding of both groups. For instance, the community may be able to better understand the danger that occurs in "routine" traffic stops. In addition, the community may be able to better understand procedural issues that occur in "routine" traffic stops. The police-citizen academy will provide a foundation for better communication between the community and law enforcement.

Conclusion

Despite the limitations, the study does provide insight into racial, gender, age, and types of moving violations in the request for a consent search of the driver. Hopefully, this study will provide support for law enforcement to develop explicit and implicit bias training, potential changes in policy and procedures regarding consent searches, and internal studies of disparities. With follow-up studies further exploring this issue, we hope this contributes to reducing the disparities of the request for consent searches.

Disclosure statement

No potential conflict of interest was reported by the authors.

Notes

1. As one reviewer pointed out, the search of a vehicle is legally justified if an officer views the contraband in plain sight.
2. A 10% random sample was chosen to reduce computational time. Further, analytics with over 1 million data points would render all analytics statistically significant, or an issue of having too much statistical power.
3. The data collection form includes four different categories to collect information on the following type of searches of the driver: Consent search requested? (Yes or No); Consent Given? (Yes or No); Search conducted? (Yes or No) Search Conducted By? (Consent or Other)
4. The tables assessing the balancing for each model are available from the lead author upon request

References

American Civil Liberteris Union. (2009). *The persistence of racial and ethnic profiling in the United States*. New York: ACLU National Office.

Armenta, A. (2017). Racializing crimmigration: Structural racism, colorblindness, and the institutional production of immigrant criminality. *Sociology of Race and Ethnicity, 3*(1), 82–95. https://doi.org/10.1177/2332649216648714

Bah, A. B. (2006). Racial profiling and the war on terror: Changing trends and perspectives. *Ethnic Studies Review, 29*(1), 76–100. https://doi.org/10.1525/esr.2006.29.1.76

Bai, H., & Clark, M. H. (2018). *Propensity score methods and applications*. Los Angeles, CA: Sage Publications.

Baumgartner, F. R., Christiani, L., Epp, D. A., Roach, K., & Shoub, K. (2017). Racial disparities in traffic stop outcomes. *Duke FL & Soc. Change, 9*, 21–53.

Baumgartner, F. R., Epp, D. A., & Shoub, K. (2018). *Suspect citizens: What 20 million traffic stops tell us about policing and race*. Cambridge: Cambridge University Press.

Bloche, M. G. (2001). Race and discretion in American medicine. *Yale Journal of Health Policy, Law, and Ethics, 1*(1), 95–131.

Briggs, S. J., & Keimig, K. A. (2017). The impact of police deployment on racial disparities in discretionary searches. *Race and Justice, 7*(3), 256–275. https://doi.org/10.1177/2153368716646163

Brinegar v. United States. (1949). 338 U.S. 160.

Schneckcloth v. Bustamonte. (1972). 412 U.S. 218.

Caliendo, M., & Kopeinig, S. (2008). Some practical guidance for the implementation of propensity score matching. *Journal of Economic Surveys, 22*(1), 31–72. https://doi.org/10.1111/j.1467-6419.2007.00527.x

Carroll, L., & Gonzalez, M. L. (2014). Out of place: Racial stereotypes and the ecology of frisks and searches following traffic stops. *Journal of Research in Crime and Delinquency, 51*(5), 559–584. https://doi.org/10.1177/0022427814523788

Check. (2021). *Check*. Retrieved from https://www.getcheckapp.com/

Close, B. R., & Mason, P. L. (2007). Searching for efficient enforcement: Officer characteristics and racially biased policing. *Review of Law & Economics, 3*(2), 263–281. https://doi.org/10.2202/1555-5879.1058

Conner, M. (2017). Traffic justice: Achieving effective and equitable traffic enforcement in the age of Vision Zero. *Fordham Urban Law Journal, 44*, 969.

Costelloe, M. T., Chiricos, T., & Gertz, M. (2009). Punitive attitudes toward criminals: Exploring the relevance of crime salience and economic insecurity. *Punishment & Society, 11*(1), 25–49. https://doi.org/10.1177/1462474508098131

Covington, J. (2001). Round up the usual suspects: Racial profiling and the war on drugs. In D. Milovanivic & K. K. Russell (Eds.), *Petit apartheid in the United States criminal justice system: The dark figure of racism* (pp. 27–42). Durham: Carolina Academic Press.

Drenth, A. R., & van Steden, R. (2020). Everyday patrol work for a data-driven flying squad: Advancing theoretical thinking on police craftsmanship in interacting with civilians. *Journal of Crime and Justice, 43*(4), 486–801. https://doi.org/10.1080/0735648X.2020.1722202

Eberhardt, J. L., Goff, P. A., Purdie, V. J., & Davies, P. G. (2004). Seeing black: Race, crime and visual processing. *Journal of Personality and Social Psychology, 87*(6), 876–893.

Engel, R. S., & Calnon, J. M. (2004). Examining the influence of drivers' characteristics during traffic stops with police: Results from a national survey. *Justice Quarterly, 21*(1), 49–90. https://doi.org/10.1080/07418820400095741

Epp, C. R., Maynard-Moody, S., & Haider-Markel, D. P. (2014). *Pulled over: How police stops define race and citizenship*. Chicago: University of Chicago Press.

Fallik, S. W. (2019). The methodological struggles of racial profiling research: A causal question that automobile stop data has yet to answer. *Criminal Justice Studies, 32*(1), 32–49. https://doi.org/10.1080/1478601X.2018.1558057

Fallik, S., & Novak, K. J. (2012). The decision to search: Is race or ethnicity important? *Journal of Contemporary Criminal Justice, 28*(2), 146–165. https://doi.org/10.1177/1043986211425734

Fried, B. (2014, February 20). *There is now doubt that automated traffic enforcement saves lives*. Streetsblog NYC. Retrieved from https://nyc.streetsblog.org/2014/02/20/there-is-no-doubt-that-automated-traffic-enforcement-save-lives/.

Forscher, P. S., Lai, C. K., Axt, J. R., Ebersole, C. R., Herman, M., Devine, P. G., & Nosek, B. A. (2019). A meta-analysis of procedures to change implicit measures. *Journal of Personality and Social Psychology, 117*(3), 522–559. https://doi.org/10.1037/pspa0000160

Gau, J. M. (2013). Consent searches as a threat to procedural justice and police legitimacy: An analysis of consent requests during traffic stops. *Criminal Justice Policy Review, 24*(6), 759–777. https://doi.org/10.1177/0887403412464547

Ghandnoosh, N. (2014). *Race and punishment: Racial perceptions of crime and support for punitive policies*. Washintgon, DC: The Sentencing Project.

Gilliam, F. D., Jr., Valentino, N. A., & Beckmann, M. N. (2002). Where you live and what you watch: The impact of racial proximity and local television news on attitudes about race and crime. *Political Research Quarterly, 55*(4), 755–780. https://doi.org/10.1177/106591290205500402

Gizzi, M. C. (2011). Pretextual stops, vehicle searches, and crime control: An examination of strategies used on the frontline of the war on drugs. *Criminal Justice Studies, 24*(2), 139–152. https://doi.org/10.1080/1478601X.2011.561644

Goff, P. A., Eberhardt, J. L., Williams, M. J., & Jackson, M. C. (2008). Not yet human: Implicit knowledge, historical dehumanization, and contemporary consequences. *Journal of Personality and Social Psychology, 94*(2), 292–306. https://doi.org/10.1037/0022-3514.94.2.292

Guo, S., & Fraser, M. W. (2014). *Propensity score analysis: Statistical methods and applications* (2nd ed.). Thousand Oaks: SAGE Publications.

Harrell, E., & Davis, E. (2020). *Contacts between police and the public, 2018 - statistical tables*. Washington, DC: U.S. Department of Justice Office of Justice Programs Bureau of Justice Statistics.

Harris, D. A. (1999). *Driving while Black: Racial profiling on our nations highways*. Washington, DC: American Civil Liberties Union.

Harris, D. A. (2002). *Profiles in injustice: Why racial profiling cannot work*. New York: New Press.

Hawkins, A. J. (2020, September 25). *Ring's traffic stop feature is about bringing more accountability to policing*. The Verge. Retrieved from https://www.theverge.com/2020/9/25/21454772/amazon-ring-car-cam-traffic-stop-police-accountability.

Heumann, M., & Cassak, L. (2003). *Good cop, bad cop: Racial profiling and competing views of justice*. New York: Peter Lang.

Higgins, G. E., Vito, G. F., & Grossi, E. L. (2012). The impact of race on the police decision to search during a traffic stop: A focal concerns theory perspective. *Journal of Contemporary Criminal Justice, 28*(2), 166-183. https://doi.org/10.1177/1043986211425725

Hurwitz, J., & Peffley, M. (1997). Public perceptions of race and crime: The role of racial stereotypes. *American Journal of Political Science, 41*(2), 375-401. https://doi.org/10.2307/2111769

Jones-Brown, D., & Maule, B. A. (2010). Racially biased policing: A review of the judicial and legislative literature. In S. K. Rice, & M. D. White, *Race, ethnicity, and policing: New and essential readings* (pp. 140-173). New York: New York University Press.

Kamalu, N. C. (2016). African Americans and racial profiling by U.S. law enforcement: An analysis of police traffic stops and searches of motorists in Nebraska (2002-2007). *African Journal of Criminology and Justice Studies, 9*(1), 187-206.

Klahm, C. F., & Tillyer, R. (2015). Rethinking the measurement of officer experience and its role in traffic stop searches. *Police Quarterly, 18*(4), 343-367. https://doi.org/10.1177/1098611115585315

Kraska, P. B. (2001). Crime control as warfare: Language matters. In P. Kraska, *Militarizing the American criminal justice system* (pp. 14-28). Boston: Northeastern University Press.

Kraska, P. B., & Kappeler, V. E. (1997). Militarizing American police: The rise and normalization of paramilitary units. *Social Problems, 44*(1), 1-117. https://doi.org/10.2307/3096870

LaFave, W. R. (2004a). *Search and seizure: A treatise on the Fourth Amendment* (Vol. 4). West Group Publishing.

LaFave, W. R. (2004b). The "routine traffic stop" from start to finish: Too much "routine," not enough Fourth Amendment. *Michigan Law Review, 102*(8), 1843-1905. https://doi.org/10.2307/4141969

Lai, C. K., Skinner, A. L., Cooley, E., Murrar, S., Brauer, M., Devos, T., ... Nosek, B. A. (2016). Reducing implicit racial preferences: II. Intervention effectiveness across time. *Journal of Experimental Psychology: General, 145*(8), 1001-1016. https://doi.org/10.1037/xge0000179

Lever, A. (2007). What's wrong with racial profiling? Another look at the problem. *Criminal Justice Ethics, 26*(1), 20-28. https://doi.org/10.1080/0731129X.2007.9992208

Levit, J. K. (1996). Pretextual traffic stops: United States v. Whren and the Death of Terry v. Ohio. *Loyola University Chicago Law Journal, 28*(1/5), 145-187.

Lundman, R. J. (2010). Are police reported driving while Black data a valid indicator of race and ethnicity of the traffic law violators police stop? A negative answer with minor qualifications. *Journal of Criminal Justice, 38*(1), 77-87. https://doi.org/10.1016/j.jcrimjus.2009.11.010

Lundman, R. J., & Kaufman, R. L. (2003). Driving while black: Effects of race, ethnicity, and gender on citizen self-reports of traffic stops and police actions. *Criminology, 41*(1), 195-219. https://doi.org/10.1111/j.1745-9125.2003.tb00986.x

McGlinchy, J. C. (2018). "Was that a yes or no?" Reviewing voluntariness in consent searches. *Virginia Law Review, 104*(2), 301-340.

Meehan, A. J., & Ponder, M. C. (2002). Race and place: The ecology of racial profiling African American motorists. *Justice Quarterly, 19*(3), 399-430. https://doi.org/10.1080/07418820200095291

Miller, K. (2008). Police stops, pretext, and racial profiling: Explaining warning and ticket stops using citizen self-reports. *Journal of Ethnicity in Criminal Justice, 6*(2), 123-149. https://doi.org/10.1080/15377930802096496

Miller, K. (2009). Race, driving, and police organization: Modeling moving and nonmoving traffic stops with citizen self-reports of driving practices. *Journal of Criminal Justice*, *37*(6), 564–575. https://doi.org/10.1016/j.jcrimjus.2009.09.005

Neil, R., & Winship, C. (2019). Methodological challenges and opportunities in testing for racial discrimination in policing. *Annual Review of Criminology*, *2*(1), 73–98. https://doi.org/10.1146/annurev-criminol-011518-024731

New York City Department of Transportation (NYC DOT). (2018a). *Automated speed enforcement program report 2014-2017*. New York: New York City Department of Transportation.

New York City Department of Transportation (NYC DOT). (2018b). *Strategic plan 2017 progress report*. New York: New York City Department of Transportation.

Novak, K. J. (2004). Disparity and racial profiling in traffic enforcement. *Police Quarterly*, *7*(1), 65–96. https://doi.org/10.1177/1098611102250359

Nowacki, J. S., & Spencer, T. (2019). Police discretion, organizational characteristics, and traffic stops: An analysis of racial disparity in Illinois. *International Journal of Police Science & Management*, *21*(1), 4–16.

Pickerill, J. M., Mosher, C., & Pratt, T. (2009). Search and seizure. racial profiling, and traffic stops: A disparate impact framework. *Law & Policy*, *31*(1), 1–31. https://doi.org/10.1111/j.1467-9930.2008.00282.x

Pryor, M., Buchanan, K. S., & Goff, P. A. (2020). Risky situations: Sources of racial disparity in police behavior. *Annual Review of Law and Social Science*, *16*(1), 343–360. https://doi.org/10.1146/annurev-lawsocsci-101518-042633

Ram, A. (2015, May 3). *It's your right to film the police. These apps can help*. Wired. Retrieved from https://www.wired.com/2015/05/right-film-police-apps-can-help/

Reisig, M. D., McCluskey, J. D., Mastrofski, S. D., & Terrill, W. (2004). Suspect disrespect toward the police. *Police Quarterly*, *21*, 241–269.

Ridgeway, G. (2006). Assessing the effect of race bias in post-traffic stop outcomes using propensity scores. *Journal of Quantitative Criminology*, *22*(1), 1–29. https://doi.org/10.1007/s10940-005-9000-9

Ridgeway, G., & MacDonald, J. (2010). Methods for assessing racially biased policing. In S. K. Rice & M. D. White, *Race, ethnicity, and policing: New and essential readings* (pp. 180–204). New York and London: NYU Press.

Roh, S., & Robinson, M. (2009). A geographic approach to racial profiling: The microanalysis and macroanalysis of racial disparity in traffic stops. *Police Quarterly*, *12*(2), 137–169. https://doi.org/10.1177/1098611109332422

Rosenbaum, P., & Rubin, D. (1985). Constructing a control group using multivariate matched sampling methods that incorporate the propensity score. *The American Statistician*, *39*(1), 33–38.

Rosenfeld, R., Rojek, J., & Decker, S. (2012). Age matters: Race differences in police searches of young and older male drivers. *Journal of Research in Crime and Delinquency*, *49*(1), 31–55. https://doi.org/10.1177/0022427810397951

Schafer, J. A., Carter, D. L., Katz-Bannister, A. J., & Wells, W. M. (2006). Decision making in traffic stop encounters: A multivariate analysis of police behavior. *Police Quarterly*, *9*(2), 184–209. https://doi.org/10.1177/1098611104264990

Skolnick, J. H., & Caplovitz, A. (2004). Guns, drugs, and profiling: Ways to target guns and minimize racial profiling. *Arizona Law Review*, *43*, 413–437.

Smith, M. R., & Alpert, G. P. (2007). Explaining police bias: A theory of social conditioning and illusory correlation. *Criminal Justice and Behavior*, *34*(10), 1262–1283. https://doi.org/10.1177/0093854807304484

Smith, M. R., & Petrocelli, M. (2001). Racial profiling? A multivariate analysis of police traffic stop data. *Police Quarterly*, *4*(1), 4–27. https://doi.org/10.1177/1098611101004001001

Smith, R. J., & Levinson, J. D. (2011). The impact of implicit racial bias on the exercise of prosecutorial discretion. *Seattle University Law Review*, *35*, 795–826.

Spencer, K. B., Charbonneau, A. K., & Glaser, J. (2016). Implicit bias and policing. *Social and Personality Psychology Compass*, *10*(1), 50–63. https://doi.org/10.1111/spc3.12210

Steinbock, D. J. (2001). The wrong line between freedom and restraint: The unreality, obscurity, and incivility of the Fourth Amendment consensual encounter doctrine. *San Diego Law Review*, *38*, 507–563.

Swencionis, J. K., & Goff, P. A. (2017). The psychological science of racial bias and policing. *Psychology, Public Policy, and Law*, *23*(4), 398–409. https://doi.org/10.1037/law0000130

Tillyer, R., & Engel, R. S. (2013). The impact of drivers' race, gender, and age during traffic stops: Assessing interaction terms and the social conditioning model. *Crime & Delinquency*, *59*(3), 369–395.

Tillyer, R., Klahm, IV, C. F., & Engel, R. S. (2012). The discretion to search: A multilevel examination of driver demographics and officer characteristics. *Journal of Contemporary Criminal Justice*, *28*(2), 184–205. https://doi.org/10.1177/1043986211425721

Transportation Alternatives. (2020). *The case for self-enforcing streets: How reallocating a portion of the NYPD budget to the DOT can reduce the harm of racial bias and improve safety for all New Yorkers*. New York: Transportation Alternatives.

Van Duizend, R., Sutton, L. P., & Carter-Ymauchi, C. A. (1985). *The search warrant process: Preconceptions, perceptions and practices*. Williamsburg, VA: National Center for State Courts.

Vito, A. G., Griffin, V. W., Vito, G. F., & Higgins, G. E. (2020). Does daylight matter"? An examination of racial bias in traffic stops by police. *Policing: An International Journal*.

Vito, A. G., Grossi, E. L., & Higgins, G. E. (2018). Analyzing racial profiling from traffic searches: Using focal concerns theory and propensity score matching. *Policing*, *41*(6), 721–733. https://doi.org/10.1108/PIJPSM-06-2017-0081

Warren, P., Tomaskovic-Devey, D., Smith, W., Zingraff, M., & Mason, M. (2006). Driving while Black: Bias processes and racial disparity in police stops. *Criminology*, *44*(3), 709–738. https://doi.org/10.1111/j.1745-9125.2006.00061.x

Whorf, R. (1997). Coercive ambiguity' in the routine traffic stop turned consent search. *Suffolk University Law Review*, *30*(2), 379–413.

Whren v. United States, 517 U.S. 806. (1996). The Supreme Court.

Withrow, B. L. (2007). When Whren won't work: The effects of a diminished capacity to initiate a pretextual stop on police officer behavior. *Police Quarterly*, *10*(4), 351–370. https://doi.org/10.1177/1098611106293681

Worden, R. E., McLean, S. J., Engel, R. S., Cochran, H., Corsaro, N., Reynolds, D., & Isaza, G. T. (2020). *The impacts of implicit bias awareness training in the NYPD*. The John F. Finn Institute for Public Safety/University of Cincinnati Center for Police Research and Policy.

"I'm afraid of cops:" black protesters' and residents' perceptions of policing in the United States

Jennifer Cobbina-Dungy

ABSTRACT
Proactive policing strategies produce a wide range of harms to African Americans. Research on attitudes towards police show that citizen distrust is more widespread among Blacks than Whites. However, we know less about how gender intersects with race and neighborhood context in determining whether and why Black people fear the police. Here, I build from the insights of previous research by providing a contextual examination of the gendered nature of fear of the police among Black protesters and residents of Ferguson, Missouri and Baltimore, Maryland. Drawing from a larger qualitative study of race, policing, and protests following Michael Brown's and Freddie Gray's deaths, I examine 155 Black men's and women's accounts of why they do or do not fear the police. Policy implications are discussed, along with concrete recommendations for reducing anti-Black racism in police policy and practice.

It is well documented that the relationship between Black people and the police has been contentious throughout American history. From the very beginning of American society, the police, first in the form of slave patrols (which were charged with capturing, terrorizing, and returning runaway slaves), and later in the form of official police departments, have historically engaged in racially biased policing and enforced unjust laws (Bass, 2001a, 2001b). As a result of police officers' long history of violence and aggression toward Black people, Blacks are more likely than Whites and Latinx to have negative encounters with the police (Brunson, 2007; Cobbina, 2019; Russell-Brown, 2009), which drives their attitudes toward law enforcement (Boyles, 2015; Weitzer & Tuch, 2005).

However, important gaps remain in our understanding of the nature of attitudes toward the police. First, most studies focus their examination of police-civilian relations on Black males and their treatment by the police. Fewer have paid specific attention to how gender intersects with race and neighborhood context in determining whether and why Black women fear the police. However, evidence suggests that the outcome of police-civilian encounters is shaped by gender (Cobbina, Conteh, & Emrich, 2019). Second, while previous research has documented that Black people distrust the police, few studies explore whether and why Black people fear the police. This is surprising because fear is an emotion that can influence attitudes and behaviors (Tannenbaum et al., 2015). While "police forces are a visible branch of state authority legally entrusted to protect society and maintain order by force when deemed necessary" (Roche & Oberwittler, 2018, p. 3), police use of deadly force, violence, and aggression against unarmed minority civilians does little to instill confidence in the police among Black people and may leave them uncertain as to what to expect when confronted by law enforcement officials. Consequently, fear of the police can exacerbate distrust between Black civilians and law enforcement authorities.

Against the backdrop of high-profile police killings that garnered national media attention, this study analyzes the accounts of Black protesters and Ferguson and Baltimore residents' perceptions of the police. Drawing from in-depth interviews, the present study investigates whether and why Ferguson and Baltimore residents and protesters fear the police. Specifically, this study examines whether there are key similarities and differences among Black men's and women's perceptions of police.

Race, gender, neighborhood characteristics, and perceptions of the police

A large body of literature on attitudes toward police shows that citizen distrust is more prevalent among Blacks than Whites (Sampson & Bartusch, 1998; Weitzer & Tuch, 2002). Research examining the relationship between civilians' perceptions and the context of interactions with law enforcement suggests that unfavorable views of the police result from negative police encounters (Boyles, 2015; Brunson, 2007; Cobbina, 2019). Personal contact with the police is a central factor that drives attitudes toward the police. Blacks are more likely to experience police-initiated contact than Whites (Harris, 1999), and negative (involuntary and voluntary) police-initiated contact, by its very nature, generally results in unfavorable views (Huebner, Schafer, & Bynum, 2004; Webb & Marshall, 1995). According to Weitzer and Tuch (2002), "net of other factors, race and personal experience with racial profiling are among the strongest and most consistent of attitudes toward the police" (p. 445). In other words, direct experiences with racial discrimination can have enduring detrimental effects on people's perception of law enforcement (Weitzer & Tuch, 2002).

In addition, police actions are ecologically patterned. Considerable research shows that African Americans reside in areas with the most concentrated disadvantage (Massey, 1995; Massey & Denton, 1993; Wilson, 1996). Large urban Black communities remain highly segregated, endure high levels of poverty, and face extreme racial isolation (Massey & Fischer, 2000). Thus, it is not surprising that crime takes place in these areas, as criminal activity thrives in areas faced with economic, social, and political isolation (Massey, 1995). It is within these enclaves where the relationship between police and civilians is at its worst, as "[t]he intensity of poverty, crime, and general disorder in the locale affects the amount, type, and quality of policing that citizens receive" (Brunson & Gau, 2015, p. 219).

Aggressive order maintenance police strategies are disproportionately concentrated in economically distressed neighborhoods (Terrill & Reisig, 2003). The US National Academies' Committee on Proactive Policing (Natl. Acad. Sci. Eng. Med. 2018, p. 1) defines proactive policing as referring to "all policing strategies that have as one of their goals the prevention or reduction of crime and disorder and that are not reactive in terms of focusing primarily on uncovering ongoing crime or on investigating or responding to crimes once they have occurred." Although such efforts are designed to control crime, policies focused on proactive intervention extend a historical pattern of racialized criminalization in the use of police stops, searches, and force (Epp, Maynard-Moody, & Haider-Markel, 2014; Jones-Brown, Gill, & Trone, 2010; Terrill & Reisig, 2003). This, in turn, shapes attitudinal responses often fueling resentment toward law enforcement (Rios, Prieto, & Ibarra, 2020). Because police practices vary by geographical location, the over-representation of Black individuals among the urban poor means that this group is more likely to experience the harsh enforcement styles of policing practiced in impoverished, disorganized, and high-crime neighborhoods (Anderson 1999; Brunson & Miller, 2006a, 2006b). Diverse experiences among individuals who reside in distressed areas include greater levels of being watched and detained (Jones-Brown, 2000), racially profiled (Weitzer & Tuch, 2005), searched and arrested (Epp, Maynard-Moody, & Haider-Markel, 2014), officer misconduct (Brunson, 2007), slower response time and less police services (Anderson, 1999), becoming the recipient of physical and deadly force (Brunson, 2007; Cobbina, 2019; Terrill & Reisig, 2003), and perceptions that police in general treat people differently based on race (Brunson, 2007; Cobbina, 2019).

Even though direct personal encounters with police shape attitudes toward law enforcement, research shows that vicarious experiences – secondhand information from other people or the media – also play a role. Vicarious encounters affect views of the police. For example, in their examination of the effects police experiences have on perceptions of the police, Rosenbaum, Schuck, Costello, Hawkins, and Ring (2005) found that vicarious interactions had an impact on attitudes toward police, and this was greater for Blacks than Whites. They also found that Blacks and Latinos were more likely to learn about adverse vicarious experiences with the police primarily through family, friends, and neighbors while Whites were more likely to receive such reports through the media. Evidence also reveals that high profile media cases of police violence increase minorities' distrust of the police (Weitzer, 2002). Yet, few studies have examined whether distrust in the police translates to fear of police.

While many studies have explored the role of race and policing, most have focused on the negative police interactions involving Black men (Brunson, 2007; Brunson & Miller, 2006a; Jones-Brown, 2007). Even though scholars have increasingly examined the plight of Black women in the criminal legal system (Collins, 2000; Jones, 2010), only a few studies examine the perceptions of and experiences that Black women have with the police. For instance, in her book, *Arrested Justice*, Beth Richie (2012) called attention to the plight of Black women, as their social location left them socially stigmatized and increasingly susceptible to male violence and criminalization. She revealed how reluctant Black women are to call police in cases of intimate partner violence because police and the rest of the legal system are focused on using criminalization to manage family crises in ways that are ultimately harmful instead of providing them with resources and tools to overcome these crises. Likewise, in her book, *Invisible No More,* Andrea Ritchie (2017) highlights the various forms of police violence with women of color, as well as how race, gender, sexual orientation, and ability shape the expression of police brutality.

A few studies have compared the experiences of Black women and men regarding the interactions with law enforcement. Brunson and Miller (2006b) underscored police-initiated involvement they had with police, which was characterized by disrespectful, combative, and hostile treatment. On the other hand, Black women frequently reported police harassment due to violation of curfew, and at times, were subject to police sexual violence. Contrary to young men, young women held that the role of the police is to protect and serve community residents and respond to victims of crime. Moreover, in their examination of how Black men and women respond to police encounters, Cobbina et al. (2019) found that the strategies civilians employed are common across both genders (i.e., question police, comply, combination of questioning and complying); however, the police–civilian outcome is demonstrably shaped by gender. That is, Black men were more likely to be recipients of arrests, incarceration, and police violence than their female counterparts. However, Black women who did not acquiesce to the instructions of law enforcement were either free to go or received a ticket for a traffic violation.

Despite these studies, what is absent from much of the research is consideration of whether and to what extent fear of the police is gendered. Specifically, we know little about how gender intersects with race and place in shaping Black people's expectations of law enforcement and the nature of police/civilian interactions. Below, I examine the extent to which Black Ferguson and Baltimore residents and protesters fear the police and whether there are key similarities and variations among Black men's and women's emotional reactions toward law enforcement.

Methods

Data for this study hail from a larger study of neighborhood violence and policing. The current investigation is based on qualitative in-depth interviews with 155 Black protesters and residents of Ferguson, Missouri and Baltimore, Maryland. Interviews were conducted in October and November 2014 in Ferguson and in July 2015 in Baltimore. Prior to the beginning of each interview, the research team[1] outlined the study objectives, obtained informed consent, assured confidentiality, and guaranteed respondents that they would be compensated $40 for their participation.

Sampling was purposive in nature. Using a maximum variation sampling strategy, the goal was to capture a wide range of varying perspectives regarding the police. Effort was made to target a heterogeneous sample of protesters and residents of Ferguson and Baltimore across race, gender, and age, which yielded a nonprobability sample. Youth were recruited to participate in the project if they lived in Ferguson/Baltimore or engaged in some form of community action (e.g., protests, marches, rallies, etc.) following Michael Brown's and Freddie Gray's deaths. Several different approaches were used to recruit participants. First, effort was made to purposefully recruit from locations where young people were present, as many protests in both Ferguson and Baltimore originated from younger activists. As a result, a flyer describing the research project was placed on my Facebook and Twitter accounts and dispersed to social justice and activist networks that were active on social media. Second, the project announcement was shared with prominent city community members with affiliations in churches, community colleges, and universities and with both newly established and long-standing citizen-led grassroots initiatives. Third, to reach Ferguson's and Baltimore's older demographic, flyers were posted and distributed at the local public library and an advertisement was placed in the employment section of a local newspaper serving the Black community.

Data collection began with a brief survey, which collected demographic information. This was followed by a digitally recorded in-depth interview where primary contextual and perceptual information was collected. The interviews were semi-structured with open-ended questions that allowed for considerable probing. Respondents were asked to describe their reaction to the news about the deaths of Michael Brown and Freddie Gray, and what had been happening in their city. This was followed by asking respondents their perceptions of how police handled the outcry from members in the community. They were then asked to discuss positive and negative interactions they had with local police before and after the deaths of Brown and Gray. They were questioned about whether they were afraid of police and their reasons for having such perceptions. The current study draws from responses to the latter question.

Interviews lasted approximately one hour. Interviews were conducted in several locations across the Greater St. Louis and Baltimore metropolitan area, including in a conference room at a local university and public library, in fast food restaurants, coffee shops, and a private office in a church. All interviews were transcribed verbatim and serve as the primary data.

Black people are the focus here because research has identified them as the group that is most likely to experience involuntary police contacts (Weitzer & Tuch, 2006). Few studies have offered an in-depth examination of the nature of Black women's perceptions of and experiences with the police (but see Brunson & Miller, 2006a, 2006b; Richie, 2012; Ritchie, 2017) and how that shapes fear of the police. This study allows for a detailed examination of these issues with Black men and women. The interviews explore their perceptions of the police and their direct and indirect experiences with officers.

To begin the analysis, all relevant data were sorted into a dataset, which included respondents' response to whether they feared the police. Inductive analytic techniques were used to identify common themes. That is, effort was made to ensure that the concepts developed and described below typify the most common patterns in respondents' accounts. This determination was achieved using grounded theory methods, including the search for and examination of outlier cases (Strauss, 1987). In addition, comparisons were made to search for potential differences across gender and place.

Table 1. Select neighborhood characteristics.

	Ferguson	St. Louis County	Baltimore	Baltimore County
Population Size	21,203	998,883	621,849	805,029
Median Family Income[a]	$40,660	$59,520	$41,819	$66,940
Percent Black	67.4	23.3	63.7	26.1
Female-headed Families w/ Children[b]	15.3	7.6	11.3	7.6
Percent Poverty	22.7	9.6	24.2	9.8
Percent Unemployment[b]	8.0	5.4	8.6	5.0

Source: US Census, 2010.

Study setting

Table 1 provides a comparison of demographic and socioeconomic indicators for residents in Ferguson and Baltimore with their surrounding counties. Two thirds of the population in both cities are Black compared to 23 and 26 percent of the population in St. Louis County and Baltimore County, respectively. Ferguson and Baltimore are characterized by high rates of female-headed households and unemployment, which exceeds those residing in the county. The proportion of poverty is two times greater in both Ferguson and Baltimore City than in St. Louis County and Baltimore County. Residents of Ferguson have a median income nearly $20,000 less than those residing in St. Louis County. Likewise, Baltimore residents have a median income $25,000 less that those living in Baltimore County. Overall, individuals residing in the cities of Ferguson and Baltimore fare worse on several socioeconomic indicators when compared to individuals living in St. Louis County and Baltimore County.

Findings

Table 2 provides a basic description of the sample. This study included 155 Black protesters from Baltimore and Ferguson. The Ferguson sample included 87 protesters (43 males and 44 females). These respondents ranged in age from 18 to 74, with a mean age of 36 years. As it relates to educational status, the modal category was some college; that is, respondents were currently in college or had taken some college coursework. Most of the respondents reported being employed either part- or full-time (N = 55) at the time of the interview. Regarding place of residence, 57 reported living in Ferguson for an average of 9 years. The rest resided in the broader St. Louis area for an average of 16 years.

The Baltimore sample included 68 protesters (27 males and 41 females). Respondents ranged in age from 19 to 86, with a mean age of 46 years. In terms of educational status, most completed a high school diploma/GED. As it relates to economic standing, 40 were unemployed while the remainder reported part- or full-time employment. In terms of place of residence, 65 were from Baltimore and lived in the city for an average of 11 years. Only 3 Baltimore protesters reported residing outside of the city, with an average residence length of 6 years.

Of the 155 participants in the study, there were five cases of missing data. The qualitative analysis as to whether Black people fear the police was based on the valid responses to questions about why people may or may not fear law enforcement; that is, 150 Black participants explained why they personally were or were not afraid of the police.

Table 2. Demographics characteristics of protesters (N = 155)

	Baltimore N = 68	Ferguson N = 87
Gender		
Male	27	43
Female	41	44
Age		
Mean	46	36
Range	19-86	18-74
*Education**		
Some elementary	10	1
Some high school	6	4
High school diploma/GED	26	21
Some college	9	43
Associate/Bachelor degree	7	13
Graduate degree	10	4
Economic standing		
Unemployed	40	32
Part/Full time	28	55
Residence		
Baltimore	65	
Non-Baltimore	3	
Ferguson		57
St. Louis area		30
*Years in residence (Mean)***		
Baltimore	11	
Non-Baltimore	6	
Ferguson		9
St. Louis area		16

Source: US Census, 2010.
*Data missing for one person in Ferguson.
**Data missing for two people in Baltimore; three people in Ferguson.

Afraid of the police

In the current study, one-quarter (N = 40) of the participants stated they were afraid of law enforcement. Of those who feared the police, twice as many women (N = 27) as men (N = 13) reported such fear. Those from Ferguson (N = 32) were much more likely to report being afraid of the police than those from Baltimore (N = 8). The common reasons given include police intimidation, previous direct negative experiences with police, and being afraid of mistreatment.

Police intimidation

One-third of those who feared the police expressed feeling a level of intimidation from law enforcement. An equivalent number of men (N = 6) and women (N = 7) expressed such sentiments with most from Ferguson (N = 10) instead of Baltimore (N = 3). Some Ferguson residents perceived that they were stereotyped by officers who viewed them as suspicious and "criminal" because of their race. Javon stated he feared being shot by the police because "I speak my mind … [the police] don't like me, and I'm a young Black male." And Latoya feared that "I will be targeted because of my demographic." This was tied to geographic location, as poor neighborhoods were more likely to be heavily policed. Baltimore resident, Donald, explained:

> Certain spots like, you know, [police can] pick you up and search you, you know in a heartbeat .... [But] .... you can go to some part of like on the Westside, you know like where there [are] real quiet neighborhoods, you know. You can walk down the street with maybe a pound of cocaine and whatnot and the police wouldn't even stop and question you or nothing. But on this side [of town] you walk in ... they're going to pick you up and search you, pat you down.

Likewise, asked if he was afraid of the police, Ferguson resident, Marquis, asserted: "Sometimes you are. Like, I would rather stay at home because this area right here is Normandy .... So you drive through here and Ferguson ... and you feel intimidation. If anything is wrong with your vehicle or something, they will find a reason to give you a ticket." And Dyshelle asserted, after having been stopped while traveling in a predominately White neighborhood, "I felt like I was pushed into the stereotype of Black people here in St. Louis." These accounts coincide with reports from the Department of Justice that the Ferguson Police Department and courts engaged in a pattern of unconstitutional police and court practices that was aimed at Black residents (DOJ, 2015). The DOJ's report concluded that police officers functioned as street-level enforcers for policies that used fines and fees to extract resources from poor communities of color and deliver them to municipal coffers. These practices were aggressively promoted by city officials.

Negative direct and indirect experiences with police

Of those who feared the police, 30 percent (N = 12), all of whom were from Ferguson except one, reported that they were afraid of police because they had experienced unfavorable encounters with them. Women (N = 10) were more likely than men (N = 2) to report prior negative encounters, which led them to fear the police. In fact, at times, participants in the study called the police for protection *but* they ended up arrested or harmed by the police. Isabelle, a Ferguson resident, asserted: "One time I did call [the police] on my ex-husband and I got arrested because I had a warrant. I did have a traffic warrant." And Crystal, a resident of Ferguson, explained a retaliatory incident she faced after calling the police for help:

> [B]ack in 2011 one morning I was on my way to work ... and there was a pit bull that was always loose .... I called the police department ... [a]nd they said, "Well, we'll send somebody out." So as I'm getting ready for work, I'm looking out the window and I see the dog across the street, and I see the police drive past .... So I called back and I said, "The police officer that just drove down the street didn't see the dog." I said, "It was a woman too." I said, "I don't think you all should send a woman here to even be bothered with this pit bull .... So as I was getting

ready, I heard a knock on the door, and they came to the door. And I said, "Yeah, the dog was across the street." And they said, "We're not here for the dog. You have a warrant. You're under arrest."

After finding out she was jailed for having been stopped a few years ago for an issue pertaining to her car muffler, Crystal lamented, "It was something so minor and so petty." She later learned what happened when she confronted the officer while being booked in jail:

> I said, "I called about a dog … [b]ecause the pound told me to call the police department." And the lady [police officer] said, "Well maybe if they would have sent a man out first, maybe you wouldn't be here." And I said, "Oh, I get it. I get it. So apparently you must have got offended." And she said, "I'm not saying nothing" …. It killed my spirit from that point on …where I don't even want to call [the police] for anything.

The retaliatory action by the police toward Crystal ultimately colored her view of law enforcement for the worst. Likewise, Rosalind from Ferguson, remarked: "I called the police one time [because] I had a dispute with a neighbor and they just came to fight, they didn't come to ask questions. Knocked at my door, just grabbed me out the house … [and] I was beat up by the police."

While some experienced police violence and misconduct after having initiated contact to receive help, others were subject to involuntary police contacts. Justin, a resident of Baltimore, explained that while walking down the street in his neighborhood with a friend and his wife:

> I heard the police again say, "get on the ground." And I'm looking back, and saying, "he's not really talking to me is he?" And so I stopped. He said, "if I tell you to get on the ground again, I'm going to shoot you in the back." A White policeman. I said, "okay. He's talking to me." So, I stopped. I've never been through this. So, he's like "get on the ground" …. I got on my knees like, and just like that down on my knees, like, "okay, like this." And he says, "no, get on the ground." So I'm like, "what do you mean?" He said, "get on the ground." It's like, it came to me. Get. On. The ground …. [He said] "if I tell you again, I'm going to shoot you in your back." So I got on the ground, completely. Stretched out, it was cold, it was wintertime, I'll never forget.

Justin and his friends were arrested for drinking beer in public, which they refuted, and were released 36 hours later without he or his friends being charged. It is worth noting that even if Justin and his friends consumed an alcoholic beverage in public, such an act is an infraction to be punishable by fine. It certainly is not worth being shot at by an officer. It is that threat of extreme force for a minor infraction, which caused Justin to fear the police more generally.

Moreover, it was not uncommon for Black men and women to be viewed with suspicion and find themselves the targets of racial profiling. Dyshelle explained that while traveling in a predominately White, affluent neighborhood in St. Louis, she was pulled over because "I had tints on my windows, it was an '04 Taurus, a pretty big car …. I was going past [the police and] she made a U-turn and pulled behind me …. She told me and my friend to get out of the car and set us on the curb in a busy intersection." When asked why she was stopped, the officer responded, "I smelt marijuana." Dyshelle was upset because not only was it impossible for the officer to smell drugs in her car since they were both in their vehicles but "I don't smoke marijuana [and] I don't let nobody smoke marijuana in my car …. [Yet, the officer called] two other cop cars and dogs and everything…. It was embarrassing." Dyshelle was especially upset because not only was she not engaging in any behavior deemed to be suspicious, but she believed that she was racially profiled because she was Black and had tints on her car windows.

While some had directly experienced unfavorable treatment from police, others witnessed abusive treatment by officers. Ferguson resident Shaniqua said that she feared the police because "on many occasions [I'm] riding past, I'll be like 'oh my God, why that police got him on the ground?' And then they always have to put their foot in the back of your neck. What is all that for? To me, the police just use excessive force." As a result, Justin from Baltimore admitted, "I'm afraid of what [the police] might do." This fear is steeped in the fact that police represent the state who are called to protect and serve. But as Ebony noted, the police are "the law [so] what can you say? Because it's usually their word against yours."

Afraid of mistreatment from police

Of those who feared the police, 23 percent (N=9), all who were from Ferguson except one, narrated that they were afraid of police mistreating them. Such statements were commonly made by Black women (N=7) rather than men (N=2).[2] There was a sense among some Black women residing in Ferguson that they would be treated unfairly when they encounter officers. For example, Leonetta stated: "it's not a fair situation that you're in with the police. I mean, you never know what's going to happen or how it's going to go down. So yes, I am afraid of the police." And Shaniqua asserted, "I'm afraid of them more so than them helping me." When asked why that was the case, she explained:

> [J]ust say if me and somebody was into it … and I called the police. Then the police come. Then he might come with an attitude for something that happened on his other call. And then, especially if it's me and a White person, then I know nine times out of ten, I'm going to be totally in the wrong to him. And then ain't no telling how he might act. The next thing I know, I'm slammed on the ground or any of that. And that's one of my fears. I hope to God the police never have to slam me on the ground because I see the way they slam people on the ground.

And some viewed the police as corrupt individuals who engage in wrongdoing. Rosalind said she was afraid of the police because "of the way they come, their attitude, [and] ... the things that they do. They place drugs on people in my community." As a result, Arlene remarked that even though "I have no warrants [and] I've never had any ... I would run before I would ask them for help." With the high-profile police killings of Michael Brown, Freddie Gray, and countless other Black individuals, some had a fear of being murdered by law enforcement. Javon acknowledged, "I'm not really afraid of [the police]. The only thing I'm afraid of is probably one of them catching me on the back street and killing me ... that they could do me like they did Mike Brown." It is worth noting that while Javon states that he's not afraid of the police, he expounds on being fearful that he could end up killed by law enforcement. No doubt, the killing of Michael Brown by Darren Wilson coupled with the fact that Wilson was not charged for Brown's death left Javon concerned that he could become a victim of police violence. For some, fear of the police is driven by their unpredictable and unreliable nature, which, in turn, left many stressed about the outcome of potential police interactions.

Not afraid of police

While some Black adults in the sample reported being afraid of the police, the majority reported not being fearful of law enforcement. In particular, of the 150 responses, 73% (N = 110) said they were not afraid of the police. An even distribution of response to this question was found, as 51 percent (N = 56) of men reported not being afraid compared to 49 percent (N = 54) of women. However, Baltimore residents were more likely than Ferguson residents to say that they did not fear the police. Specifically, of the 110 respondents who reported not being afraid of the police, 54 percent (N = 59) were from Baltimore and 46 percent (N = 51) were from Ferguson.[3]

While the vast majority of respondents stated that they were not afraid of the police, their explanation for not being afraid varied. For example, the most common reasons given include police are human, respondents follow the law, they know how to behave if stopped by police, and they remain hyper-aware of police.

Police are "human just like me"

Of those respondents who were not afraid of the police, 28 percent (N = 31) reported that police were human just like them, which was evenly split among Ferguson (N = 15) and Baltimore (N = 16) residents. Specifically, 61 percent (N = 19) of men and 39 percent of women (N = 12) emphasized the humanity of officers. Nekeisha from Ferguson asserted, "I'm not afraid of police officers because they're human just like me, they bleed just like I bleed. They put their pants on one leg at a time everyday just like I do …. They're no gods, so I don't fear them. I would never fear them." For some, they feared no one but God. Ferguson resident Keanu explained:

> First, being spiritual, I don't fear anyone but God Himself. If you mean I understand what they can do, what some of them can do – because what they think they can do as far as the law is concerned and how the law backs them up as far as me getting hurt and them accusing me of doing something, I fear that. As far as what they can do on paper. But as far as a man concerned, I don't fear them at all.

While he reported not fearing anyone but God, Keanu did admit having concerns as to what the police could potentially do. His focus was not on a generalized fear of police officers themselves but a reasonable perception of becoming the recipient of police injury and having a system that backs the behavior of state officials if he is accused of a crime by the police.

Others reported not being fearful of anyone. Keston, a resident of Ferguson, stated, "I'm not afraid of the police … because they're human just like I am. I am not afraid of any man." Some made a conscious decision not to live in fear despite being confronted with the reality that there were reasons to be apprehensive of the police. Nia, from Ferguson, noted that "my ego won't allow me to say that I'm afraid of the police…. I can't walk on this earth allowing myself to be fearful of that." Notwithstanding, she admitted, "I am afraid for us as a community because of what happens with the police. I'm afraid for my African American son because of what they can do, and what they have done, and the reasons why they do it." Yet even still, Nia refused "to teach my son to live" in fear of the police. In a similar vein, Jerry, who resided in Baltimore, explained: "I'm not afraid of police. But that's a decision. I think fear is a decision you know. I'm not afraid. I've decided not to be afraid of the police. But that does not erase the reality that I have to fear the police." As a visible branch of state authority in which police act with relative impunity, some Black people realized they have much to fear. Yet, despite the larger pattern of police violence depicted throughout the nation, some Black men and women actively chose not to live in fear of the police.

Obey the law
Another common theme reported among those who said they were not afraid of the police was they were not involved in crime. Specifically, 18 percent (N = 20) of respondents felt they had no reason to fear the police because they obey the law. This sentiment was slightly more

common among men (N = 12) than women (N = 8) and common among both Ferguson (N = 9) and Baltimore (N = 11) residents in the sample. Perhaps not surprising, most believed that if they followed the law, then there was no reason to fear law enforcement. Of his perceptions of the police, Alex from Baltimore said, "I don't do nothing wrong to like affiliate myself with them wanting to bother me ... [so] I have no fear of them." When asked why she is not afraid of police, Ranisha, from Baltimore, said point blank "because I'm an upstanding citizen." Reginald, a Ferguson resident, explained: "I don't pose a threat beyond my race and ethnicity, so I have nothing to be fearful of .... If I haven't done anything that justifies police to take action on me, I don't feel like I have anything to worry about." Reginald's point is illustrative, as his statement indicates that he's well aware that his race alone can warrant suspicion from the police. Yet, even with that, he believed that prosocial behavior would not evoke attention of the police while criminal behavior would do so.

In fact, a few Baltimore residents discussed having a criminal past and their efforts to stay on the straight and narrow path precluded them from being apprehensive of law enforcement. Eddie, admitted that "when I was into drugs and stuff ... I used to [avoid police]." But now he states he is not fearful of the officers because "I try not to do anything where the law is going to even have to come into my life." Similarly, speaking of his criminal past, Jeffrey asserted, "I'm not living like I used to live ... So [I am] not afraid of them." Overall, many found solace in the belief that operating within the boundaries of the law would prevent them from encountering law enforcement; thus, they did not fear them.

Know how to act when confronted by police
Although many assumed that they would not be targeted by police because of their compliance with the law, they also believed that should they encounter law enforcement they know how to behave. In particular, 13 percent (N = 14) of people from Ferguson and Baltimore reported not being afraid of the police because they remained aware of how to comport themselves when they interact with officers. Specifically, 64 percent (N = 9) of men and 36 percent (N = 5) of women made such statements. Respecting state officials was commonly reported among participants for not being fearful of them. Asked if she was afraid of the police, Ferguson resident Nekeisha responded, "I'm not afraid of anyone. I respect the police and I will continue to respect them." In a similar fashion, Dennis, a Baltimore resident, lives by the principal that "an answer when mild turns away rage." He explained how his reactions have ultimately shaped interactions with the police:

> I was driving my car and I didn't know my license was expired because I had tickets I didn't pay and I was stopped. And the first thing the police told me when he stopped me after he had checked my ID and everything. He said, "I'm going to write here that you are very cooperative." He said, "I'm going to put that you did not give me any resistance, didn't give me any problem at all." He said, "I'm going to make sure I put that here in the report." So that, you know basically has been my whole experience with the police.

As a result, Dennis' interactions with the police have been positive because according to him, "the way I answer them, the way I talk to them it's respectful." Likewise, Clayton, a resident of Ferguson, understood his response to encounters with officers could shape police-civilian outcomes, as he asserted: "I'm not going to do something where it's going to risk my life or something like that." If stopped by the police, he said, "I can be calm, chill, keep my composure and be respectful and leave after that." Extant literature document that civilian response to police can shape the outcome of police-civilian interactions (Cobbina et al., 2019).

While Black men and women both emphasized the need to be respectful, some men in the sample underscored the need to be particularly deferential toward the police when stopped. Omar from Baltimore asserted that he was not afraid of police because "I'm articulate enough to address them and speak in a professional manner, so there's no way they're going to intimidate me." Likewise, Malik, a resident of Ferguson, asserted that if stopped by police it is important to "know how to phrase your words … [and say] 'yes sir, no sir' … [to] make this ordeal [end]." In a similar vein, Darius, a resident of Baltimore, claimed, "I wouldn't say I'm afraid, but I have to act a certain way to the police." When asked to clarify, he responded, "I've got to turn on my proper voice and [say] 'yes sir, no sir, yes ma'am, no ma'am,' and all that other sh*t." Though he understood how to negotiate police encounters, Darius was quite resentful about having to resort to such mannerism because "I don't say that on a regular basis so why would I say it to an officer?" Some, like Darius, felt it was necessary to subscribe to a social code of behavioral conduct to neutralize the presumption of guilt and/or threat that officers may associate with young Black individuals.

A few women also noted the need to silence their voice in order to avoid escalating a police encounter. Kayla, a Baltimore resident, noted that with "me being humble … I know how to keep my mouth closed and keep my thoughts to myself" when interacting with the police. Similarly, Edith, a resident of Baltimore, asserted that in the aftermath of Freddie Gray's death, "it makes me think of how to respond to [police]." She continued: "[I need] to be more humble for fear that I might just be one that they slang or twist on. There is a fear now of how do I respond to them. If I let them know I know my rights, will that be accepted, or will they disregard that and punish me for knowing my rights?" Both Edith and Kayla spoke about the need to be humble as well as silence one's voice as a strategy for navigating encounters with law enforcement. Understanding the stereotype that women should be silent and not answer back, a few women in the study were aware that violating such gender norms could result in being viewed as "difficult" by law enforcement. Overall, even though some asserted that they did not have a fear of officers, their concerns about police contact shaped their behavior.

Police have a job to protect and serve
Although many reported not being afraid of the police because officers were human, and respondents follow the law and know how to behave when confronted by the police, 14 percent (N = 15) reported not being afraid because they believe that police are simply doing their job. While an equivalent number of men (N = 7) and women (N = 8) made this assertion, such sentiments were common among Baltimore residents (N = 12) compared to Ferguson residents (N = 3). Interestingly, this statement was particularly common among older Black participants in the study. In fact, of the 15 respondents who reported this as a common theme, all were over the age of 40 years except for three people. Older participants perceived that officer's primary job is to protect the innocent and serve community residents by providing aid when needed. For example, 50-year-old Willie, a resident of Ferguson, said "most of the police officers believe in that oath." Of police, Candice from Baltimore said, "I look at them as a protector not as they are going to do me harm." Though as a 60-year-old woman, Candice admitted, "I mean I'm not 18 years old so maybe 18-year-olds have a different perspective. In my age category they are not – what are they going to do?"

As older respondents, they perceived themselves in need of protection by the police and expected officers to assist them when needed. And 54-year-old Lorraine from Baltimore asserted that she was not afraid of the police because "when the police come, they probably trying to do their job anyway." Likewise, Morris, a 58-year-old Baltimore resident, stated that "if someone tries to break into my house I'm going to call the police, [and] I expect them to serve." Overall, older participants were much more likely to report that the mission of police is to protect and serve residents.

Hyper-aware of police

While most reported not being afraid of the police, a smaller number (N = 7; 6 percent) noted being aware of police presence. A similar number of men (N = 4) and women (N = 3) reported being hyper-aware of law enforcement. Such sentiments were common among Ferguson (N = 4) and Baltimore (N = 3) residents. Often when asked if they fear the police, participants responded no but were quick to qualify their feelings toward police. For instance, of police, Baltimore resident Breeann stated, she has "a healthy aware[ness]" of law enforcement. And Chaundrise from Baltimore admitted, "I am more aware. Before if something happened, I would call them. And now, I would still probably call them, I'm just more aware [of their presence]."

However, Black men from Ferguson were more likely to be on high alert of the police. Dwan stated that even though he is not afraid of the police, "I do be cautious about dealing with them." And Maurice stated that his negative encounter with the police "made me more aware of, 'okay, that's how it is.' It just made me more focused. More so on my toes about police officers." Even though they reported being unafraid of police, a few remained conscious of police presence and cognizant of what they were capable of doing.

Discussion

Previous research on minorities and the police has consistently shown that Black civilians report more distrust in the police than any other racial/ethnic group (Gabbidon & Higgins, 2009). In addition, Black people disproportionately report being the recipient of aggressive police tactics and disproportionately experiencing a range of additional negative police actions (Weitzer & Tuch, 2006). Most research on race and policing has primarily focused on Black males because they are routinely at the receiving end of aggressive crime control efforts (Anderson, 1999; Brunson, 2007; Rios, 2011). Although several studies have shown patterns of distrust among Black civilians, especially who reside in distressed urban communities, research on whether they fear the police is limited, and few consider how gender intersects with race and place in determining whether and why Black women fear the police. The current study extends previous research through a comparative qualitative analysis of the emotional reactions of Black men and women – a group who disproportionately are targeted, stopped, and surveilled – toward the police. The goal was to offer a contextual examination of whether and why they fear the police in their everyday lives. Moreover, by sampling men and women from Ferguson and Baltimore, this study provides insights into Black individuals' perceptions of both race and place in shaping their emotional reaction toward the police.

Overall, the findings suggest that the sample of Black participants held a rather complex understanding of fear toward the police. Indeed, the vast majority (73%) of men and women in the study reported that they did not fear the police. There did not appear to be qualitative differences between Black men and women who reported not being afraid of the police. However, most who reported not being fearful of the police resided in the city of Baltimore. In explaining their views about not being afraid of law enforcement, four key themes arose: police are human, respondents follow the law, they know how to behave if stopped by police, and they remain hyper-aware of law enforcement. Those who reported not fearing the police because they are human asserted that they were not afraid of anyone and refused to live in fear. Yet, despite a conscious decision not to fear the police this did not mean that Black people did not have a reason to fear. In fact, there were often contradictory statements in that even as some Black participants reported not being afraid of the police, there were admissions that they were afraid as to what the police might do and that the law would back them up even if they were in the wrong. Thus, findings illustrate that the fear is more subtle than overt but still present.

Some pointed to the fact that they obey the law, which precludes them from fearing the police. There was a belief among many that there was no reason to be afraid of state officials when one complies with the law. And even if stopped by police, some believed that their respectful mannerism and deferential demeanor would shield them from any potential problems. There was a common perception, particularly among Black men, that such reverential behavior needed to be displayed to neutralize any presumption of guilt or threat officers may associate with Black individuals. This is grounded in respectability politics, which is rooted in the belief that if only marginalized groups would behave better in public, present a better image to the outside world, and subscribe to mainstream values, then their lot in life would improve. This self-presentation strategy was historically adopted by enslaved Blacks where effort was made to fall in line with being good slaves in order to avoid punishments, such as physical and sexual assault, being separated or sold, and execution (Rodgers, 2017). In this contemporary day, "respectability focuses squarely on what one is not to do or say and with whom they are not to do it" (Kerrison, Cobbina, & Bender, 2018, p. 3). Because accepted norms for behavior are deeply racialized, gendered, and class-based, poor respectability performance can cast individuals as being criminally other (da Silva, 2013). In the current study, there was an awareness that any divergence from showing deference to officers could become a lethal event. In fact, even though reports were made of not fearing the police, some were certainly hyper-aware of the police, which stemmed from distrust. Aware of the broad powers to intervene and control their activities, even those who reported not being afraid of the police described experiencing policing in a way that restricts and limits their use of public space. This is a modern kind of enslavement or restricted liberty not suffered by Whites, and illustrates that public space remains unwelcoming to Black bodies.

In contrast, older Black respondents, especially from Baltimore, were more likely to characterize the police as doing their jobs to protect and serve; hence, they were less likely to report being afraid of the police. Police action in distressed neighborhoods are distinct from those operating in middle-class and more affluent neighborhoods (Terrill & Reisig, 2003). Drugs and gang suppression efforts are often focused in urban neighborhoods. As a result of the visibility of such illegal activities, proactive aggressive police tactics are more acceptable to some neighborhood residents.

The study also found that Black people fear the police. While not as prevalent as those who reported not being afraid of the police, one-quarter noted that they were indeed afraid of law enforcement. Such comments were more common among women and those residing in Ferguson. Several in the study said that aggressive policing strategies left them feeling intimidated. Respondents believed that the police served as an occupying force in their communities because they assumed those residing in these neighborhoods were "criminals." Black civilians reported often being viewed with suspicion by police. Recall Dyshelle who was accused of smoking marijuana in her vehicle by an officer who she was driving by even though there was no evidence of this. And remember Justin's account explaining that a police officer threatened to shoot him and his friend if they did not get on the ground after being accused of drinking in public, which they refuted. They tied this most explicitly to race but also to geographical location, as those residing in economically distressed neighborhoods were more likely to come under police surveillance and control. Moreover, fear of the police stemmed from prior negative interactions, especially among Black woman in the study. Consistent with prior studies, Black women reported being the recipient of police misconduct, mistreatment, and violence (Ritchie, 2017). Involuntary police contact coupled with mistreatment during such contacts initiated an accrued body of lived experiences that shaped Black civilian's distrust toward and fear of the police. Even when Black women in the study called the police for help because they needed protection and service, some found themselves arrested. Consequently, police were viewed by some study participants as the face of larger systems of inequality because they interact in Black communities daily.

The current study provides evidence that Black residents of urban cities have justifiable negative feelings toward police and police practices. This includes both overt and subtle fear of police. These feelings make it difficult to expect that community members and law enforcement officers will be able to work together to solve crimes or prevent violence. As a result, there have been many activists demanding fewer interactions with the police. Rather than having police respond to situations, such as traffic violations, some are calling for the implementation of alternative first responder teams to handle such situations. There have been many calls to defund the police in which funding is reallocated away from police departments to human centered services in marginalized communities, such as education, employment, housing, and healthcare. Defunding the police offers a solution to addressing the root causes of crime by ameliorating the conditions that give rise to high levels of crime and making investments that increase economic mobility. Many cities have made moves to defund the police. For example, the School District of Minneapolis, Minnesota terminated its contract with the Minneapolis Police Department and will use these funds for mentoring its students (Beckett, 2020). The city of Los Angeles has made steps to cut $100 million dollars to its police force and use those dollars to invest in marginalized communities (Cowan, 2020). The New York City Council announced that it would cut the NYPD budget by $1 billion and many cities are following suit (Associated Press, 2020). As cities restructure public spending priorities, evaluation studies must be conducted to examine the effects of defunding police on crime rates and community resident's ability to secure affordable housing, quality jobs, and health services.

Moreover, there are some innovative approaches that communities have been exploring to promote safety and wellbeing outside of policing. Advance Peace is a nonprofit organization committed to ending cyclical gun violence by investing in the development, health, and wellbeing of individuals who are most likely to be perpetrators of gun violence (Corburn, Boggan, & Muttaqi, 2020). Recognizing that unhealed trauma often contribute to firearm use, the organization understands that people who engage in and are harmed by urban gun violence are young individuals of color living in communities with long histories of structural racism, divestment, and isolation from law enforcement, social services, and education (Corburn et al., 2020). Rather than rely on law enforcement to communicate messages against gun violence, Advance Peace relies on street outreach workers and formerly incarcerated individuals to use their skills to build meaningful relationships while also working with community-based organizations. Outcome evaluations of Advance Peace show positive results. For instance, both Stockton and Sacramento, California have experienced a 21 percent reduction in gun homicides and assaults in 2018 and 2019 (Corburn & Fukutome, 2021; Corburn & Fukutome-Lopez, 2020).

The prevention and reduction of over-policing of Black bodies requires thwarting racial bias at the heart of punitive policing practices. Shifting the culture of policing such that defunding the police and utilizing street outreach workers to curb gun violence are alternative approaches to ensure public safety and reduce fear of state-sanctioned and civilian violence.

Notes

1. The interview team consisted of four people. Three of the four individuals were Black, and one was White. They included two Black female university professors, a White female professor, and a Black male PhD student. The entire research team was in their 30s.
2. Of the nine participants who reported police mistreatment as a theme, all were Ferguson residents with the exception of one from Baltimore. Justin, who was from Baltimore, had a negative police encounter, which drove him to fear that he and/or others would become the recipient of mistreatment from law enforcement.
3. This includes those who protested in Baltimore and Ferguson but may not have resided within these cities.

References

Anderson, E. (1999). *Code of the street: Decency, violence and the moral life of the inner city*. New York, NY: W.W. Norton & Company.

Associated Press. (2020, July 1). New York City Council approves $1-billion cut to NYPD. *Los Angeles Times*. https://www.latimes.com/world-nation/story/2020-07-01/new-york-billion-dollar-cut-nypd.

Bass, S. (2001a). Policing space, policing race: Social control imperatives and police discretionary decisions. *Social Justice*, 28, 156–176.

Bass, S. (2001b). Out of place: Petit apartheid and the police. In Dragan Milovanovic and Katheryn K. Russell (Eds.), *Petit apartheid in the U. S. criminal justice system*. Durham, NC: Carolina Academic Press.

Beckett, L. (2020, June 2). Minneapolis public school board votes to terminate its contract with police. *The Guardian*. https://www.theguardian.com/us-news/2020/jun/01/minneapolis-public-school-end-police-contract.

Boyles, A. S. (2015). *Race, place, and suburban policing: Too close for comfort*. Oakland: University of California Press.

Brunson, R.K. (2007). Police don't like black people: African-American young men's accumulated police experiences. *Criminology & Public Policy*, 6(1), 71–102. doi:10.1111/j.1745-9133.2007.00423.x

Brunson, R. K., & Gau, J. M. (2015). Officer race versus macro-level context: A test of competing hypotheses about black citizens' experiences with and perceptions of black police officers. *Crime & Delinquency*, 61(2), 213–242. doi:10.1177/0011128711398027

Brunson, R., & Miller, J. (2006a). Young black men and urban policing in the United States. *The British Journal of Criminology*, 46(4), 613–640. doi:10.1093/bjc/azi093

Brunson, R. K., & Miller, J. (2006b). Gender, race, and urban policing: The experience of African American youths. *Gender & Society, 20*(4), 531–552. doi:10.1177/0891243206287727

Cobbina, J. E. (2019). *Hands up, don't shoot: Why the protests in Ferguson and Baltimore matter, and how they changed America*. New York, NY: New York University Press.

Cobbina, J. E., Conteh, M., & Emrich, C. (2019). Race, gender, and responses to the police among Ferguson residents and protesters. *Race and Justice, 9*(3), 276–303. doi:10.1177/2153368717699673

Collins, P. H. (2000). *Black feminist thought: Knowledge, consciousness, and the politics of empowerment* (2nd ed.). New York, NY: Routledge.

Corburn, J., Boggan, D., & Muttaqi, K. (2020). *Advance peace and focused deterrence: What are the differences?* California: Advance Peace & UC Berkeley.

Corburn, J., & Fukutome, A. (2021). *Advance Peace Stockton, 2018-20 Evaluation Report*. Berkeley, CA: Center for Global Healthy Cities. www.healthycities.berkeley.edu.

Cowan, J, (June 12, 2020). What to Know About Calls to Defund the Police in California. *The New YorkTimes*. https://www.nytimes.com/2020/06/09/us/ca-defund-police.html.

da Silva, D. F. (2013). To be announced: Radical praxis or knowing (at) the limits of justice. *Social Text, 31*(1), 43–62. doi:10.1215/01642472-1958890

Epp, C.R., Maynard-Moody, S., & Haider-Markel, D. (2014). *Pulled over: How police stops define race and citizenship*. Chicago, IL: University of Chicago Press.

Gabbidon, S.L., & Higgins, G.E. (2009). The role of race/ethnicity and race relations on public opinion related to the treatment of blacks by the police. *Police Quarterly, 12*(1), 102–115. doi:10.1177/1098611108329692

Harris, D. A. (1999). Stories, the statistics, and the law: Why 'driving while black' matters. *Minnesota Law Review, 84*, 265–325.

Huebner, B. M., Schafer, J.A., & Bynum, T.S. (2004). African American and white perceptions of police service: Within- and between-group variation. *Journal of Criminal Justice, 32*(2), 123–135. doi:10.1016/j.jcrimjus.2003.12.003

Jones, N. (2010). *Between good and ghetto: African American girls and inner-city violence*. New Brunswick, NJ: Rutgers University Press.

Jones-Brown, D. (2007). Forever the Symbolic Assailant: The More Things Change, the More They Remain the Same. *Criminology & Public Policy, 6*(1), 103–121. doi:10.1111/j.1745-9133.2007.00424.x

Jones-Brown, D. (2000). Debunking the myth of officer friendly: How African American males experience community policing. *Journal of Contemporary Criminal Justice, 16*(2), 209–229. doi:10.1177/1043986200016002006

Jones-Brown, D., Gill, J., & Trone, J. (2010). *Stop, question and frisk: Policing practices in New York city: A primer*. New York, NY: Center on Race, Crime and Justice, John Jay College of Criminal Justice.

Kerrison, E., Cobbina, J.E., & Bender, K. (2018). Your pants won't save you: Why black youth challenge the demands of respectability politics and race-based police surveillance. *Race and Justice, 8*(1), 7–26. doi:10.1177/2153368717734291

Massey, D. S. (1995). Getting away with murder: Segregation and violent crime in urban America. *University of Pennsylvania Law Review, 143*(5), 1203–1232. doi:10.2307/3312474

Massey, D. S., & Denton, N. A. (1993). *American apartheid*. Cambridge, MA: Harvard University Press.

Massey, D. S., & Fischer, M. J. (2000). How segregation concentrated poverty. *Ethnic and Racial Studies, 23*(4), 670–691. doi:10.1080/01419870050033676

National Academy of Science, Engineering, and Medicine. (2018). *Proactive policing: Effects on crime and communities*. Washington, DC: National Academy Press.

Richie, B. (2012). *Arrested justice: Black women, violence, and America's prison nation*. New York: New York University Press.

Rios, V.M. (2011). *Punished: Policing the lives of black and Latino boys*. New York: NYU Press.

Rios, V.M., Prieto, G., & Ibarra, J.M. (2020). Mano suave–mano dura: Legitimacy policing and Latino stop-and-frisk. *American Sociological Review*, 85(1), 58–75. doi:10.1177/0003122419897348

Ritchie, A. (2017). *Invisible no more: Police violence against black women and women of color*. Boston, MA: Beacon Press.

Roche, S., & Oberwittler, D. (2018). Towards a broader view of police–citizen relations How societal cleavages and political contexts shape trust and distrust, legitimacy and illegitimacy. In D. Oberwittler & S. Roche (Eds.), *Police-citizen relations across the world: Comparing sources and contexts of trust and legitimacy* (pp. 3–26). London: Routledge.

Rodgers, S. (2017, June 19). How Respectability Politics Stifle Black Self Expression. *Medium*. https://medium.com/@sheneversleeps/how-respectability-politics-stifle-black-self-expression-c162d9418ff.

Rosenbaum, D.P., Schuck, A.M., Costello, S.K., Hawkins, D.F., & Ring, M.K. (2005). Attitudes toward the police: The effects of direct and vicarious experience. *Police Quarterly*, 8(3), 343–365. doi:10.1177/1098611104271085

Russell-Brown, K. (2009). *The color of crime* (2nd ed.). New York, NY: New York University Press.

Sampson, R. J., & Bartusch, D. J. (1998). Legal cynicism and (subcultural?) tolerance of deviance: The neighborhood context of racial differences. *Law & Society Review*, 32(4), 777–804. doi:10.2307/827739

Strauss, A. (1987). *Qualitative analysis for social scientists*. New York, NY: Cambridge Univ. Press.

Tannenbaum, M.B., Hepler, J., Zimmerman, R.S., Lindsey, S., Jacobs, S., Wilson, K., & Albarracín, D. (2015). Appealing to fear: A meta-analysis of fear appeal effectiveness and theories. *Psychological Bulletin*, 141(6), 1178–1204. doi:10.1037/a0039729

Terrill, W., & Reisig, M. (2003). Neighborhood context and police use of force. *Journal of Research in Crime and Delinquency*, 40(3), 291–321. doi:10.1177/0022427803253800

US Department of Justice. (2015). Department of Justice Report Regarding the Criminal Investigation into the Shooting Death of Michael Brown by Ferguson, Missouri Police Officer Darren Wilson. https://www.justice.gov.

van der Merwe, H., & Lamb, G, Africa. International Center for Transitional Justice. (2009). Transitional justice and DDR: The case of South. www.ictj.org.

Webb, V.J., & Marshall, C.E. (1995). The relative importance of race and ethnicity on citizen attitudes toward the police. *American Journal of Police*, 14(2), 45–66. doi:10.1108/07358549510102749

Weitzer, R. (2002). Incidents of police misconduct and public opinion. *Journal of Criminal Justice*, 30(5), 397–408. doi:10.1016/S0047-2352(02)00150-2

Weitzer, R., & Tuch, S.A. (2002). Perceptions of racial profiling: Race, class and personal experience. *Criminology*, 40(2), 435–457. doi:10.1111/j.1745-9125.2002.tb00962.x

Weitzer, R., & Tuch, S.A. (2005). *Racially Biased Policing: Determinants of Citizen Perceptions*. Social Forces, 83, 1009–1030.

Weitzer, R., & Tuch, S.A. (2006). *Race and policing in America: Conflict and reform*. New York, NY: Cambridge University Press.

Wilson, W.J. (1996). *When work disappears: The world of the new urban poor*. New York, NY: Knopf.

U.S. policing as racialized violence and control: a qualitative assessment of black narratives from Ferguson, Missouri

Jason M. Williams

ABSTRACT
U.S. policing has long been captured within a master narrative of colorblind consensus; however, distinct lived experiences between community groups depict grave disparities in law enforcement experiences and perceptions. Orthodox conceptions of law enforcement ultimately silence marginalized voices disproportionately affected by negative contacts with law enforcement. Centering data in critical theory, this study will present thematic results from semi-interviews gathered in Ferguson, M.O., during a critical ethnographic research project. Themes reveal experiences and perceptions of racialized and violent policing, the unique position of Black officers, and regard for the impact police have on children. Results also help to foreground new epistemic frameworks for contextualizing U.S. policing along racial and geographic contours.

Introduction

U.S. policing has long been captured within a colorblind narrative that distorts the lived reality of many who are subjected to adverse effects of law enforcement administration. While U.S. citizens are indoctrinated to believe that governing institutions are impartial and theoretically equal, especially in the post-1960s and Obama eras, consistent expressions of resistance to the institution of policing affirm an oppositional reality. Policing, in particular, has continued, for the most part, to be that singular prong within the U.S. social control complex that has continued to affect the lives of the oppressed (Williams, 2017). Moreover, some have argued that the institution has meandered within the lives of the powerless precisely for expressed purposes of maintaining the status quo of white supremacy and caste (Tatum, 1994). According to a national poll, about 65% of Americans believe that law enforcement officers should be held civilly liable for their indiscretions and overuse of force (Pew Research

Center, 2020). The same poll indicated stark racial differences as well. For instance, nearly 85% of those identifying as Black adults believed that citizens should be able to sue law enforcement officers, "as do 75% Hispanics adults and 60% of white adults" (p. 1). This poll represents the rallying cry for change that has come about during the aftermath of what appeared to be ceremonious police-involved deaths and displays of excessive force around the nation.

However, for some citizens, civil liability may not be enough. Since the police-involved deaths of George Floyd, Breonna Taylor, Toni McDade, and others, abolitionist affirmations around the reconfiguration of law enforcement have reemerged astoundingly (see Lartey & Griffin, 2020). Despite abolitionist calls, the Pew Research Center (2020) reported that over 70% of Americans believe that police agencies' expenditures should remain the same. Although Blacks were likely to favor cuts, close to half of those Blacks recorded in the poll noted that budgets should be reduced. Meanwhile, just over 20% of whites favored cutting police budgets. The poll indicated that age was a significant factor, underscoring that people under 50 years old were more likely to support defunding than those who were older. Lastly, "90% of the public favors a federal government database to track officers accused of misconduct" (p. 4).

Through the bifurcation of law enforcement administration and citizens' experiences, a keen comprehension of intersectional realities can be ascertained that readily exposes the foundational, theoretical indoctrinations that underlie and sustain contemporary policing against the voices of those whose very lives know better—victims of police brutality. Consistent deaths of Black Americans at the hands of law enforcement have cultivated mass movements across the U.S. and the world in hopes of ushering change in institutions charged with keeping the peace. Despite the outcries of Black Americans and their allies, substantial change has yet to materialize in ways that eradicate root causes of police brutality. Despite minimal changes in the administration of justice, the voices of those most affected by police murder and violence have not fully influenced changes being made by legislators.

The quantitative literature continues to report evident disparities regarding experiences and perceptions with the police based on race/ethnicity (Berg, Stewart, Intravia, Warren, & Simons, 2016; Decker, 1981; Epp, Maynard-Moody, & Haider-Markel, 2014; Gabbidon & Higgins, 2009; Graziano & Gauthier, 2019; Rice, Reitzel, & Piquero, 2005; Stewart, Baumer, Brunson, & Simons, 2009; Weitzer & Tuch, 2002). While those studies are crucial, we argue that it is the voices that are most important in both academic and political discourses. Some qualitative research has also reported unnerving findings regarding citizen perceptions and police experiences (Brunson, 2007; Brunson & Miller, 2006a, 2006b; Brunson & Weitzer, 2009; Cobbina, Owusu-Bempah, & Bender, 2016; Gau & Brunson, 2010; Weitzer & Brunson, 2013). However, lacking throughout much of the literature (quantitative and qualitative) are assessments that contextualize Black American experiences within critical theory consistent with their historical and contemporary lived reality.

Thus, this article uses qualitative methodology to investigate the perceptions and experiences of Black American citizens' interactions with police in Ferguson, Missouri. Narratives were collected during the aftermath of the police-involved murder of Michael Brown. This article attempts to respond to arguments that criminological scholarship fails to capture the narrative of those affected by state violence fully by using analytical frameworks most appropriate for Black Americans navigating racialized policing. The colonial model is the chosen framework for this inquiry since it not only responds intricately to the Black American condition, but it does so in ways that build on a genealogy of critical theory developed by Black radical scholars. Using critical theories developed by Black scholars to unpack Black American narratives, we argue, is most epistemically ethical and suitable for the current study.

Theoretical framework: the colonial model

The colonial model has been an underused framework within criminal justice and criminological contexts, although it has been around for some time. For purposes of the current study, we rely on Staples' (1975) and Tatum's (1994) depiction of this model concerning race and policing.

Staples (1975) largely contextualized the colonial model as a framework within which Black Americans are continuously racially subjugated. He states:

> Race is a political identity because it defines the way in which an individual is to be treated by the political state and the conditions of one's oppression. It is cultural in the sense that white cultural values always have ascendancy over black cultural values, thus what is "good" or "bad," "criminal" or "legitimate" behavior is always defined in terms favorable to the ruling class. The result is that crime by blacks in America is structured by their relationship to the colonial structure, which is based on racial inequality and perpetuated by the political state (p. 14–15).

Thus, social control is a political mechanism by which racial groups are sorted—and minoritized people are beneath the majority group. This theory is similar to (and predates) Critical Race Theory (see, Bell, 1992; Crenshaw, Gotanda, Peller, & Thomas, 1995; Delgado & Stefancic, 2012), which unequivocally accepts white supremacy as foundational to the functionality of American society and its institutions—especially those charged with governance.

The colonial model has roots in various critical works such as Fanon's (1961) seminal book, *The Wretched of the Earth*, Blauner's (1969) essay, *Internal Colonialism and Ghetto Revolt*, Cruse's (1968) essay, *Revolutionary Nationalism and the Afro-American,* and many other canonical works particularly during the Freedom Movement era—a time in which radical thought was sought and embraced. Nevertheless, these earlier works intricately helped to contextualize Black life in the U.S. under the confines of oppression and repression[1], particularly during a period of overt racialized uproar. These theoretical frameworks are also more ethically applicable to Blacks as a group, given their historical experiences along the socio-political continuum. Similarly, Staples (1975) contention is that one's lived experience largely marks colonialism through society's structural political machinery, which keeps the Black community "as an underdeveloped colony whose economics and politics are controlled by leaders of the racially dominant group" (p. 14).

In the current study, we analyze Black residents' narratives regarding their sense of position within the Ferguson, Missouri community following immense tension with the police after Michael Brown's death. Many of the Ferguson Resistance suppositions were grounded in longstanding perceptions of general governmental unfairness, neglect, and police misconduct (Boyles, 2019; Cobbina, 2019; Williams, 2017). Given the above reality in Ferguson, it becomes necessary to foreground our analysis within theoretical contours that pays close attention to the lived reality and perceptions of those whose narratives are being analyzed. Tatum (1994) lamented that police play an essential role in the degradation of Black citizens by upholding the status quo of white supremacy. For instance, she writes, "the police…maintain frequent and direct contact with the native. Their role in the colonial social system is to put oppression and domination into practice" (as noted in, Gabbidon, Greene, & Young, 2002, p. 311). Tatum (1994) argued that police engage in these processes knowingly; therefore, implying that law enforcement should not be given the benefit of events like Ferguson. Tatum's suppositions are in agreement with a host of viewpoints that are covered in the next section.

Policing as racialized social control

Lawrence-McIntyre (1992) purported that policing misconduct is part and parcel of a two-tiered social control system. She argued that it was through a process of criminalizing Black Americans that wider white society, and thus the system was able to effectuate its harsh mistreatment of Blacks.

In the aftermath of slavery, she explains, policing became a distinct institution of social control that sought to maintain the status quo, as well as an impetus for utter revenge at the behest of whites who were upset at newfound Black freedoms.

Moreover, Balbus (1973) defined the criminal legal system as a program of legal repression. He also redefined the "riots" of the earlier Twentieth Century as revolts. In doing so, he charts those revolts that occurred primarily in Los Angeles, Detroit, and Chicago, painstakingly through a racial-structural lens—essentially arguing that these revolts set the impetus for a racially charged social control mechanism via the courts that played a significant role in instituting repression. For example, many demonstrators, now known as political prisoners (see, James, 2003), were summarily sought and charged by the judicial system for engaging in the fight for Black liberation. It should be noted that these demonstrators under the U.S. Constitution should have had the right to engage in protest. However, Balbus (1973), with surgical precision, unpacks what he terms as the *dialectics of legal repression* to show how revolutionaries were essentially punished as examples to others who would want to follow, but also how these targeted prosecutions served the purpose of upholding white supremacy and the current social order. Policing was a principal in this new age formation of social control.

Issues surrounding policing today stem from the early 1990s, primarily with the Rodney King incident. He was beaten in 1991 by the Los Angeles Police Department after a rapid chase, under the suspicion of being under the influence of a controlled substance. Following the stop, King was summarily beaten, and the footage recorded by George Holliday (a passerby) was depicted on news screens across the globe. Although his initial charge was dropped, the officers involved in the beating were eventually charged for excessive force. At the state level, the officers were acquitted, yet two were convicted and imprisoned following a federal probe into the violation of King's civil rights. King also won a civil court judgment for punitive damages resulting in 3.8 million dollars (Mydans, 1994). The reaction to the first trial caused a major uprising in Los Angeles that resulted in a robust racial outbreak.

While the acquittal in the Zimmerman trial gave birth to Black Lives Matter (BLM), this case was different because unlike state-sanctioned murder, Trayvon Martin (Zimmerman's victim) was murdered in a vigilante fashion. Furthermore, Eric Garner, Sandra Bland, and many other Black Americans who were murdered by police (or state-agents) helped build the momentum that would catapult social movements around Black liberation and freedom into high-speed. While BLM came about during the aftermath of the Zimmerman acquittal, Michael Brown's death at the hands of Officer Darren Wilson in Ferguson, Missouri, engraved BLM as an organization in homes around the world (Nummi, Jennings, & Feagin, 2019). BLM has called attention to anti-Black state-sanctioned violence and has done so in ways that are hugely intersectional and deeply radical, unlike past movements (Fleming & Morris, 2015; Nummi et al., 2019). While BLM certainly has similarities to former civil rights efforts, activists operating within and around BLM benefit from many technological advents today that helps to bolster their message and reach, such that change can be made (Fleming & Morris, 2015).

The suppositions made by activists today are well documented by empirical research. One such area of corroboration is ecological studies in policing (Klinger, 1997). Building from foundational arguments of police behavior in ecological explanations, research has shown that police malpractice is racially distributed (Mastrofski, Reisig, & McCluskey, 2002). Moreover, ecological contexts also underscore the importance of disaggregating geographies of policing and race (Boyles, 2015, 2019), as geography can often serve as a proxy for other social identifiers (i.e., race, class, etc.). Boyles (2015) underscores the core importance of intersectionalizing geographic terrains such as the suburban against the "expected Black urban space." In her study, she depicts strenuous accounts of police misconduct from participants in suburban Ferguson, Missouri, and provides a counter-canvas from which to compare urban policing and Blacks. Also, the Investigation of the Ferguson Police Department further unearthed a pattern and practice of pervasive racial discrimination and repression in the suburban town that subjected Black residents to mere caste (Department of Justice (DOJ), 2015; Williams, 2017). In fact, Black residents experienced much of the same kind of surveillance and social control tactics as those in urban districts (Fagan & Davies, 2000; Hurst & Frank, 2000). Therefore, critical ecological understandings of policing illuminate contemporary racial discourses of police misconduct and racialized social control.

Through the conflation of geographies of policing—with race as a proxy, the symbolic assailant became a mainstay within law enforcement administration. Skolnick (2011) developed the term symbolic assailant, who purported that the assailant represents the quintessential enemy to law enforcement. The archetype assailant is primarily based on stereotypical depictions of "criminals" officers have observed on patrol and those whom they have come to associate with danger and criminality: Black men. This terminology was further explored by Black criminologists who sought to contextualize the term in contemporary discourses of racialized policing (see, Jones-Brown, 2007; Russell-Brown, 2008). Brunson and Miller (2006a) conducted qualitative research using in-depth interviews with 40 participants from an oppressed neighborhood. They found that, for the most part, the young men in the study believed themselves to be symbolic assailants. Their sense of self was, in large part, based on their interaction with police. Thus, their interfacing with police played a direct role in how they depicted themselves within the eyes of the law. The authors conclude that the overarching impact of continuous negative interactions with police must be taken to account if procedural justice is to be achieved. Their research and suggestions corroborate neighboring research around Black citizens and community policing relations, which suggest that lived experiences and perception of fairness must be foregrounded (Brandl, Stroshine, & Frank, 2001; Phillips & Bowling, 2003; Williams, 2019).

Qualitative research has underscored the importance of nominating people's lived experiences as viable sources of knowledge around policing. The argument to foreground qualitative research is particularly keen given the historical positionality of law enforcement as a counter to Black liberty and freedom in the U.S. (Balbus, 1973; Civil Rights Congress, 1952; Lawrence-McIntyre, 1992). While quantitative analyses serve as significant sources of impact and provide the frequency with which racialized policing is executed, qualitative research unearths the human component, which is sorely missing within policing literature. Similar to the study mentioned above, Brunson and Miller (2006b) conducted another qualitative inquiry into Black citizens' experiences and perceptions with police, and this time they foreground gender differences. While most accounts pointed to police violence against young Black men, they found that Black women often felt under-protected by police, particularly in instances when they needed intervention regarding sexual assault. In cases when respondents were appropriately inquiring from police, they experienced excessive force, arrest, or received no information at all. Collectively, these experiences are congruent with arguments mentioned in the theoretical framework that describe the Black condition as one consistent with colonization.

Cobbina et al. (2016) conducted qualitative research in Ferguson, Missouri, focusing on perceptions of race, crime, and policing among protesters. They found that nearly 60% of respondents believed that police viewed Blacks as criminals—a remark consistent with the symbolic assailant concept. Participants noted reasons were grounded in stereotypical logics that constructs Blackness and Black space as criminal-prone because of expected social disorganization and lack of education (among others). Some participants noted that slavery was a core factor for the divergent kinds of policing Blacks experienced in Ferguson. Meanwhile, others simply believed that police were genuinely afraid of Black residents and viewed them as threats. These perceptions are consistent with Lawrence-McIntyre (1992) thesis around the criminalization of Blackness as a precursor for the destruction of Black bodies and geographies via systems of social control like that of policing.

Methods

While the researcher was employed at another institution (Fairleigh Dickinson University) at the start of data collection, we submitted the protocol to Montclair State University's Institutional Review Board in August 2016 for subsequent approval (IRB-FY16-17-329).

Research question

This study sought to investigate lived experiences and perceptions regarding police interactions with Black Americans living in Ferguson Missouri during the aftermath of Michael Brown's death. More specifically, we wanted to know the details around participants' experiences, their perceptions of those experiences, and any relevant ensuing remarks that would naturally come from the semi-structured interviewing process. Semi-structured interviewing allows for a free-flowing conversation between the participant and the researcher (Bhattacharya, 2017), thus breaking down traditional hierarchies of power dynamics inherent in field research. This modality often caused us to stray away from certain questions as the participant took control over the conversation (albeit while still responding to our general inquiries).

Study setting

Narratives from this study are the result of critical ethnographic research in Ferguson, Missouri. This research began during the aftermath of the police-involved shooting of Michael Brown. The researcher made several trips to Ferguson starting in the fall of 2014. During these trips, the researcher engaged in participant observation while also collecting narratives via semi-structured interviews with Black American adult community members. Some participant observation examples included attending demonstrations, organizing meetings, and other activities congruent with boots-on-the-ground oriented research.

According to 2019 figures, Blacks account for nearly 70% of Ferguson, Missouri's population (U.S. Census, 2020). Meanwhile, whites account for about 24% of those residing in Ferguson (U.S. Census, 2020). Just over half of residents owned their homes from 2014 to 2018, while the median gross rent was $900.00 (U.S. Census, 2020). While close to 90% of residents graduate from high school, just under 20% enter post-secondary education (U.S. Census, 2020). Moreover, poverty affects 20% of the population, as the per capita income rests at $21,000, and the median household income is an estimated 41,600^2(U.S. Census, 2020). People without health insurance represent 12% of the population (U.S. Census, 2020).

In 2015, the Department of Justice released a report detailing its investigation into the Ferguson Police Department (DOJ, 2015) after the police-involved murder of Michael Brown, which created a revolt captured across the world. Primarily Black residents were horrified that their quest for justice had been sabotaged by the system, as Officer Darren Wilson failed to be indicted. Wilson's non-indictment precipitated massive protest from residents who sought to partake in their First Amendment rights, resulting in multiple clashes with police immediately after the grand jury decision. The anniversary of Brown's death would often reignite revolts as emotions about the non-indictment would often enflame feelings of injustice.

Nevertheless, the Department of Justice's report (DOJ, 2015) detailed a series of longstanding unlawful practices that disproportionately affected Black American residents. For instance, the weaponization of courts to induce additional harms onto Ferguson's most desperate and poverty-stricken citizens (DOJ, 2015). They noted how law enforcement acted as a revenue-generating machine to the detriment of public safety, thus further decimating trust between police and the community (DOJ, 2015). These examples and more, they concluded, resulted in the wholesale violation of several Constitutional rights granted to the residents of Ferguson. The report also mentioned that many of these gross infractions were avoidable. The current study is grounded in the above setting.

Participants

The sample (n = 10) consists of four Black women and six Black men. Most have lived in Ferguson, Missouri, for over five years, while one participant has resided there her entire life (27 years). Only two participants lived there for under five years. The majority of them are parents (7), ranging from having 2–4 children. Also, each was single except for one participant who was engaged. Ages ranged from the early twenties up to sixty years-old.

Procedures

The current study consists of narratives drawn from critical ethnographic research. The study took place over a series of trips to Ferguson, Missouri starting in fall 2014. Critical ethnographic research typically consists of mixed qualitative methodologies that are ideologically consistent with the issue under investigation (Bhattacharya, 2017). Critical ethnography is fully inclusive to the standpoint epistemologies of participants' lived realities, perspectives, and expectations during the research process. Under this framework, respondents are collaborators in the knowledge production process—their expressions are viable units of data (Haraway, 1988; Harding, 1991; Hill Collins, 2013; Smith, 1990). More importantly, such methodologies are accountable to ideological undercurrents that govern the sociological setting under analysis (Bhattacharya, 2017). For example, this research sought to investigate the phenomenon of police interactions with Black American residents in Ferguson, Missouri—but through the residents' vantage point. The study also took place during the aftermath of the police-involved shooting of Michael Brown, a Black male resident of said town. Therefore, utilizing critical ethnography was a fundamental all-encompassing methodology that allowed the researcher to engage various qualitative tools that genuinely and unapologetically foregrounded participants' lived experiences.

One such tool was the use of semi-structured interviews. Interviewees were recruited during demonstrations and ethnographic canvasing of the community. The study relied mostly on snowball sampling, since the targeted population is a hard-to-reach group (Bhattacharya, 2017). Upon starting audio-recorded interviews, informed consent was established, and participants were ensured that they could stop the interview if they should become uncomfortable. Respondents earned $10.00 for their engagement after the interview. Interviews lasted 25 min on average. Through the collection of interviews, the researcher developed a holistic phenomenological inference around participants' experiences and perceptions with police in Ferguson (Saldana, 2014). Also, interviews allowed for additional triangulation avenues with other qualitative data collection methods such as participant observation, photos, archival sources, etc. (Bhattacharya, 2017).

Participant observation was another method utilized, which allowed the researcher to become immersed within the phenomenon of community and police relations. The study took place during the aftermath of Michael Brown's death and various hostile demonstrations between the community and police. Participant observation provides yet another window through which to observe and experience participants' culture and lived experiences (Saldana, 2014). Various memos, photos, and recordings were taken as additional datasets during these moments. Moreover, the researcher's positionality as a Black American male helped establish further rapport during all the research process stages. Rapport building is an essential and necessary process in qualitative research (Prior, 2018). Rapport building is especially crucial with research around hard-to-reach populations (Bhattacharya, 2017). Consistent with the tradition of critical ethnography, the researcher's lived knowledges around the Black experience and history played an essential role in navigating the research site, understanding cultural cues, and deciphering narratives, gestures, and expressions. Thus, the researcher's role as a conscious actor during data collection helped improve the accuracy of said data by establishing unfiltered trust with interviewees and the surrounding community.

Analysis

We utilized MAXQDA for data analysis. Transcripts were entered into the program and scanned for repetition as typical in phenomenological assessments (Saldana, 2014). First, the researcher engaged open coding, which allowed for the initial comprehension of interview data (Saldana, 2014). Open coding allowed for the building of initial themes. Next, axial coding helped develop broader categories into which the open coding could fit (Bhattacharya, 2017). Axial coding provided an impetus to establish patterned concepts, and understandings of those patterns began to emerge from the interview data through several rounds of coding. Both processes were vital because they allowed the researcher to thoroughly comb through the data such that repetition in patterns can be achieved. To build rigor, interview data were triangulated against other relevant collected data sources, primarily participant observation notes, memos, and photos. This allowed the researcher to control for a level of qualitative validity (Saldana, 2014). Once patterns began to develop, they were narrowed down to specific themes for presentation in this article.

In alignment with critical ethnography, this study reports emerged patterns within a theoretical framework (the colonial model) that is epistemically ethical and appropriate for the issue under investigation. Thus, below, we provide results on the three most relevant emerging themes from the study: *the police, tolerating community violence, and the children.*

Results

The themes below depicted a recurring theme of colonial control and racialized policing in Ferguson, Missouri. While Michael Brown's death facilitated tremendous pushback from community members, the narratives below show that these issues were long occurring before Brown was shot. Below we share various accounts that capture Black community members' lived experiences and perceptions from Ferguson, Missouri, as they interface with their police department.

The police

Consistent with policing's ecological theories and the symbolic assailant, as noted above, many respondents purported feeling hunted by police.

Ecological policing has often institutionalized stereotypical and racist practices in law enforcement (Mastrofski et al., 2002), leading to severe malpractice (DOJ, 2015). For instance, Cephas, 60, talked about how he avoids police precisely because of the profiling he has experienced, *"I don't have any felonies or warrants, but when they stop you that's what they're looking for, you know. But like I said, in some situations, you just gotta know that you can't win with them, so you gotta avoid them."* At 60 years old, Cephas talked about the various bouts he has had with police over the years, even recalling some of the more overt forms of racist policing he witnessed as a youth. Yet, he laments, *"the kids today have it much worse than we did. Police today are far more racist from what I can see."* Interestingly enough, as an elder, Cephas did not seem to believe that advancements in civil rights have been sufficient to suffice true freedom for Black Americans. Again, recalling how youth today have it worse than his generation, alongside other chronic unemployment, tolerated poor-performing schools, and other social issues, he seemed to believe that Blacks in his community existed within a reality intentionally built for repression. According to Tatum's (1994) conception of colonial policing, law enforcement would play a key role in instituting repression—which goes in hand with Cephas' expressions about his community.

Others readily agreed with Cephas. Tyrone, 29, lamented, *"this shit's been going on for how many years now? Since we [Blacks] came over here on ships."* While Tyrone's sentiments are more pessimistic, he firmly believed that his feelings were grounded in historical fact, as he did not think the system was capable of helping his community. Tyrone said of the system, *"fuck them, I don't care about nobody in the judicial system because they don't give a fuck about us. It's about their money and hanging us."* Bennie, 23, revealed multiple stories about the harassment he has experienced at the police's hands. He says that he no longer feels comfortable calling on them for help. Bennie shared, *"so when I see a cop ride pass, I look at them like, okay, if you have the opportunity, you're gonna hit me or look for a reason to charge me. That's how I feel about them."* Their cumulative negative experiences underscored many participants' pessimism about police in Ferguson.

Consistent with the colonial model, colonizing people includes installing hopelessness and helplessness upon them—and respondents summarily showed signs of both. For instance, Dominique, 18, who had been active in the demonstrations, feared that police were not paying attention:

> *It's [protests] not going to make a difference. It is not because the police are not listening to anything we have to say, because if they were, they would have given us our justice. But that's the point, we over here talking to them, and they don't care. That's what the people don't understand; the police do not care what we're saying.*

Dominque was deeply committed to her perception that police were not listening: *"They [police] keep on killing little kids, we're going to keep on talking, and we're going to keep on acting a 'fool.' If you keep on killing, we're going to keep on doing what we do."* Despite some participant's sense of hopelessness and helplessness, they believed all they had was their voice.

All participants noted blatant negative interactions with police, and each believed that policing in Ferguson was mostly motivated by race. Tyesha, 20, had experienced gender-based profiling where she felt police had sexually harassed she and her friends after stopping them and letting them go without incident. She shared, *"we were walking down the street, and they asked us to get on the wall, they flashed the lights on our backside then asked us to turn around and show our hands. One of my girls was pregnant, too, no respect for her. It just felt weird like they were undressing us or something."* She also believed the issue of racial profiling in Ferguson was most explicit on young Black men, noting an incident with her brother:

> *People get pulled over for nothing here. It happened to me, but it happens all the time to my brother. My brother is a Black man, and he has dreds. They pulled him over, claiming he didn't signal, but he did. I saw him do it.*

They overwhelmingly reported that police openly used racial epithets. For instance, Dominique recalled an incident during a protest, *"they were calling us niggers, knowing we couldn't do anything 'cause they got the shield, and they have guns, tear gas, and all that stuff. We couldn't do anything but cuss them out."* Mark, 32, corroborates, with his testimony, *"...you can't walk down the street when police pull up and fucking with you for no reason and all that bullshit."* While residents report typical harassment from law enforcement, *"all that bullshit,"* as Mark describes, materializes as extra-legal harassment[3], such as verbal assault and other indignities that serves to dehumanize their personhood and sense of freedom. Interviewees report that this added harassment enflames the negative perception and feeling of their interactions with police.

Taking the colonial models to account, participants' experiences with police provide credence for many of the arguments made by earlier theorists on the colonial model (Tatum, 1994; Staples, 1975). Moreover, their feelings of not having control over their bodies and not having freedom of movement is crucial toward understanding the association of their narratives alongside the colonial model. They note actively avoiding the police simply because they do not believe the police are there to protect them but rather to harm them—an argument made in Tatum's (1994) framing of law enforcement's function on oppressed people. Moreover, through the above narratives a gendered distinction is made visible, which is consistent with historical practices of colonization, particularly as a means of installing more hopelessness and helplessness among targeted groups (Collins, 2002; Cruse, 1968; Davis, 2011).

Black police officers

Furthermore, a clear majority of subjects expressed clear condemnation of Black police officers. Generally, they believed that Black officers are acculturated into the system and would not step up to protect Blacks or enforce the law equally because their foremost goal is to impress white officers and the broader system of white supremacy. For instance, Jennifer, 53, noted differential treatment between a few white officers who were with a sole Black colleague:

> *I think the Black one was trying to impress them [white officers]. Because they [white officers] treated me like I'm an older woman, you know, but he [Black officer] didn't, and I believe that was a show-off moment for him. So, I gave most of it back. When you know better, you do better.*

Being an elder, Jennifer expressed discontent with the sole Black officer, who seemed unable to show her a level of respect consistent with her age. Meanwhile, his white colleagues were able to materialize respect. As a result, she chastised him without incident. Bennie said, "*I feel as if they're under a leash...there's only so much that a Black officer can say and do, you know?*"

A single participant, Tyesha, noted that she did not have direct issues with Black officers, yet she still had concerns: "*I don't really have any problems with the Black cops. But I still don't like cops, period. I'm not a racist at all. So, it doesn't matter about their color. If you wear a badge, I don't like you.*" She furthered lamented, "*They [Black officers] represent the system, too...they are allowing it, so it has nothing to do with color to me.*" Residents were not bought by diversity and inclusion discourses in law enforcement. For example, Tyrone uttered, "*just 'cause you hire a couple of Black cops and a police chief, he still gotta do what the fuck they all say. He's a puppet.*" Johnny agrees, "*they [Black officers] just run with the system. Period.*"

Under the system of slavery (America's first system of policing), enslaved Blacks often served as overseers which resulted in status gains (Wiethoff, 2006). Moreover, media reports consistently depict misconduct in majority Black police agencies that oversee Black communities (Lussenhop, 2018). The narratives above show how Blacks can be tools of colonial policing. More important, Black Americans, who are living under differential racialized policing, are depicting Black officers as part of the very system that their Blackness is supposed to neutralize. Residents did not seem to buy the hiring of BIPOC officers as a remedy, as they see the entire institution of policing as illegitimate. Yet, this depiction has much to do with their experiences of policing under a colonial model, which also includes Black officers.

Tolerating community violence

Colonial frameworks predict extreme disarray within colonized communities. Such disorganization may include intra-community and racial violence along with other behaviors that are perceived as self-sabotaging impediments. These displays of violence and broader "anti-social" behavior further underscore stereotypical archetypes of people living in these communities. Some forms of policing practices, including community policing, intelligence-led policing, and others are likely to be instituted. Such depictions are byproducts of grander structural barriers and racisms bestowed onto marginalized geographies, however. Incidentally, these factors are often left out of discourses that attempt to theorize on the development of "anti-social" behavior in historically oppressed and repressed communities.

Interviewees recalled concurrently witnessing violence in the community and inaction from the police. Johnny, 27, spoke about a shootout that happened in which two opposing sides were on the attack near innocent bystanders, yet the police sat back and did not intervene:

> *Well, to me, I think they're [police] real crooked. The system allows racism. Like the shooting I spoke about, the police let that go on. Them dudes shot over fifty rounds, and they were running back and forth while innocent people, including kids, were in the way. The cops ain't do shit but sit on the side. They don't give a fuck about the violence either.*

Three additional people witnessed and spoke about the above incident, corroborating Johnny's testimony.

In addition to witnessing the above incident, Tyrone accented that, *"gun battles—all this shit is nothing, I'm used to it now."* Some participants exhibited signs of desensitization to violence and other oppression-induced-community abnormalities, all of which are symptoms of colonization that can manifest mental illness. Additionally, Cephas added, *"you gotta grow up fast out here. You get hip to the game early."* They spoke to their community's positionality as ripe for crime precisely due to the sustained lack of resources and political power. Travis, 29, points to structural economic inequality: *"We're going to need more jobs, more hiring, so people are not just sitting around every day. Otherwise, negativity is going to catch on."*

According to some respondents, when police take action against violence, they are often aggressive, and victims are treated like culprits. Dominique recalled an incident in which a man was shot by an assailant and yet approached by the police as a criminal:

> *So, the police ran over there and was trying to beat on the boy because he was still walking. I guess they thought he was running from the police. I ran over there and was like, 'No, no no, he's been shot!' They threw him down, dragged him by the thread, going toward this dumpster. I was fuming like, 'Y'all gonna throw his body in the dumpster?" They proceeded to put cuffs on him, and all I could see was his crazy breathing and blinking eyes. I was so scared for the boy, he needed help and they cuffing him, why?!*

A majority of participants spoke about intra-racial violence in the community. They mostly believed that such violence was the result of community disarray and political abandonment. Dominque also believed that Black-on-Black violence served a discursive purpose of legitimating institutional anti-Black violence:

> *Black people fighting Black people is bad because all that does is make the police laugh. Last night there were so many kids fighting each other, and the police was just laughing. That's what they like to see. They like to see us not getting along with each other; they're trying to break us. That's the whole problem.*

They believed that intra-community violence sent messages to the broader public that residents did not care about each other. Counter to mainstream anti-Black narratives, there was a resounding condemnation of violence within the Ferguson community. Dominque opined, *"we're not supposed to give the police a show…or they [the police] will then say, 'we can take them one by one.'"*

Some believed it to be an uphill battle fighting the violence within the community concurrently with the state-sanctioned variety. However, a few subjects explained community-based violence within colonial frameworks, fully understanding how each feeds off the other. Under a colonial model of governance, it benefits the dominate group tremendously to position its subordinate as viciously dangerous and helplessly untamable. For African Americans, this has been the label since slavery—and it was supercharged during Radical Reconstruction with the use of racially designed draconian laws that helped to mass incarcerate African Americans. In the contemporary context, such labels or tropes serve a distinct purpose in legitimating colonized geographies such that the deaths that occur therein are easily diminished and forgotten. Meanwhile, all activity within such spaces are the result of how the people within interface with mainstream society—whether it be through the lack of resources, political abandonment, or other structural/institutional influences. The ability for dominate society to be cleared from its culpability of the conditions in colonized geographies is not by mistake. Ideologies of personal responsibility and hyper-individualism are at the foundation of the ideological positioning that is required for maintaining internal colonies (Staples, 1975; Cruse, 1968) in pluralistic societies in which all are said to have equal opportunity to aspire.

The children

Participants provided narratives about the impact community violence and policing had on the children of Ferguson. Additionally, they also offered advice for children that they believed would shield them from the pain that they have experienced.

They noted lots of trauma with community children. For instance, Brown's death brought about shockwaves of fear, especially with Black youth, according to respondents. Meanwhile, some say they wish reality were different. For instance, Tyesha said, *"I have a four-year-old daughter. I don't want my daughter to think that the police is not good because one day she might need the police."* But Cindy, 27, adds, *"It's sad they're growing up not to trust cops."* Meanwhile, Dominique has witnessed youth having hostile altercations with police:

> *I've seen kids at ten-years-old, cussing out police after they've been in their face. The kids are mad too. But that's the problem; the cops don't understand. These kids [Black youth] just saw someone like them get killed, and they don't want to be killed either. The cops should back away.*

Tyrone spoke about his childhood contextualizing how hard it was to reconcile living as a Black youth in a racist society. Tyrone believed this experience caused him severe mental distress, saying, *"it's growing up in a society that you feel don't give a fuck about you."* Many were afraid for today's Black youth because they believed they lacked guidance and a sense of pride. These sentiments, in many ways, tie back to the colonial model because respondents note the distinct reality Black children face in their community. Such feelings should be not be normal for anyone growing up in a society where everyone is treated equal. Yet, these participants inhabit particular space and racial categories that puts them at risk of harboring such experiences.

Regarding advice, they overwhelmingly encouraged Black youth to remain in school. Education was offered as a quintessential equalizer and protector. Some believed it best for children to leave the community, too. For instance, Tyrone uttered:

> *Love school, get a job, get the fuck away from here. Know that these people here don't look out for you. These people don't give a fuck about you. They want you to kill each other. They want a genocide. They want us to slaughter each other off. Don't give them what they want.*

Dominique added, *"don't do drugs, don't act bad, and don't do anything illegal. Just stay a child as long as you can."* Lastly, many believed that children needed a sense of pride in their heritage because knowing themselves can bring about encouragement and determination. For instance, Tyrone concluded, *"this is our city. This is our country. We are the backbone of this country—and they know that. But as long as they feel like they can brainwash us and keep us against each other, we'll always be in the dark. It's time to wake up!"* Because interviewees felt political figures largely abandoned them, advice to children were often hyper-individualized and slightly pivoted against reliance on the state. Such advice illuminates the extent to which Black youth in such locales are neglected by the state and are socialized to become desensitized to said neglect. For some, this unusual reaction to state neglect can be a form of motivation, whereas, for others, it can induce mental illness. Overall, the uncertain and disoriented advice is on part with operating under the colonial model.

Discussion

This article contextualizes Black American residents' experiences and perceptions in Ferguson, Missouri, with police. The colonial model serves as a most applicable framework through which to contextualize the provided narratives fully. For instance, Staples (1975) contended that under the colonial model, Black Americans are continuously subjugated under a system of colonization. Meanwhile, Tatum (1994) purported that the police act as a sustaining force of oppression and repression such that their activities are equivalent to colonization. Moreover, Tatum argues that institutional policing actively serves in a support capacity to the color caste system. Thus, given these core tenets, Black Americans face a peculiar kind of social control and policing—one that is particularly cruel and racialized. Extenuating circumstances also color these forms of control within the broader social structure.

Regarding participants' experiences with police, results depict damning corroboration with the colonial model. Residents mostly believed that they were abandoned by political figures and the system writ large. Police served an illustrative purpose of keeping them in place and subjecting them to harm. The use of extra-legal harassment by officers enflamed their sense of detachment and dehumanization. There was a strong sense that policing today is far more problematic from the elders and underscored by deeply entrenched institutional inequities. Such perceptions are congruent with the colonial model, as colonized geographies are often minimized to mere nonexistence, and residents are offered below minimum services via the social safety net. Blacks in Ferguson are inundated in chronic unemployment, poor-performing schools (Hannah-Jones, 2014; Kneebone, 2014), and other social abnormalities that hinder them from participating productively in society. Consequently, these manufactured impediments result in Black residents lacking political will and power to change their reality and reach self-determination. Within colonial contexts such as Black Ferguson, community efficacy is obliterated before it has even begun through the installation of institutional hopelessness and helplessness.

Moreover, when social institutions fail within oppressed and repressed Black communities, law enforcement is often deployed as a mechanism of social control to upkeep the status quo (Lawrence-McIntyre, 1992; Tatum, 1994). Through this lens, the colonial model reigns supreme insofar that Blacks are conceived as out-of-control captives in need of taming. Through the ecological model of policing, such communities are viewed as open-air prisons, and they are likewise experienced that way by residents. Recall some of the narratives provided by subjects that underscored the desensitization to violence which is equivalent to that which one would experience in traditional prisons (see Boxer, Middlemass, & Delorenzo, 2009). The cultivation and proliferation of mental illness become a real prospect for many living in such spaces, starting during youth, as noted by Tyrone.

Also, gender-based differences were clearly articulated by interviewees. Women noted a lack of respect for their bodies and their age. During slavery, Reconstruction, and Jim Crow, Black women were routinely treated like inanimate objects, without the capacity of receiving genuine justice in the judicial system. Interviewees note a qualitatively similar experience to their ancestors, who lived through the terror of those past eras. Thus, consciousness around how officers deploy customer service matters and their interaction with citizens should be intersectionally purposeful. Procedural justice was a constant theme in this study, and from the vantage point of those interviewed, it was lacking. Yet, procedural justice, from a colonial model perspective, would be lacking; its absence is intentional, as those living within such a model are merely enemy combatants.

The toleration of violence within the community painted a depressing daily reality for participants. As many of them noted, grander structural inequities largely foregrounded daily setbacks for community members. They understood that chronic unemployment and overall institutional neglect created an atmosphere of hopelessness, helplessness, and criminality that legitimated racialized policing. Living in such a state is the hallmark of living under colonial rule, as it induces an anomic state from which the target cannot escape. Moreover, feelings of pride are nonexistent, and people begin to lose attachment to their neighborhood, as shame becomes the norm and the program under which people operate. This is realized through the narratives that underscored advice to youth. Some believed that kids would do well to leave Ferguson. The current trend of people leaving such areas makes it easier for gentrification efforts to settle in as remaining residents find it hard to fight outsiders encroaching on their turf. Nevertheless, narratives around crime and overall community decay drive both gentrification and the navigation of educated people outside these communities.

Respondents gave credence to underscoring the geographies of policing and race (Boyles, 2015). While Ferguson, Missouri is categorized as a suburb, Black residents live as if they exist in the inner city. Thus, the concentric zone conception of social disorganization does not seem to suffice for Ferguson's underprivileged. In fact, Blackness is most salient and continues to be a master status under which participants are mistreated and presumed criminal. Anderson (2011) argued that the modern-day color-line question revolves around the never-ending association of the ghetto with Blackness of all kinds—and, therefore, the assumption that all Blacks carry with them the stereotypical baggage of the ghetto. Those in this study encapsulated the sentiments of Anderson's supposition. They firmly believed that race played an overarching lead in how police patrolled their community and how resources were distributed. Importantly, they also did not trust Black officers, primarily based on negative experiences. They saw Black officers as a part of the system and, therefore, against the community.

However, the study is not without limitations. For instance, its small sample size is consistent with the nature of qualitative inquiry, which focuses on micro context and thick description of social issues (Bhattacharya, 2017). Unlike quantitative analysis, this study does not use a representative analysis of the wider Black community in Ferguson Missouri, which would have provided a more holistic depiction. Therefore, results from this study cannot be generalized, as the data collected is limited to those who self-selected themselves into the study.

Nevertheless, results corroborate many findings noted in the Investigation of the Ferguson Police Department report (DOJ, 2015). The report revealed a pattern and practice of pervasive racialized policing that amounted to extreme Constitutional violations that disproportionately affected Black residents. The fact that these residents had to live in such a harsh, racist reality for so long begs the question as to why such differential treatment was allowed and tolerated for long and why it took a police-involved murder to uncover such egregious practices. The triangulation of the Department of Justice findings alongside narratives from this study shows that the colonial model may be the most appropriate and epistemically ethical framework for analyzing policing in Black communities. Yet, the focus must not be on policing solely. Structural inequities inclusive to the entirety of the community's lived experiences must be triangulated into the discourses if Black people's truth is ever to be fully comprehended and policing decolonized.

Notes

1. Oppression is used to underscore attention given to the prolonged maltreatment and subjugation of African Americans as a matter of policy and custom. Whereas repression is used to make clear how even during the aftermath of groundbreaking policies such as the Civil Rights Acts of the 60s, there are still attempts at stifling the economic and socio-political upward mobility of African Americans. Thus, repression acts as a mechanism of holding subordinate groups in their place.
2. Each in 2018 dollars and ranging from 2014 to 2018.
3. We define extra-legal harassment as those forms of harassment and violence experienced or perceived by community members that fall outside the boundaries of legally defined and physical duties of law enforcement. Examples are but not limited to the use of, racial epithets, uncomfortable gestures, and overall disrespectful disposition. BIPOCs are typically the victims of such experiences with law enforcement and the broader judicial system.

ORCID

Jason M. Williams http://orcid.org/0000-0003-4663-8993

References

Anderson, E. (2011). *The cosmopolitan canopy: Race and civility in everyday life*. New York: W. W. Norton & Company.
Balbus, I. D. (1973). *The dialectics of legal repression: Black rebels before the American Criminal Courts*. New York: Russell Sage Foundation.
Bell, D. (1992). *Faces At The Bottom Of The Well: The Permanence Of Racism*. New York: Basic Books.
Berg, M. T., Stewart, E. A., Intravia, J., Warren, P. Y., & Simons, R. L. (2016). Cynical streets: Neighborhood social processes and perceptions of criminal injustice. *Criminology*, 54(3), 520–547. doi:10.1111/1745-9125.12113
Bhattacharya, K. (2017). *Fundamentals of qualitative research: A practical guide*. New York: Routledge.
Boxer, P., Middlemass, K., & Delorenzo, T. (2009). Exposure to violent crime during incarceration: Effects on psychological adjustment following release. *Criminal Justice and Behavior*, 36(8), 793–807. doi:10.1177/0093854809336453

Boyles, A. S. (2015). *Race, place, and suburban policing: Too close for comfort*. Berkely: University of California Press.

Boyles, A. S. (2019). *You can't stop the revolution: Community disorder and social ties in post-Ferguson America*. Berkely: University of California Press.

Brandl, S., Stroshine, M., & Frank, J. (2001). Who are the complaint-prone officers?: An examination of the relationship between police officers' attributes, arrest activity, assignment, and citizens' complaints about excessive force. *Journal of Criminal Justice*, *29*(6), 521–529. doi:10.1016/S0047-2352(01)00114-3

Brunson, R. K. (2007). Police don't like black people": African-American young men's accumulated police experiences. *Criminology & Public Policy*, *6*(1), 71–101. doi:10.1111/j.1745-9133.2007.00423.x

Brunson, R. K., & Miller, J. (2006a). Young black men and urban policing in the United States. *The British Journal of Criminology*, *46*(4), 613–640. doi:10.1093/bjc/azi093

Brunson, R. K., & Miller, J. (2006b). Gender, race, and urban policing: The experience of African-American youths. *Gender & Society*, *20*(4), 531–552. doi:10.1177/0891243206287727

Brunson, R. K., & Weitzer, R. (2009). Police relations with black and white youths in different urban neighborhoods. *Urban Affairs Review*, *44*(6), 858–885. doi:10.1177/1078087408326973

Civil Rights Congress. (1952). We charge genocide: The historic petition to the United Nations for relief from a crime of the United States Government against the negro people. Civil Rights Congress.

Crenshaw, K., Gotanda, N., Peller, G., & Thomas, K. (Eds.). (1995). *Critical race theory: The key writings that formed the movement*. New York: The New Press.

Cruse, H. (1968). *Rebellion Or Revolution?*. Minneapolis: University of Minnesota Press.

Cobbina, J. E. (2019). *Hands up, don't shoot: Why the protests in Ferguson and Baltimore matter, and how they changed America*. New York: NYU Press.

Cobbina, J. E., Owusu-Bempah, A., & Bender, K. (2016). Perceptions of race, crime, and policing among Ferguson protesters. *Journal of Crime and Justice*, *39*(1), 210–229. doi:10.1080/0735648X.2015.1119950

Collins, P. H. (2002). *Black feminist thought: Knowledge, consciousness, and the politics of empowerment*. New York: Routledge.

Davis, A. Y. (2011). *Women, race, & class*. New York: Knopf Doubleday Publishing Group.

Decker, S. H. (1981). Citizen attitudes toward the police: A review of past findings and suggestions for future policy. *Journal of Police Science and Administration*, *9*, 80–87.

Delgado, R. & Stefancic, J. (2012). *Critical Race Theory: An Introduction, Second Edition*. New York: NYU Press.

Department of Justice (DOJ). (2015, March 4). *Justice department announces findings of two civil rights investigations in Ferguson, Missouri*. https://www.justice.gov/opa/pr/justice-department-announces-findings-two-civil-rights-investigations-ferguson-missouri.

Epp, C. R., Maynard-Moody, S., & Haider-Markel, D. P. (2014). *Pulled over: How police stops define race and citizenship*. Chicago: University of Chicago Press.

Fagan, J., & Davies, G. (2000). Street stops and broken windows: Terry, race, and disorder in New York City. *Fordham Urban Law Journal*, *28*(2), 457–504.

Fleming, C. M., & Morris, A. (2015). Theorizing ethnic and racial movements in the global age: Lessons from the civil rights movement. *Sociology of Race and Ethnicity*, *1*(1), 105–126. doi:10.1177/2332649214562473

Gabbidon, S. L., Greene, H. T., & Young, V. D. (2002). *African-American classics in criminology and criminal justice*. Thousand Oaks: SAGE.

Gabbidon, S. L., & Higgins, G. E. (2009). The role of race/ethnicity and race relations on public opinion related to the treatment of blacks by the police. *Police Quarterly*, *12*(1), 102–115. doi:10.1177/1098611108329692

Gau, J. M., & Brunson, R. K. (2010). Procedural justice and order maintenance policing: A study of inner-city young men's perceptions of police legitimacy. *Justice Quarterly*, *27*(2), 255–279. doi:10.1080/07418820902763889

Graziano, L. M., & Gauthier, J. F. (2019). Examining the racial-ethnic continuum and perceptions of police misconduct. *Policing and Society*, *29*(6), 657–672. doi:10.1080/10439463.2017.1310859

Hannah-Jones, N. (2014). School segregation, the continuing tragedy of Ferguson. *ProPublica*. https://www.propublica.org/article/ferguson-school-segregation?token=2Afda3_4a5kZwuyUcu2dePYQjk2YB3DX.

Haraway, D. (1988). Situated knowledges: The science question in feminism and the privilege of partial perspective. *Feminist Studies*, *14*(3), 575–599. doi:10.2307/3178066

Harding, S. (1991). *Whose science? Whose knowledge?: Thinking from women's Lives*. Ithaca: Cornell University Press.

Hill Collins, P. (2013). *On intellectual activism*. Philadelphia: Temple University Press.

Hurst, Y. G., & Frank, J. (2000). How kids view cops: The nature of juvenile attitudes toward the police. *Journal of Criminal Justice*, *28*(3), 189–202. doi:10.1016/S0047-2352(00)00035-0

James, J. (Ed.). (2003). *Imprisoned intellectuals: America's political prisoners write on life, liberation, and rebellion*. Lanham: Rowman & Littlefield Publishers.

Jones-Brown, D. (2007). Forever the symbolic assailant: The more things change, the more they remain the same. *Criminology & Public Policy*, *6*(1), 103–121. doi:10.1111/j.1745-9133.2007.00424.x

Klinger, D. A. (1997). Negotiating order in patrol work: An ecological theory of police response to deviance. *Criminology*, *35*(2), 277–306. doi:10.1111/j.1745-9125.1997.tb00877.x

Kneebone, E. (2014). Ferguson, Mo. emblematic of growing suburban poverty. *Brookings*. https://www.brookings.edu/blog/the-avenue/2014/08/15/ferguson-mo-emblematic-of-growing-suburban-poverty/.

Lartey, J., & Griffin, A. (2020). The System: The Future of Policing. *The Marshall Project*. https://www.themarshallproject.org/2020/10/23/the-future-of-policing.

Lawrence-McIntyre, C. C. (1992). *Criminalizing a race: Free blacks during slavery*. New York: Kayode.

Lussenhop, J. (2018, February 13). Who were the corrupt Baltimore police officers? BBC News. https://www.bbc.com/news/world-us-canada-43035628.

Mastrofski, S. D., Reisig, M. D., & McCluskey, J. D. (2002). Police disrespect toward the public: An encounter-based analysis. *Criminology*, *40*(3), 519–552. doi:10.1111/j.1745-9125.2002.tb00965.x

Mydans, S. (1994, April 20). Rodney King is awarded $3.8 million (Published 1994). The New York Times. https://www.nytimes.com/1994/04/20/us/rodney-king-is-awarded-3.8-million.html.

Nummi, J., Jennings, C., & Feagin, J. (2019). #BlackLivesMatter: Innovative black resistance. *Sociological Forum*, *34*(S1), 1042–1064. doi:10.1111/socf.12540

Pew Research Center. (2020, July 9). Majority of Public Favors Giving Civilians the Power to Sue Police Officers for Misconduct. Pew Research Center - U.S. Politics; *Policy*. https://www.pewresearch.org/politics/2020/07/09/majority-of-public-favors-giving-civiliansthe-power-to-sue-police-officers-for-misconduct/.

Phillips, C., & Bowling, B. (2003). Racism, ethnicity, and criminology: Developing minority perspectives. *British Journal of Criminology*, *43*(2), 269–290. doi:10.1093/bjc/43.2.269

Prior, M. (2018). Accomplishing "rapport" in qualitative research interviews: Empathic moments in interaction. *Applied Linguistics Review*, *9*(4), 487–511. doi:10.1515/applirev-2017-0029

Rice, S. K., Reitzel, J. D., & Piquero, A. R. (2005). Shades of brown. *Journal of Ethnicity in Criminal Justice*, *3*(1-2), 47–70. doi:10.1300/J222v03n01_03

Russell-Brown, K. (2008). *The color of crime* (2nd ed.). NewYork: NYU Press.

Saldana, J. (2014). *Thinking qualitatively: Methods of mind*. Thousand Oaks: SAGE Publications.

Staples, R. (1975). White Racism, Black Crime, and American Justice: An Application of the Colonial Model to Explain Crime and Race. *Phylon*. (1960), *36*(1), 14–22. https://doi.org/10.2307/274841.

Stewart, E. A., Baumer, E. P., Brunson, R. K., & Simons, R. L. (2009). Neighborhood racial context and perceptions of police-based racial discrimination among black youth. *Criminology*, *47*(3), 847–887. doi:10.1111/j.1745-9125.2009.00159.x

Skolnick, J. H. (2011). *Justice without trial: Law enforcement in democratic society*. New Orleans: Quid Pro Books.

Smith, D. E. (1990). *The conceptual practices of power: A feminist sociology of knowledge*. Toronto: University of Toronto Press.

Tatum, B. (1994). The colonial model as a theoretical explanation of crime and delinquency. In A. T. Sulton (Ed.), *African-American perspectives on crime causation, criminal justice administration, and crime prevention*. Boston: Butterworth-Heinemann.

U.S. Census. (2020). *U.S. Census Bureau QuickFacts: Ferguson city, Missouri*. https://www.census.gov/quickfacts/fergusoncitymissouri.

Weitzer, R., & Brunson, R. K. (2013). African-American perceptions of police misconduct and accountability. *Journal of Qualitative Criminal Justice & Criminology*, *1*(2). 243–266. doi:10.21428/88de04a1.413bb0cd

Weitzer, R., & Tuch, S. A. (2002). Perceptions of racial profiling: Race, class, and personal experience. *Criminology*, *40*(2), 435–456. doi:10.1111/j.1745-9125.2002.tb00962.x

Wiethoff, W. E. (2006). Enslaved Africans' rivalry with white overseers in plantation culture: An unconventional interpretation. *Journal of Black Studies*, *36*(3), 429–455. doi:10.1177/0021934704273958

Williams, J. (2017). Race and justice outcomes: Contextualizing racial discrimination and Ferguson. *Ralph Bunche Journal of Public Affairs*, *6*(1). https://digitalscholarship.tsu.edu/rbjpa/vol6/iss1/5.

Williams, J. M. (2019). Black males and their experiences with policing under the "Iconic Ghetto" in Ferguson, Missouri. In J. M. Williams & S. Kniffley (Eds.), *Black males and the criminal justice system* (pp. 11–20). New York: Routledge.

Is it a rally or a riot? Racialized media framing of 2020 protests in the United States

Jonathan C. Reid and Miltonette O. Craig

ABSTRACT
This article draws on race relations arguments to explore the nexus between the media, race, and protest policing. The media's coverage of Black Lives Matter (BLM) and protests opposing COVID-19 restrictions bring to light differences in police intervention at these events. How the media portrays this apparent imbalance is the focus of the current study. Using news reports from major U.S. outlets (e.g., New York Times, Washington Post), we find that protests anchored to racial justice issues are more often framed as a threat to the public interests. Our results highlight the media's role in promoting notions of racial threat and exacerbating state repression. We discuss the implications of these findings for constitutional rights, social control, and journalism.

Introduction

Does the racial character of social movements influence how they come to be policed? Davenport and colleagues (2011) draw on the protest policing literature and theories of race relations to answer this question. In their novel assessment, the authors find that Black protesters are more likely to draw police presence, be arrested, and experience police violence compared to other racial groups. For Davenport and colleagues, a deep-rooted conflict between White and Black Americans embodies an ideological context where Black political mobilization is viewed as a threat to White socio-political ascendancies. Therefore, to quell the "racial threat," Whites use control of the police force and broader justice system to repress Black political claims (Oliver, 2017). Davenport and colleagues find evidence supporting a "Protesting While Black" phenomenon, affirming that race affects how police respond to protest events. Research examining the dynamics between the media and social movements suggests that the public's perception of protesters as dangerous or threatening is primarily attributed to how the media frames the protest event (Cottle, 2008; Rosie

& Gorringe 2009; Umamaheswar, 2020). In theory, the media's coverage of social protests should reduce protesters' exposure to unwarranted state intervention because when the nation is watching, the state will be less likely to engage in repression so as "to avoid losing legitimacy and support. In the absence of such publicity, then, states are expected to be more repressive (Reynolds-Stenson, 2018, p. 50)."[1] In practice, however, this is sometimes not the case. Despite mass media coverage of 2020 nationwide demonstrations, such as Black Lives Matter (BLM), some argue that police intervention at such protests is tyrannical and unwarranted (Booker, 2021).

The recent proliferation of the BLM movement has galvanized demonstrations across Americas' cities, towns, public squares, and public streets, yet the politics that animate such assemblies are "demonstrated" in and through the media (Banks, 2018; Leopold & Bell, 2017). In part, BLM is a response to the pattern of lethal interactions between police and unarmed Black citizens (Della Porta & Diani, 2020). Although the vast majority of BLM protests have been peaceful assemblies (Chenoweth & Pressman, 2020; Leopold & Bell, 2017), the movement is routinely portrayed in a damaging manner in the mainstream news coverage (Banks, 2018; Umamaheswar, 2020). Scholars have primarily used the "protest paradigm" to explain this sort of media coverage. Broadly, the paradigm argues that social protests are "predestined to be covered negatively" (McCurdy, 2012, p. 245) due to the practices, conventions, and characteristics inherent in journalism and the media system. This includes news frames that minimize the social issue being protested to highlight the elements of protests that are more sensational, such as the "carnival frame" (Leopold & Bell, 2017, p. 721; Veneti et al., 2016). The protest paradigm is viewed as a pattern of news coverage that expresses disapproval toward protest and dissent (Umamaheswar, 2020). Overall, qualitative analyses of BLM news coverage have consistently found the protest paradigm to be at work (Kilgo et al., 2019; Mourão et al., 2018).

Indeed, the protest paradigm offers a useful framework for understating the contexts within which BLM operates. However, the paradigm overlooks a critical insight that has been central to race scholarship—namely, that race is built into the very organization of American society (Alexander, 2010; Bonilla-Silva, 2015; Feagin, 2000; Omi & Winant, 2015; Wacquant, 2002). This arrangement implies that social institutions like the media and law enforcement are themselves racialized in critical ways. The racial structure of society underscores the need to evaluate the media's illustration of social protests using theories sensitive to America's racial dynamics (Bracey, 2016; Davenport et al., 2011; Oliver, 2017). The racial conflict interpretations employed by Davenport and colleagues (2011) offer a valuable framework for exploring the media's role in promoting and concretizing public perceptions of threat. Furthermore, examining the media in this manner is critical to understanding the state repression of BLM protests. Failing to consider the racial context within which BLM functions, combined with its followers' political claims-making, can obscure our interpretation of how collective action initiated by Black Americans comes to be policed.[2]

We contribute to the social movement tradition by employing race relations and stratification arguments for understanding the media politics of dissent. Drawing on research from systemic racism and racial threat (e.g., Blalock, 1967; Blauner, 1971; Blumer, 1958; Bonilla-Silva, 2015), we argue that public protest events initiated by racial minority group members are likely to be portrayed in the mainstream news media as "threatening" irrespective of its peaceful nature. Furthermore, such media representation will reinforce perceptions that these events require police presence and extensive formal social control. We also argue that public protest events initiated by racial majority group members are likely to be represented in the mainstream news media as "non-threatening" irrespective of its violent nature and will reinforce perceptions that these protests do not require intervention by the authorities. To this end, we use news reports from major U.S. outlets (e.g., *New York Times*, *Washington Post*) in 2020 to qualitatively analyze the relationship between protest subject matter, the policing of those protests, and the news media's framing of protesters and police conduct. The implications of our analysis for theory, research, and policy are discussed.

Literature review

BLM is considered "one of the most powerful movements against racial injustice" in American history (Umamaheswar, 2020, p. 2). The movement developed relatively recently as a response to the death of 17-year-old Trayvon Martin. As Trayvon walked home from a nearby store, he was pursued and killed by George Zimmerman, a civilian who claimed to be protecting his neighborhood. Zimmerman was acquitted while Trayvon's character was questioned, and he was assigned blame for his own death (Banks, 2018). Instead of a direct response to Trayvon's death or any single judicial failure, BLM is a call to action against the criminal justice system's devaluation of Black lives (Umamaheswar, 2020). The movement uses public protest events as a central tactic in its quest for criminal justice reform and its push for racial equality across American society (Della Porta & Diani 2020). To this end, the mass media performs an essential function—it offers a far-reaching medium to communicate BLMs' message beyond its immediate audience, which can help the movement gain allies and further influence its political and social agenda (Amenta et al., 2017; Banks, 2018). Given BLM protests' widescale media coverage, scholars do not expect unwarranted state repression at these events (see Earl et al., 2003; Earl & Soule, 2006; Wisler & Giugni, 1999). In a context where "the media spotlight" allows the world to see protests unfold, authorities are likely to refrain from undue repressive conduct to avoid losing legitimacy and public support (Wisler & Giugni, 1999, p. 173). Nevertheless, for almost a decade, the BLM movement and protests that emanate from it have experienced numerous episodes of disproportionate social control handed out by police (Arnaud, 2016; Eick, 2016).

Scholarship on police-protester interactions (i.e., protest policing) maintains that "weaker" movements are more likely to be over-policed because they lack the necessary socio-political resources to resist or overcome state repression (Earl et al., 2003; Gamson, 1990 [1975]; Oliver, 2017; Reynolds-Stenson, 2018). According to Oliver (2017), movements organized around Black social advancement, such as BLM, are undermined by the lack of political power and the consequent dearth of protection afforded by media coverage. The media's ability to shape the public perception of a movement (Banks, 2018; Cottle, 2008; Updegrove et al., 2020), combined with its tendency to support state interests (Oliver, 2017), may increase a movements' vulnerability to repression and, therefore incidences of police violence (Earl et al., 2003; Reynolds-Stenson, 2018). Wisler and Giugni (1999) argue that police response to protests is rooted in public opinion as defined by repeated statements expressed in the public domain. If most mainstream news outlets adopt rhetoric emphasizing law and order, the police will likely interpret public opinion to support more aggressive protest policing tactics. In contrast, if rhetoric stresses the protection of protesters' civil rights, the police will be more likely to show restraint to protect their public image (Wisler & Giugni, 1999). In short, the media's representation of a social movement or protest will likely influence how police perceive dissidents, what to expect on the ground, and ultimately the choice of policing tactics to be used against protesters (Della Porta & Fillieule, 2004; Gorringe & Rosie, 2008; Rosie & Gorringe, 2009).

In light of the media's potential role in the over-policing of protests, some scholars have attended to the media's portrayal of social movements such as BLM. Scholarship in this area is informed mainly by the protest paradigm, which draws from the foundational work of Chan and Lee (1984). This paradigm emphasizes the "social control function" of the media in weakening marginalized groups' efforts to protest the status quo (Boyle & Schmierbach, 2009, p. 6). Therefore, media sociologists maintain that protests aligned with the paradigm are fated to negative media attention. Specifically, the protest paradigm is delineated by:

(1) news frames that either emphasize the criminal behavior of protesters or trivialize the protesters' work; (2) a reliance on official sources and official definitions, instead of those of the protesters; (3) a reliance on bystanders' (rather than protesters') voices; (4) delegitimization of the protest, where the protest's goals are emphasized far less than specific protest events; and (5) demonization of protesters through an emphasis on protester-police conflict or on protesters' disruptive/criminal behavior. (Umamaheswar, 2020, p. 4).

In short, media coverage employing the protest paradigm will likely illustrate protesters as deviant and delegitimize their aims and politics by emphasizing drama, spectacle, and violence when they challenge the established state of affairs (Cottle, 2008). Research using content analyses demonstrates the mainstream news media's tendency to ostracize BLM in their coverage, adhering to the predicted paradigm (Kilgo et al., 2019; Leopold & Bell, 2017; Mourão et al., 2018; Umamaheswar, 2020). For example, Leopold and Bell (2017) find that mainstream news articles marginalize protesters through the "racialization" of coverage. Kilgo and colleagues (2019) find that journalists marginalize BLM by focusing on violence and confrontation incidents rather than protesters' demands and agendas. When paired with similar evidence gleaned from previous coverage of Black protest events, such as the "Million Man March" (Watkins, 2001), research findings consistently indicate that protests concerning Black Americans "challenge the status quo in such a way that the paradigm remains intact regardless of the protesters' actions, tactics, or demands" (Kilgo & Mourão, 2019, p. 4290).

The media's framing of BLM may influence the degree of formal social control meted out at public protest events. Racial conflict interpretations, such as Blalock's (1967) racial threat thesis, have been used to explicate unjust police actions at Black protests (Davenport et al., 2011). However, studies focused on media coverage of Black movements, like BLM, have failed to incorporate these conflict-based interpretations. This exclusion is surprising given the established scholarship on race and stratification in the U.S., which suggests that challenges to the status quo by a racial minority group will be perceived as a threat to White socio-political dominance. In turn, Whites will mobilize their resources across various social institutions (such as law enforcement) to suppress growing racial competition (Blalock, 1967). We argue that the mainstream news media functions to maintain White privilege and Black disadvantage in their coverage of racialized protest events. Negative media framing of BLM protests is likely to represent and reinforce a sense of racial threat on the part of Whites—with consequences for how these protests are policed. In the following section, we describe and incorporate arguments from racial conflict literature to explain the mainstream media's portrayal of contemporary social protests.

Theoretical framework: BLM, racial threat, and mainstream news coverage

The salience of race in our discussion of news coverage and social protest is rooted in arguments advanced by the racial threat and systemic racism literature. We do not aim to arbitrate between these two perspectives. However, we argue that these two aspects of racial conflict explain why we expect Black social protests to be treated differently than other protests in mainstream media.

The foundations of the racial threat perspective, also referred to as minority group threat and power threat, lie within conflict theory, which asserts that society is characterized by conflicting interests and competition for valuable yet unevenly distributed resources (Stults & Swagar, 2018). In turn, dominant groups, such as those with more economic and political resources, exercise their control to exploit and oppress subordinate groups (Liska, 1992).[3] The threat perspective, first proposed by sociologist Herbert Blalock (1967), posits that the majority group will impose various forms of coercive, formal social control on the minority group when the latter grows in size and is consequently viewed as threatening (or dangerous) to the existing social order. Blalock (1967) argued that following initial increases in minority group size or power, there is a rapid and forceful amplification in formal social control intended to suppress the threat. Thus, this framework proposes that criminal justice system outcomes represent the formal social control mechanisms used to penalize minority groups who disturb the status quo (Crawford et al., 1998; Eitle & Monahan, 2009; Wang & Mears, 2010). The presence of a racialized "other" is said to increase fear and hostility among the dominant group, which then increases support for and employment of punitive initiatives, such as arrests, convictions, executions, incarceration, police use of force, prosecutions, and stop and frisk policies (Stults & Swagar, 2018).

Many scholars have argued that the U.S. is characterized by a hierarchical racial structure, where Whites are ascribed a dominant status relative to Blacks. Wacquant (2002) advances that this racial dynamic was initiated by chattel slavery and continues due to systemic racism (see also Bonilla-Silva, 2014, 2015; Feagin, 2000; Reskin, 2012). Bonilla-Silva (2015) defines systemic racism as "a network of social relations at social, political, economic, and ideological levels that shapes the life chances of the various races. This structure is responsible for the production and reproduction of systemic racial advantages for some (the dominant racial group) and disadvantages for others (the subordinate races)" (p. 1360). In this racially structured reality, racial disparities are self-perpetuating as groups receiving varying rewards have distinct group interests (Feagin, 2000). Therefore, through institutional discrimination, Whites act to maintain their dominant position by preserving rather than challenging the status quo (Alexander, 2010; Feagin, 2000; Hill, 2016; Omi & Winant, 2015). BLM protests are a clear example of a "hierarchical interaction" (Feagin, 2000, p. 21) between a subjugated group and its oppressor. Social protests harnessed to Black advancement are likely to be viewed as a threat to the ideological White supremacist project that is characteristic of systemic racism (Davenport et al., 2011). Consequently, Whites and the institutions they control—such as the police force—mobilize to suppress Black political claims (Davenport et al., 2011).

However, not all forms of socio-political control are carried out by the police. The systemic racism and racial threat literature suggest that mainstream news media, which is controlled by Whites (Oliver, 2017), can be weaponized against the claims-making efforts of Black social movements. In this context, we argue that mainstream news coverage of Black social protests will be distinguished by content that emphasizes racial threat. In particular, BLM represents collective political action that challenges systemic racism and racial inequality in American society. This movement's political claims are likely to engender a sense of racial competition and racial threat on the part of Whites (Updegrove et al., 2020). According to Oliver (2017), the mainstream media mirrors the racial character of American society and thus functions to perpetuate the interest of the White majority. Similar to law enforcement, mainstream news outlets "operate under assumptions and practices that automatically and invisibly privilege the [White] majority [and disadvantage the Black minority], even without overt discrimination" (Oliver, 2017, p. 397-398). Hence, the media portrayal of BLM is likely to reflect and support the status quo by casting a negative light on the movement and its protest activities.

Based on systemic racism and racial threat reasoning, we expect social protests initiated by Black Americans to elicit relatively hostile and invalidating news coverage. Our research strategy, described in detail in a later section, compares BLM protests with protests by other movements. We ask whether protests centered around Black socio-political advancement are more likely to be framed in a dangerous and threatening manner. To date, no research has explored the salience of racial-conflict interpretations in media coverage of BLM. Furthermore, our analysis covers a critical period in the media landscape—the months following the police killing of George Floyd and the months preceding the 2020 presidential election. While Floyd's death sparked perhaps the most widespread mobilization of BLM up to that point, the impending election has intensified political partisanship in the presence of well-institutionalized racially coded campaign strategies and rhetoric. Indeed, incumbent President Donald Trump's political rhetoric centers primarily on preserving the status quo, most clearly expressed in his campaign slogan: Keep America Great. In contrast, BLM calls for a reimagined social system that is antithetical to the current American reality. Consequently, the racial politics related to Trump's rise to power (see Bobo, 2017), coupled with racially laden partisan media coverage, makes racial conflict interpretations especially pertinent to this study.

Materials and methods

The primary data sources in this study include articles from the following newspapers: *Atlanta Journal-Constitution, New York Times, Oregonian, Wall Street Journal, Washington Post,* and *USA Today.* These newspapers are appropriate for this study because they are in high circulation in the U.S., and they represent significant outlets across the political spectrum.[4] Moreover, most of these newspapers are based in cities/states that have had numerous demonstrations within the specified timespan. For example, there were 100 consecutive days of BLM protests in Portland, Oregon, beginning in May. Also, stay-at-home-order protests drew thousands of people, some of whom were armed militia members in Georgia (Fuller, 2020; Ray, 2020). The articles were published from March 1, 2020, to August 31, 2020. This six-month time period captures the most news coverage about recent protests on COVID-19 guidelines and social/criminal justice reform in the U.S.

The articles were gathered during 12 separate searches. Most articles were obtained using the ProQuest newspaper search engine. The Oregonian Journal was not available through that database, so we gathered these articles from the paper's website. The first set of searches for each newspaper included terms such as *Black Lives Matter* and the last names of victims of high-profile, fatal police-involved deaths covered in the news during the specified timespan: *Rayshard Brooks, George Floyd,* and *Breonna Taylor*— deaths that signify the most recent cruxes of demonstrations on police reform.[5] The second set of searches for each newspaper included terms such as *mask mandate* and *stay at home order.*[6] The searches resulted in 55,568 newspaper articles. However, our analyses did not include all results, as we omitted duplicate articles and then randomly selected ten articles from each newspaper search. This resulted in 120 articles for analysis.

Analytical strategy

Four individuals conducted thematic content analyses of the newspaper articles using NVivo, a qualitative data analysis program.[7] Content analysis is employed to classify, summarize, and tabulate verbal data, and identify themes, patterns, and relationships in the data (Saldaña, 2016). The current study's coding approach included exploratory methods (i.e., provisional and hypothesis) using a coding scheme that consisted of key phrases and themes from the frameworks applied in this study. The scheme included codes to identify: (1) Media framing of the events (e.g., violent, peaceful); (2) Media framing of official responses at the events (e.g., force, arrests); and (3) Media framing of the protesters (e.g., dangerous, threatening). Additionally, open coding was utilized by the research team to allow for inductive exploration and ongoing enhancement of the coding scheme. The results are organized by the themes within the data and divided by protest topic: Black Lives Matter (BLM) and Mask Mandate/Stay at Home Order (MSH). The results also include direct quotes to demonstrate support for the theoretical foundation.

Results

Our content analyses of the news articles were performed to explore how the media portrays the two most prominent protests of 2020 (up to the end of August). Through this assessment, we were able to determine whether there are differences in media framing based on the protests' subject matter.

BLM protests/demonstrations

Framing of Events: For BLM protests, articles frequently recounted protest events as entirely disorderly and/or violent, although some acknowledged the calm nature of a protest's beginnings that then became rebellious. For instance:

> But as the march frayed, small bands of violent actors on its fringes began escalating. First, they threw trash cans into the street. Soon, they lit piles of trash on fire, eventually igniting scaffolding on an apartment building near the Strand bookstore. By the time the stragglers had reached the stretch of Fifth Avenue between 14th Street and the Flatiron Building, they were smashing almost any glass in sight. (New York Times, June 2, 2020)

> Hundreds of protesters attempting to topple the city's Christopher Columbus statue faced off with dozens of Chicago police Friday evening in an encounter that turned violent. [Criminal charges included] battery to an officer, mob action or other felonies ... after some protesters began throwing objects at officers ... About 18 officers were injured. (USA Today, July 18, 2020)

A recurring theme was the media's portrayal of a peaceful demonstration needing to involve displays of joy and cheerfulness on the part of the protesters. For example:

> In Washington, the scene outside Lafayette Square, where federal security officers had forcibly evicted peaceful protesters last week, was something closer to a music festival Saturday. Cookies and Cool Ranch Doritos were arrayed on folding tables and face masks emblazoned with "I can't breathe" were on sale along with Black Lives Matter T-shirts. Even portable toilets were on hand. Marchers on 16th Street did a coordinated dance, "the wobble," as rapper V.I.C. blared through speakers. (New York Times, June 6, 2020)
>
> People of all ages and races strolled around, listening to music, eating at barbecue tents and an ice cream kiosk, and buying T-shirts from the many vendors still on hand. The protest was still happening - it was just happening casually... (*Washington Post*, June 20, 2020)
>
> The moments of tension followed weeks of mostly peaceful protests. The carnival-like atmosphere in recent days stood in contrast to looting and clashes between protesters and police. that marked the opening days of the protests that followed the slaying of Floyd, an unarmed black man who died in police custody in Minneapolis. (*Washington Post*, June 23, 2020)

In contrast, the articles' description of negativity in protests centered on the distortion of critical messages such as justice, equality, and anti-racism. With protester-interviewees' assistance, acts of theft/looting and other property damage incidents were often labeled as hurtful and detracting.

> As the [tear gas filled the air, she began to cry]. "I understand that everybody is angry. What I want to say please stop hurting other people ... Do not destroy our city. We built it." [The] day was made up of two separate events, tied together only by shared feelings of outrage. There was the orderly protest ... then there was what took place afterwards, when people started fires, broke windows, and looted stores. (*Atlanta Journal-Constitution*, May 31, 2020)

However, there were some exceptions, as a few articles discussed the perspectives of protesters who viewed property damage as a legitimate form of protest that includes outward expressions of rage and frustration. For example:

> Not everyone reveled in the tone of non-violence emphasized during Tuesday's rally. [He] sees violence as a simple and effective tool to protect the community against police brutality. "Bad people who use violence can and will only be stopped by good people who are better at violence," he said. "This isn't a game; there are people's lives at stake." (*USA Today*, June 3, 2020)

Framing of Official Responses: The portrayals of official responses primarily encompassed descriptions of formal social control by police, such as arrests, intimidation, and especially the use of force. Several accounts detailed what appeared to be disproportional actions used against protesters. For example, the news accounts of police use of force included the following:

[The student] stood in front of a crowd of hundreds near Howard University. [They] stepped onto a brick platform, grabbed the megaphone and started speaking. "We are the face of this movement" ... We will not let this stand. Enough is enough." Hours later, [they] coughed and wheezed in a cloud of chemical gas [and] ran as federal law enforcement officers fired rubber bullets to clear demonstrators from Lafayette Square. (*Washington Post*, June 7, 2020)

Photos and videos of the incident shared to social media showed protesters bleeding from the mouth. At least one protester ... had her teeth knocked out when an officer punched her, according to video of the assault. (*USA Today*, July 18, 2020)

Other accounts described either the minimization of harmful police actions. In our sample, multiple articles referred to a disturbing incident at a New York City protest when police vehicles appeared to drive toward a crowd. One journalist account described the incident as "two police SUVs plowed into protesters Saturday evening," while another labeled the officers' actions as "two police vehicles surged forward into a crowd of demonstrators, some of whom were blocking the street and pelting the cars with debris" (*New York Times*, June 1, 2020). These reports also offered "explanations" for the use of force by centering on alleged provocation by protesters. For example:

After continuing to ask protesters to remove themselves from the road, Detroit police boxed them in from all sides and began making arrests about an hour after the citywide curfew. Officers used zip ties to detain protesters and put water in the eyes of those hit by pepper spray. They lined up the arrested, while seated, on the sidewalk. (*USA Today*, June 3, 2020)

In a chaotic scene, a helicopter flew low over the park [as] police moved through the park. Officers used a chemical irritant to disperse protesters and sweep them back ... Protesters did smash the wooden wheels of four replica cannons at the base of the Jackson statue. Protesters threw things at police as they retreated, and officers shoved people in the melee. One woman hurled a folding chair, striking an officer, who staggered away from a police line. (*Washington Post*, June 29, 2020)

Still, others pointed to a lack of police responsiveness or cooperativeness, which is a stark contrast to the corresponding accounts and the information that the mass media institution has portrayed.

Police officers also remained largely distant from the marchers as they made their way through downtown. Many marchers stopped together at a fence on Fifth Avenue, blocks away from the Justice Center, where they kneeled and chanted, "Hands up, don't shoot." Police tweeted at 8:30 that officers were going to talk with demonstrators, after they said some people in the crowd asked to meet. Protesters listened as the officer talked into the microphone. (*Oregonian*, June 1, 2020)

Demonstrations were continuing in Minneapolis on Saturday, still large in size but carried out in a considerably calmer and more organized fashion. Police officers hung back or did not appear at all at the rallies — a marked difference from the clashes between officers and protesters last weekend. (*New York Times*, June 6, 2020)

Framing of Protesters: Here, we chose to focus on portrayals of individual protesters in discussions with, or observations by, journalists on the scene. Expectedly, several protesters were described as threatening and dangerous to others in the area, but a unique theme that emerged was the description of protesters who were described as either feeling inspired and purposeful in their participation.

> "That mural isn't enough" ... I don't want to be a hashtag. [I] want to be able to live and feel safe and not have to worry about racist police officers profiling me." (*USA Today*, June 6, 2020)

> [The woman] said she normally doesn't protest but said she could no longer stay at home. ... "I'm tired. I'm tired of seeing our people killed" .... "I'm just at my limit." (*USA Today*, June 8, 2020)

> She had come straight from work [and] didn't have time to change. "My feet hurt, but you know what? George Floyd was hurting when that police officer had his knee on his neck for [8 minutes 46 seconds, so to me], being here is more important than being comfortable." (*Washington Post*, July 1, 2020)

The news articles also identified and described the actions of counter-protesters and other "agitators" during the demonstrations.

> Dozens of drivers have plowed into crowds of protesters marching in roadways ... [Some] of the vehicle incidents appear to be targeted and politically motivated; others appear to be situations in which the driver became frightened or enraged by protesters surrounding their vehicle. ... There have been at least 104 incidents of people driving vehicles into protests from May 27 through Sept. 5, including 96 by civilians and eight by police ... at least 43 of the incidents were malicious, and 39 drivers have been charged. (*New York Times*, July 9, 2020)

> This was the first Black Lives Matter rally that White, rural, Republican Rocky Mount had ever seen. ... "F--- y'all," said a low voice, and [she] turned to see a White face leaning from the window of a black pickup truck, and a middle finger thrust into the air. "Y'all are disrespecting my statue." (*Washington Post*, August 2, 2020)

> Some demonstrations happened elsewhere in Oregon as well. A small Black Lives Matter protest in Salem gathered near the Capitol with counter-protesters across the street. In Eugene, the Register Guard reported, a protest for the Black Lives Matter movement held in solidarity with Portland protesters Saturday night in Eugene almost immediately devolved into confrontation with counter protesters and later property destruction downtown. (*Oregonian*, August 6, 2020)

Mask mandate/stay at home order (MSH) protests/demonstrations

Framing of Events: The articles on COVID-19-related protests were often couched within a larger argument about the need to restart the economy and get things back to the status quo. For instance:

"I think there's a boiling point that has been reached and exceeded" ... "I call these people the modern-day Rosa Parks - they are protesting against injustice and a loss of liberties" he said of the protesters. (*Washington Post*, April 18, 2020)

A small-business owner helped organize a rally in Frankfort loud enough to disrupt the governor's daily news conference. She argued that the vulnerable could stay home, but that the state shouldn't smother people and businesses who want to operate. Protesters walked around the capital chanting "Open up Kentucky" ... [they] said the governor was jeopardizing liberty in choosing winners and losers among businesses. (*USA Today*, April 23, 2020)

Framing of Official Responses: The articles discussed official responses to protesters very rarely—since there were not many—even as related to enforcement of the mandates that are the subject of these protests. This absence of formal social intervention appeared to be grounded in free speech and assembly rights. For example:

[He organized the event but said] that he's "not going to be going around with a yard stick." He said the gathering would spread the virus "no more or less than going to work or to the grocery store or any other activity that we do in our lives. This isn't an old-fashioned chickenpox party where we are trying to get sick to get over it," he said. "We are intending to follow all CDC guidelines as much as practical, while at the same time not sacrificing our fundamental principles of liberty and constitutional law." Such gatherings were not violations of the stay-at-home orders in many states. (*Washington Post*, April 19, 2020)

Cyclists zipped across bike paths that were supposed to be off limits. Protesters shouted at police and passersby, denouncing Gov. Gavin Newsom's order to close the beaches ... Scenes across Orange County this weekend revealed both the simmering tension over the lockdown orders and the challenge of keeping people away from the ocean. (*Wall Street Journal*, May 3, 2020)

Framing of Protesters: Although the MSH protesters were not portrayed as dangerous or presenting a physical threat to authorities, the news articles did describe a few of these protesters as disorderly and/or intimidating.

[The nurse stood] silent, her facial expressions partly hidden behind her medical mask, her body rigid in surgical scrubs. She heard a stream of insults from rallygoers. People accused her of being an actor or, if a real nurse, one who performed dentistry or abortions. They were not keeping apart from each other. Most did not wear masks. She was surprised at the anger directed at her. (*USA Today*, April 23, 2020)

"Surfing is not a crime!" ... [He only left when] a police boat warned him he would be fined if he didn't leave the beach. He called the coronavirus outbreak a 'scamdemic' and said only those with compromised immune systems would get sick. (*Wall Street Journal*, May 4, 2020)

About half of the articles covering MSH demonstrations portrayed protesters as patriotic, passionate, and dedicated to the cause, rather than explicitly labeling any of their actions or thoughts as unreasonable considering the significant impact of the pandemic on Americans' health and well-being. For instance:

> Glamour Salon in downtown Salem reopened for business Tuesday morning — one client at a time — in defiance of Gov. Kate Brown's order that such businesses must remain closed to avoid making the COVID-19 pandemic worse. About 40 protesters waving signs and American flags showed up at 195 Liberty St. SE to show their support for owner Lindsey Graham, who could face significant fines from the Oregon Occupational Safety and Health Division. She and her husband own six businesses, all of which have been closed because of the virus, Graham said. This was the only business she believed she could open safely at this time. "I want (people) to understand I'm doing this to provide for my family," she said. "No other reason." (*Oregonian*, May 5, 2020)

> As photographs of gun-carrying protesters in Michigan's Capitol building made the rounds nationally, one has emerged as a defining image of last week's demonstration over the governor's orders amid the coronavirus pandemic. An unmasked man, mid-scream, yelling within inches of two police officers. ... "I was there chanting, 'Let us in,' and I saw that guy and [I just] kind of lost it a little bit" ... But the photo was criticized online. "These are the same people who tell you to 'respect the police,'" one Twitter user posted. Another wrote: "Would officers show this much restraint if [Black] men were yelling in their faces?" (*USA Today*, May 5, 2020)

Discussion

Our examination contributes to the social movement, racial threat, and media sociology literatures by using race as a lens to comprehend the media's depictions of the politics of dissent. The findings illustrate the ways in which public demonstrations harnessed to the social advancement of racial minorities are portrayed in the mainstream news media as "threatening" regardless of their nonviolent characteristics (see Chenoweth & Pressman, 2020). Moreover, such framing reifies notions that these events need police intervention. The results also indicate that public demonstrations with white privilege at their foundation are likely to be represented in the mainstream news media as "non-threatening" regardless of their violent nature (Shepherd, 2020)—reinforcing ideas that these protests do not require state-sponsored repression.

We found three major themes in the news articles' discussions of BLM protests. First, these events were characterized as violent even when legitimate protesters expressed that the looting and property damage was due to the actions of fringe groups. Media portrayals functioned to suppress and delegitimize the critical messages of equality, justice, and respect for constitutional rights. Second, although we saw descriptions of excessive force instances as well as the bodily harm they inflicted, we also found that journalists used verbiage that minimized the extent of police violence, as evidenced by referring to a vehicular assault by police as a simple "surge" into the BLM protesters. Third, the articles included language that framed protesters as part of a group that threatens the public interests in safety and property—one that primarily employs looting, destruction, and disruption in the embodiment of their "untenable" message. In contrast, the COVID-19-related protesters were portrayed as patriotic citizens seeking to uphold their rights and freedoms, even with their disorderly and aggressive approaches. However, the underlying consequences of such portrayals reflect and support the deeply-rooted racial hierarchy in American society. Furthermore, media coverage that emphasizes *threat* may influence the general purview of BLM (Banks, 2018; Updegrove et al., 2020), and with salient consequences for how these protesters will be policed.

Our theoretical framework proposes that increases in Black political mobilization will be viewed as a threat to White political ascendancy. From our analyses, we find that the media is an institution that, like other social institutions, reflects the American racial stratification system (Oliver, 2017), as it operates under the assumptions and practices that protect whiteness and simultaneously encumbers Black advancement. With this understanding, the media's skewed framing of BLM as dangerous serves as a social control mechanism that invalidates this movement's political claims. Moreover, the consequences tied to such media descriptions is three-fold as it: hinders BLM's efforts to effect racial justice changes; elicits public stereotyping of BLM protests as violent (for example, the derogatory hashtag #BurnLootMurder that saturates social media platforms); and provokes a more aggressive law enforcement response.[8] In the end, negative media coverage of BLM, like that observed in our findings, perpetuates an undercurrent of racial threat that compromises the success of Black collective action.

In terms of theoretical implications, our analysis highlights the need to use an interdisciplinary lens to fully understand race effects in social institutions even beyond the criminal justice system (Bracey, 2016). As we seek to recognize the over-policing of Black bodies, we must not look at social institutions singularly. Instead, we should acknowledge the symbiotic nature of their contributions to the racial discrimination system (Reskin, 2012). For example, the operation of the media may have consequences for the operation of state coercive forces—through decisions by criminal justice system administrators (e.g., invest more in military-grade equipment to handle "riots") and members of the public in their voting decisions (e.g., desire to elect officials who support "law and order" initiatives) (Arnaud, 2016; Updegrove et al., 2020).

In terms of policy implications, we call for more diversity and minority representation in the media leadership as well as the recognition of racial bias in reporting. Media organizations need to "deal directly with racism and stereotyping among journalists and editors, who are embedded in the entrenched race discrimination system that spurred BLM" (Leopold &

Bell, 2017, p. 732). Beyond hiring, reporters should be trained to identify their own implicit biases and understand that threat-related themes can, and do, perpetuate racism in American news reporting. We also call for equal treatment in the exercise of constitutional rights. Engaging in protest is an essential thread in America's social fabric, and denying this freedom to those who have been historically marginalized only further underscores Feagin's (2000) observation of America as a "total racist society" (p. 26).

When we turn specifically to the problematic over-policing of Black bodies, we first call for law enforcement's unequivocal recognition that many of its strategies are racially-biased and inflict substantial trauma in Black communities—from the stamp of criminality by way of the vestiges of slavery, to the unnecessary and tragic loss of life due to discriminatory police action (Epp et al., 2014; Kendi, 2016; Mears et al., 2017). Once that acknowledgment is made, then the pathway to a profound transformation of the policing institution can be forged.

Furthermore, although police officers assert that they are stringently following orders and rules from their administrators, they can still be influenced by damaging, racist tropes portrayed in the media, which can then go into their required rapid decision-making when policing in general, and policing protests, specifically. To help resolve this problem, we implore law enforcement agencies to implement more comprehensive screening of applicants at both the recruitment and hiring phases. They must also mandate regular, continuous, evidence-based training throughout officers' tenure (e.g., implicit bias training on a quarterly basis), especially as they move up in the ranks and/or move to special weapons and tactics teams. We also call on police agencies to work more intensely with community leaders and advocacy organizations in Black neighborhoods. These residents need to be heard and have their experiences validated to improve police-community relations and police legitimacy. Such conversations—in town hall meetings or church gatherings, for example—can facilitate discussions of necessary changes to ensure equality in police treatment (e.g., ending hyper-surveillance and hot spots techniques, allowing Black residents to protest without fear) and establish reciprocally beneficial relationships.

These findings and conclusions must be considered in light of the study's limitations. The analyses herein are based on data from a limited number of national, largely distributed newspapers and are also based on a fraction of the articles that each paper publishes. Additionally, the time period of the examination does not include all instances of racial bias (or lack thereof) in the media as it relates to the BLM movement. Future research should discuss the media's representation of over-policing and racism by police agencies at the local level, which has more immediate effects in Black communities.

Notes

1. For example, in a broad study of protest policing in Switzerland, Wisler and Giugni (1999) found that, over a three-decade period, increases in media attention during protest campaigns are associated with diminished state repression by law enforcement (e.g. fewer weapons discharges).
2. It is important to note that the historical policing of collective action initiated by Black Americans (e.g., slave rebellions in antebellum society, the Civil Rights movement in Jim Crow society, and contemporary demonstrations prompted by police killings of Black civilians) have all been met with police violence against those seeking racial equality (Davenport et al., 2011; Umamaheswar, 2020;). In contrast, when armed White civilians gather and march (e.g., KKK rallies from the Reconstruction Era up until now, maskless protests during a global pandemic), they face only minimal police interference even though the risk of harm is tangible and omnipresent (Tolnay & Beck, 1995; Ray, 2020).
3. In accordance with America's changing demographics, the threat hypothesis also encompasses "ethnic threat" and "immigrant threat" (Stults & Swagar, 2018).
4. Information on the political leanings and media polarization of various U.S. newspaper outlets comes from The Pew Research Center (https://www.journalism.org/2020/01/24/media-polarization-methodology/). For instance, *The New York Times* is widely regarded as left-leaning whereas *The Wall Street Journal* is widely regarded as right-leaning.
5. The exact search terms and Boolean operators were: "Black Lives Matter" AND Floyd OR Taylor OR Brooks AND riot (title) OR rally (title) OR protest (title) OR demonstration (title).
6. The exact search terms and Boolean operators were: coronavirus AND "stay at home" OR "stay at home order" OR mask OR "mask mandate" AND riot (title) OR rally (title) OR protest (title) OR demonstration (title).
7. The co-author and three graduate students formed the coding team. The assistants, from Illinois State University's Anthropology, Criminal Justice Sciences, and Sociology departments, completed coding training covering operational definitions, and coding categories, and data analysis. Intercoder reliability was at least 75% on all articles coded by the team.
8. The media's depiction of BLM as dangerous has prompted forceful police presence at the sites of scheduled demonstrations. In contrast, the media's depiction of protests centered around whiteness has resulted in insufficient responses by law enforcement. For instance, the violent insurrection on January 6, 2021, at the U.S. Capitol, prompted by misinformation about the 2020 presidential election results, was in part a function of minimal law enforcement presence. According to statements by the Capitol Police, they did not anticipate such riotous behavior from the "Stop the Steal" dissidents (Durst et al., 2021). This lack of preparedness is reflective of the mainstream media's signals that such social movements are safe and nonthreatening.

References

Alexander, M. (2010). *The new Jim Crow: Mass incarceration in the age of colorblindness*. New York: The New Press.

Amenta, E., Elliott, T. A., Shortt, N., Tierney, A. C., Türkoğlu, D., & Vann Jr, B. (2017). From bias to coverage: What explains how news organizations treat social movements. *Sociology Compass, 11*(3), e12460. doi:10.1111/soc4.12460

Arnaud, E. (2016). Dismantling of dissent: Militarization and the right to peaceable assemble. *Cornell Law Review, 101*(3), 777–812.

Banks, C. (2018). Disciplining Black activism: Post-racial rhetoric, public memory and decorum in news media framing of the Black Lives Matter movement. *Continuum, 32*(6), 709–720. doi:10.1080/10304312.2018.1525920

Blalock, H. M. (1967). *Toward a theory of minority-group relations* (Vol. 325). New York, NY: Wiley.

Blauner, R. (1971). *Racial oppression in America*. New York, NY: Harper & Row

Blumer, H. (1958). Race prejudice as a sense of group position. *The Pacific Sociological Review, 1*(1), 3–7. doi:10.2307/1388607

Bobo, L. D. (2017). Racism in Trump's America: Reflections on culture, sociology, and the 2016 US presidential election. *The British Journal of Sociology, 68*, S85–S104. doi:10.1111/1468-4446.12324

Bonilla-Silva, E. (2014). *Racism without racists: Color-blind racism and the persistence of racial inequality in America* (4th ed.). Lanham, MD: Rowman & Littlefield.

Bonilla-Silva, E. (2015). The structure of racism in color-blind, "post-racial" America. *American Behavioral Scientist, 59*(11), 1358–1376. doi:10.1177/0002764215586826

Booker, B. (2021, January 7). Protests in White and Black, and the different response of law enforcement. *NPR*. https://n.pr/3v1XtIq.

Boyle, M. P., & Schmierbach, M. (2009). Media use and protest: The role of mainstream and alternative media use in predicting traditional and protest participation. *Communication Quarterly, 57*(1), 1–17. doi:10.1080/01463370802662424

Bracey, G. E. (2016). Black movements need Black theorizing: Exposing implicit whiteness in Political Process Theory. *Sociological Focus, 49*(1), 11–27. doi:10.1080/00380237.2015.1067569 .

Chan, J. M., & Lee, C. C. (1984). The journalistic paradigm on civil protests: A case study of Hong Kong. In A. Arno and W. Dissanayake (Eds.), *The news media in national and international conflict* (pp. 183–202). Boulder, CO: Westview Press.

Chenoweth, E., & Pressman, J. (2020, October 20). Black Lives Matter protesters were overwhelmingly peaceful, our research finds. *Harvard Radcliffe Institute*.https://www.radcliffe.harvard.edu/news-and-ideas/black-lives-matter-protesters-were-overwhelmingly-peaceful-our-research-finds.

Cottle, S. (2008). Reporting demonstrations: The changing media politics of dissent. *Media, Culture & Society, 30*(6), 853–872. doi:10.1177/0163443708096097

Crawford, C., Chiricos, T., & Kleck, G. (1998). Race, racial threat, and sentencing of habitual offenders. *Criminology, 36*(3), 481–512. doi:10.1111/j.1745-9125.1998.tb01256.x

Davenport, C., Soule, S. A., & Armstrong, D. A. (2011). Protesting while Black? The differential policing of American activism, 1960 to 1990. *American Sociological Review, 76*(1), 152–178. doi:10.1177/0003122410395370[Mismatch] https://doi.org/10.1177/0163443708096097.

Della Porta, D., & Diani, M. (2020). *Social movements: An introduction*. West Sussex, UK: John Wiley & Sons .

Della Porta, D., & Fillieule, O. (2004). Policing social protest. In D. A. Snow, S. A. Soule, & H. Kriesi, *The Blackwell companion to social movements* (pp. 217–241). Oxford, UK: Blackwell.

Durst, D., Mansfield, E., & Penzenstadler, N. (2021, January 26). 'It was a horrible scene': Capitol Police have a $500M budget. Why were they unprepared at the Jan. 6 riot?. *USA Today*. https://www.usatoday.com/story/news/investigations/2021/01/26/insurrection-capitol-police-riot-gear-officer-equipment/4231075001/.

Earl, J., & Soule, S. (2006). Seeing blue: A police-centered explanation of protest policing. *Mobilization: An International Quarterly*, 11(2), 145–164. doi:10.17813/maiq.11.2.u1wj8w41n301627u

Earl, J., Soule, S., & McCarthy, J. (2003). Protest under Fire? Explaining the Policing of Protest. *American Sociological Review*, 68(4), 581–606. Retrieved September 30, 2020, from http://www.jstor.org/stable/1519740. doi:10.2307/1519740

Eick, A. M. (2016). Forging ahead from ferguson: Re-evaluating the right to assemble in the face of police militarization. *William & Mary Bill of Rights Journal*, 24(4), 1235–1258.

Eitle, D., & Monahan, S. (2009). Revisiting the racial threat thesis: The role of police organizational characteristics in predicting race-specific drug arrest rates. *Justice Quarterly*, 26(3), 528–561. doi:10.1080/07418820802427817

Epp, C., Maynard-Moody, S., & Haider-Markel, D. (2014). *Pulled over: How police stops define race and citizenship*. Chicago, IL: University of Chicago Press .

Feagin, J. R. (2000). *Racist America: Roots. current realities, and future reparations*. New York, NY: Routledge.

Fuller, T. (2020, September 11). 100 days of protest: A chasm grows between Portland and the rest of Oregon. *The New York Times*. Retrieved from https://nyti.ms/2GfRps3.

Gamson, W.A. (1990 [1975]). *The strategy of social protest*. Homewood, IL: Dorsey.

Gorringe, H., & Rosie, M. (2008). It's a long way to Auchterarder! 'Negotiated management' and mismanagement in the policing of G8 protests . *The British Journal of Sociology*, 59(2), 187–205. doi:10.1111/j.1468-4446.2008.00189.x

Kendi, I. (2016). *Stamped from the beginning: The definitive history of racist ideas in America*. New York, NY: Bold Type Books.

Kilgo, D., & Mourão, R. R. (2019). Media effects and marginalized ideas: Relationships among media consumption and support for Black Lives Matter. *International Journal of Communication*, 13, 4287–4305. Retrieved from https://ijoc.org/index.php/ijoc/article/view/10518.

Kilgo, D. K., Mourao, R. R., & Sylvie, G. (2019). Martin to Brown: How time and platform impact coverage of the Black Lives Matter movement. *Journalism Practice*, 13(4), 413–430. doi:10.1080/17512786.2018.1507680

Leopold, J., & Bell, M. P. (2017). News media and the racialization of protest: An analysis of Black Lives Matter articles. *Equality, Diversity and Inclusion: An International Journal*, 36(8), 720–735. doi:10.1108/EDI-01-2017-0010 .

Liska, A. E. (Ed.). (1992). *Social threat and social control*. Albany, NY: SUNY Press

McCurdy, P. (2012). Social movements, protest and mainstream media. *Sociology Compass*, 6(3), 244–255. doi:10.1111/j.1751-9020.2011.00448.x

Mears, D., Craig, M., Stewart, E., & Warren, P. (2017). Thinking fast, not slow: How cognitive biases may contribute to racial disparities in the use of force in police-citizen encounters. *Journal of Criminal Justice*, 53, 12–24. doi:10.1016/j.jcrimjus.2017.09.001

Mourão, R. R., Kilgo, D. K., & Sylvie, G. (2018). Framing Ferguson: The interplay of advocacy and journalistic frames in local and national newspaper coverage of Michael Brown. *Journalism*, 22(2), 320–340. doi:10.1177/1464884918778722

Oliver, P. (2017). The ethnic dimensions in social movements. *Mobilization: An International Quarterly, 22*(4), 395–416. doi:10.17813/1086-671X-22-4-395

Omi, M., & Winant, H. (2015). *Racial formation in the United States: From the 1960s to the 1990s.* New York, NY: Routledge.

Ray, R. (2020, May 8). In Wisconsin, stay-at-home orders have become a flash point. *The Washington Post.* https://wapo.st/3492GT6.

Reskin, B. (2012). The race discrimination system. *Annual Review of Sociology, 38*(1), 17–35. doi:10.1146/annurev-soc-071811-145508 .

Reynolds-Stenson, H. (2018). Protesting the police: Anti-police brutality claims as a predictor of police repression of protest. *Social Movement Studies, 17*(1), 48–63. doi:10.1080/14742837.2017.1381592 .

Rosie, M., & Gorringe, H. (2009). The anarchists' world cup': Respectable protest and media panics. *Social Movement Studies, 8*(1), 35–53. doi:10.1080/14742830802591135

Saldaña, J. (2016). *The coding manual for qualitative researchers* (3rd ed.). Thousand Oaks, CA: Sage.

Shepherd, K. (2020, May 13). Tensions over restrictions spark violence and defiance among protesters as Trump pushes states to reopen. *The Washington Post.* https://wapo.st/3rC0xuu.

Stults, B., & Swagar, N. (2018). Racial and ethnic threat: Theory, research, and new directions. In R. Martinez, M. Hollis, & J. Stowell (Eds.), *The Handbook of Race, Ethnicity, Crime, and Justice* (pp. 147–171), Hoboken, NJ: Wiley . doi:10.1002/9781119113799.ch7

Tolnay, S., & Beck, E. (1995). *A festival of violence: An analysis of Southern Lynchings, 1882-1930.* Chicago. IL: University of Illinois Press.

Umamaheswar, J. (2020). Policing and racial (In) justice in the media: Newspaper portrayals of the "Black Lives Matter" movement. *Civic Sociology, 1*(1): 1–13. doi:10.1525/001c.12143

Updegrove, A. H., Cooper, M. N., Orrick, E. A., & Piquero, A. R. (2020). Red states and Black lives: Applying the racial threat hypothesis to the Black Lives Matter movement. *Justice Quarterly, 37*(1), 85–108. doi:10.1080/07418825.2018.1516797

Veneti, A., Karadimitriou, A., & Poulakidakos, S. (2016). Media ecology and the politics of dissent: Representations of the Hong Kong protests in *The Guardian* and *China Daily. Social Media + Society, 2*(3), 205630511666217–205630511666213. doi:10.1177/2056305116662175

Wacquant, L. (2002). From slavery to mass incarceration. *New Left Review, 13,* 14–60.

Wang, X., & Mears, D. P. (2010). Examining the direct and interactive effects of changes in racial and ethnic threat on sentencing decisions. *Journal of Research in Crime and Delinquency, 47*(4), 522–557. doi:10.1177/0022427810375576

Watkins, S. C. (2001). Framing protest: News media frames of the Million Man March. *Critical Studies in Media Communication, 18*(1), 83–101. doi:10.1080/15295030109367125

Wisler, D., & Giugni, M. (1999). Under the spotlight: The impact of media attention on protest policing. *Mobilization: An International Quarterly, 4*(2), 171–187. doi:10.17813/maiq.4.2.e02v758487330131 .

Why we should stop using the term "Black-on-Black crime": an analysis across disciplines

Delores Jones-Brown, Kenethia McIntosh Fuller, Paul Reck and Waverly Duck

ABSTRACT
Official statistics document that the majority of all crime committed in the U.S. is intra-racial. Only crimes involving victims and offenders of Black racial identity have been assigned an explicitly racialized label. Drawing on work from multiple disciplines, this paper traces the historical origins of racialized crime statistics. It examines how official statistics are manipulated, through racial disproportionality analysis, to mask the amount of crime committed by Whites and to support a view that Black crime is more prevalent and dangerous than other criminal offending. We trace the origin of the term "Black on Black crime" to unsuccessful efforts by Black leaders to protect the Black community from victimization or gain equitable treatment for Black defendants. We argue that the use of the term should be abandoned, in part, because of its current use in public discourse to legitimize police and civilian violence against Blacks. Recommendations for addressing and eliminating the use of this racially charged term in public discourse, policy, and criminal justice practice are provided.

Introduction

According to official crime statistics, each year Whites make up roughly 70% of those who are arrested, while Blacks and other persons of color make up the remaining 30%.[1] This seventy/thirty split has been documented since the late 1800s, when according to historian Khalil Gibran Muhammad, "[W]ith the publication of the 1890 census, prison statistics for the first time became the basis of a national discussion about blacks[2] as a distinct and dangerous criminal population" (Muhammad, 2010, p. 3). In his book, aptly titled, *The Condemnation of Blackness: Race, Crime, and the Making of Modern Urban America*, Muhammad (2010) notes that:

> New statistical and racial identities forged out of raw census data showed that African Americans as 12 percent of the population, made up 30 percent of the nation's prison population... From that moment forward, notions about blacks as criminals materialized in national debates about the fundamental racial and cultural differences between African-Americans and native-born whites and European immigrants... For white Americans of every ideological stripe...*African American criminality became one of the most widely accepted bases for justifying prejudicial thinking, discriminatory treatment, and/or racial violence* [against blacks] *as an instrument of public safety.* (p. 4) [emphasis added]

He adds that, "white social scientists presented the new crime data as objective, color-blind, and incontrovertible" (Muhammad, 2010, p. 4). The manipulation, interpretation and presentation of these statistical data would prove to be anything but neutral,[3] as race-coded crime data would become a mainstay of modern criminology and an important contributor to the criminalization and over-policing of Black bodies and the spaces they occupy.

Overview

In this article we draw heavily on the work of thought leaders across multiple disciplines, but especially the work of Black scholars, critical race theorist, and scholars of intersectionality to critique, understand and explain how Black racial identity became the center of understandings and fears about crime. We note here that the work of such scholars is often ignored in mainstream criminological analyses and research (see Gabbidon et al., 2004; Taylor Greene et al., 2018; Young & Sulton, 1991), though the topic of crime committed by Black perpetrators has been studied and reported ad nauseum.

By tracing race-coded crime statistics to their racist origins, we argue that all racialized statistical representations of crime are invalid and should be eliminated because they promote the idea that one's racial identity- as defined by socially recognizable physiological traits—has a direct causal connection to crime. We show that while, annually, a greater number of persons identified as "White" are reported in crime statistics, racial disproportionality analysis supports a myth that Black racial identity has a greater causal connection to crime than does White racial identity—a myth that manifests in the belief that Black people commit more crime than White people (see Robinson, 2000). We contend that this thinking is a contributor to beliefs that Black intra-racial violence is particularly prevalent and pernicious. Through examining 40 years of national homicide data reported to the FBI, we find no support for concluding that intra-racial violence among the Black population, represents a more peculiar social phenomenon than does intra-racial violence among Whites.

Our call for the elimination of the term "Black-on-Black crime" from social science, crime policy and popular discourse is, in part, an attempt to uncouple Black images from criminal images in the public imagination; and, to jumpstart a paradigm shift away from legitimizing the collection of race-coded crime statistics as directly empirically relevant to understanding crime. To be clear, the focus of this paper is not about racial disparities in the criminal justice system. It is the racialization of crime—a practice that we contend has contributed significantly to such disparities, including racial disparity in police contact.

Through our research, we discovered that the term "Black-on-Black crime" was developed as a call for resources to promote safety and equitable justice within Black urban spaces but, our review of internet media sources confirms that the term is currently being used to undermine the movement for the protection of Black lives—a movement sparked and reinforced by numerous highly publicized incidents of police violence against Black victims and of Black deaths at the hands of racist civilians. For these and other reasons we conclude this article by calling for the elimination of racial categories in national crime statistics because their inclusion and aggregate statistical manipulation, including racial disproportionality analysis (RDA), the reporting of racial crime rates, and the labeling of crime as either Black or White, unwittingly and intentionally serves to fuel and reinforce centuries old racist understandings of who is criminal, who is dangerous, and who is not.

An exhaustive discussion of how the social scientific world was convinced to concentrate its resources on attempting to explain the numerically least amount of crime occurrence (30%) rather than the majority amount of crime occurrence (70%) is a lesson in politics and human behavior that is far beyond the scope of this paper to adequately address.[4] However, here we contend that the time has come to acknowledge: 1) the harm done by the presentation of racialized crime statistics; and, 2) the urgent need to take corrective action.

Race and crime assumptions: a lesson in historical and contemporary racism

In 1928, just shy of forty years after race-coded prison data emerged as a basis for the modern 'scientific' study of "race and crime" in the United States, the prominent University of Pennsylvania sociologist, Thorsten Sellin, in his article, "The Negro Criminal: A Statistical Note" made the following observation about Black racial identity and crime:

> The colored criminal does not ... enjoy the racial anonymity which cloaks the offenses of individuals of the white race. The press is almost certain to brand him,

and the more revolting his crime proves to be the more likely it is that his race will be advertised... his individuality is ... submerged, and instead of a mere thief, robber, or murderer, he becomes a representative of his race, which in its turn is made to suffer for his sins (as cited in Muhammad, 2010, p. 2).

Sellin and others[5] urged social scientists to uncouple black racial identity from criminality but were largely unsuccessful as evidenced by contemporary one-sided racial references to "Black criminality" and "Black-on-Black crime" in both, popular discourse (see Robinson, 2000) and social scientific work. In her ground-breaking book, *"The Color of Crime: Racial Hoaxes, White Fear, Black Protectionism, Police Harassment, and other Macroaggressions,"* legal scholar, Katheryn Russell-Brown addresses the myth of the *criminalblackman*—that is, the popularly held erroneous belief that most Black men are criminal and dangerous (Russell, 1998).

Muhammad (2010) traces the social scientific support for this belief back to the reporting and analysis of the 1890 census data. In a nation not already marred by nearly three centuries of anti-Black racism, the fact that the majority of persons in prison were White, should have led thought leaders to believe that the physical or social environments of this numerical majority needed to be studied in order to determine the factors that were contributing to their criminality. Or, in the alternative, colorblind logic would have suggested that studying the prison population, as a whole, would yield meaningful information about all inmates' path to prison. Instead, the focus on Blacks as if there was some direct and independent connection between Black racial identity and crime, left nearly seventy percent of crime unexplained and unexamined.

Muhammad (2010) documents, that when criminality among Whites was studied, its causes were determined by White researchers to be outside of the White body. That is, the causes of White crime were deemed to be rooted in the social structure, "the stresses and strains of modern civilization"; "the total amount of misery and vice prevailing in a given community"; and "the state of society into which the individual is thrown" (p. 40, citing Hoffman, 1896). The criminal and self-destructive behavior of Whites was deemed to be a function of economic inequality - "a consequence of a diseased *society* [emphasis added], not of 'diseased manhood or womanhood'" (Muhammad, 2010, p. 41). These were the 'findings' of a Newark, New Jersey based actuary and statistician named Frederick L. Hoffman (1896). Using this logic, Hoffman and other influential racists of his time, called for economic intervention and social programs to address the needs and prolong the lives of White youth and adults.

For Blacks, who represented 30% of the prison population, Hoffman and others[6] took a different approach, assigning their criminal behavior to "racial proclivity" toward crime (Muhammad, 2010, p. 41). By locating the cause(s) of crime among Blacks inside the Black body and within Black "culture," Hoffman suggested that it would be a "waste of the nation's resources" to provide Blacks with the types of interventions afforded to Whites because Blacks were a "vanishing race" as evidenced by their self-destructive behavior (Muhammad, 2010, p. 40). To support the "racial proclivity" position, White statisticians developed and emphasized a racial disproportionality analysis (RDA) of race and crime. Under RDA then, Whites who comprised roughly 80% of the general population were under-represented in crime statistics because they represented 'only' 70% of the national prison population. Conversely, under this politically-motivated grouping by race,[7] Blacks were substantially over-represented as criminals since they comprised 30% of prisoners, while 'only' 12% of the population as a whole. This proportional difference was read to mean that Blacks were more criminal than their White counterparts (see e.g., Feagin, 2009).

Under RDA, Blackness became *the* public signifier of criminality, though European ethnics, such as the Irish and Italians, had also previously been known as the criminal classes (Gibson & Rafter, 2006; Webster, 2008). The proposition that Irish, Italian, German or Jewish identity was a main contributor to individual criminality diminished as social structural explanations for their crime gained prominence and the binary racial categorization of official crime statistics into columns labeled "White" or "Black" emerged (see Knepper, 2000). These binary columns ignored ethnic differences within each grouping. In addition, the substantial difference in the raw number of offenders in each of these two racial categories–with Blacks comprising the lower number–was masked by resort to aggregate rather than individualized comparative measures of crime—a practice that continues today.

In addition to reporting different causal explanations for White versus Black peoples' inclusion within the crime statistics available at the time, as Sellin later noted, the data in the race-coded columns were presented publicly through a racial disproportionality interpretative lens that served to minimize and distract from crime committed by ethnics who came to be labeled as "White" but emphasized that committed by "Blacks". RDA has carried over to the modern day, with arrest statistics replacing prison statistics as its basis. It erroneously and myopically centers Black racial identity as a biological or cultural cause of crime and has become a dominant criminalizing narrative in the discussion of crime in America, including among some people of color (see, e.g., Gabbidon et al., 2013).

Debunking the myth of crime as innately "Black"

Though the federal government's official reporting of arrests by race in the *Uniform Crime Reports* (*UCR*), has expanded the number of racial categories from two to five,[8] here we focus on the" White"/"Black" binary. Like the prison data from 1890, arrest data are an imperfect, socially[9] biased measure of crime that has a long history of use in criminological analyses. Similarly, though current studies of race and crime treat the Latinx population as a racial category, federal statistics treat this identity as an ethnic group, which, in some cases, is also subdivided into categories labeled "Black" or "White".[10] Because UCR data are submitted by law enforcement agencies across the country, it is impossible to know for certain how Latinx individuals are represented within Table 43 which annually reports arrests in the United States by race. Here we assume that they are likely assigned to racial categories based on appearance such as skin-tone, hair texture and other stereotyped physical features.

With these caveats in mind, we draw on arrest data from the UCR to illustrate the wrong-headedness of primarily seeing crime in Blackface (Russell, 1998). In 2019, the most recent year reported at the time of this writing, the raw number of arrests reported under the racial category labeled "White" was 2.6 times greater than that reported in the category labeled "Black". (See Table 1). The number of arrests where the person arrested was reported as White represented 69.4% of all arrests, while 26.6% of arrests were reported as involving a person who was assigned the racial identity of Black. Whites represented more than two-thirds of property crime arrests for burglary (68.2%), larceny (66.3%), car theft (67.6%) and arson (70.8%). A person labeled White also outnumbered Blacks in two of the four violent crime categories—forcible rape (at 69.8%) and aggravated assault (at 61.8%).

Table 1. Total UCR reported arrests in the United States 2019 by race, raw number and percentage.

	Whites arrested	Blacks arrested	%White	%Black
Total	4,729,290	1,815,144	69.4	26.6
Property crime				
Burglary	81,104	34,188	68.2	28.8
Larceny-theft	393,719	178,937	66.3	30.2
Motor vehicle theft	38,719	16,409	67.6	28.6
Arson	4,453	1,553	70.8	24.7
Violent crime				
Homicide[a]	3,650	4,078	45.8	51.2
Forcible rape	11,588	4,427	69.8	26.7
Robbery	25,143	29,677	44.7	52.7
Aggravated assault	169,467	91,164	61.8	33.2

Source: Uniform Crime Reports, Crime in the United States 2019, Table 43A.
https://ucr.fbi.gov/crime-in-the-u.s/2019/crime-in-the-u.s.-2019/topic-pages/tables/table-43
[a]Murder and non-negligent manslaughter.

In the two violent crime categories where those who are labeled Black represented the greater number and percentage of arrests—homicide (51.2%) and robbery (52.7%), we contend that the difference across race for these offenses are not as stark as RDA and other aggregate analyses might suggest. The 70/30 split in the racial identity of those arrested has been reported within UCR data dating back at least 30 years.[11] They do not support a view that Blacks commit greater than 50% of crime in the United States—the amount that would be needed to constitute "the majority" or "the most" crime, as commonly believed (Robinson, 2000). We recognize that criminologists and the public are not trained to read official crime statistics in this straightforward way and many are likely unaware or not fully cognizant of the racist history that is responsible for RDA and other aggregate analyses that normalize racial comparisons without questioning the reason for doing so. Those analyses confound the understanding of criminal behavior by focusing on racial difference among offenders rather than the criminal risk factors that they have in common. RDA skews in favor of Whites who racially comprise a significant majority of the general population and the group for whom social support (see Cullen, 1994) has unevenly been made available.

Having established that official crime statistics do not support the idea that Black perpetrators of crime outnumber those who are White, we turn to the question of whether official statistics support a claim that intra-racial offending among Blacks is more prevalent and dangerous than intra-racial offending among Whites such that it warrants a special race-coded label. To address these questions, we examined 40 years of intra-racial homicide data. (See Table 2). We found that from 1979 through 2019 the majority of *all* homicides were intra-racial. On average, roughly 92% of

Table 2. Percentage of intra-racial homicides 1979 to 2019.

	1979	1980	1981	1982	1983	1984	1985	1986	1988	1989	1990
Black-on-Black	94.74	94.84	94.96	94.69	94.41	94.22	93.76	94.68	94.45	93.62	93.46
White-on-White	87.86	87.7	87.63	88.99	88.24	88.22	87.88	87.84	86.42	85.73	86.00
	1991	1992	1993	1994	1995	1996	1997	1998	1999	2000	
Black-on-Black	92.67	93.52	93.27	92.38	92.82	92.42	92.92	92.69	93.2	93.03	
White-on-White	84.69	82.98	82.97	82.76	83.24	83.83	84.07	85.97	83.3	85.32	
	2001	2002	2003	2004	2005	2006	2007	2008	2009	2010	
Black-on-Black	90.76	90.91	91.00	90.77	90.72	91.85	90.18	90.01	90.82	90.4	
White-on-White	83.94	83.75	83.73	83.79	83.22	81.59	81.34	83.33	84.22	83.47	
	2011	2012	2013	2014	2015	2016	2017	2018	2019		
Black-on-Black	90.79	91.09	90.12	89.96	89.34	89.54	88.45	88.88	88.58		
White-on-White	82.91	83.57	83.49	82.36	81.28	81.57	80.2	80.75	78.63		

Source: Uniform Crime Reports, Crime in the United States, Supplementary Homicide Reports.
Notes. The data provided the race of both the offender and the victim, for all homicides in which the race of the offender is known. These incidents also include only offenses that have one victim and one offender. Data is included for every year for which the data are publicly available. Once the raw count for race of offenders and victims was obtained, those numbers were converted to the actual percentages for each group. For the purposes of this paper, the focus remains on Black and White offenders and victims.

homicides against Black victims were committed by Black offenders and 84% of White victims were killed by a perpetrator who was White. Also on average, the annual difference in homicides that involved Black perpetrators and Black victims and those that involved White perpetrators and White victims was 7%. Researchers from different academic disciplines might disagree over the threshold at which these annual differences might validly denote a "problem" worthy of intense study and focus. In our view, these data debunk the notion that "Black-on-Black" homicide is a unique social phenomenon; and the relative closeness of the figures suggests that homicidal violence in Black communities is not due to innate race-based pathology requiring a distinct label.[12]

Shifting the focus from homicides to self-reported violent victimization, National Crime Victimization Survey (NCVS) data show that more than half of all reported non-homicide violent victimizations are intra-racial. A Bureau of Justice Statistics (BJS) analysis for the years 2012 to 2015 places violent victimizations between Whites at 56.6% and that between Blacks at 63.2% (Morgan, 2017). Intra-racial violent victimization reported for 2018 and 2019 showed an increase in this statistic. For both years, the victimization involving Black perpetrators and Black victims was reported as roughly 70% and that involving White perpetrators and White victims was reported as roughly 62% (Morgan & Oudekerk, 2019; Morgan & Truman, 2020). Again, the difference in Black intra-racial offending and that of White intra-racial offending averaged out to about 7%. This difference hardly seems sufficient empirical justification for arguing that the pattern of violent intra-racial victimization among Blacks is an anomaly that warrants a special label, while the pattern of White intra-racial victimization does not. These data debunk the notion that violent crime perpetrated by Black individuals against others within their racial group is a unique social phenomenon, since those who are socially recognized as "White" engage is these behaviors too. These numbers also counter the media images noted by Robinson (2000)—images that tend to exaggerate the amount of violence committed by Blacks and to present Blacks as society's most dangerous and criminal group. They call for closer examination of how public attention continues to be drawn, sometimes almost exclusively, to "Black crime" and intra-racial offending among the group.

Origins of the term "Black-on-Black crime"

The acceptance of "Black crime" as a distinct social phenomenon set the stage for the development of a term that would also distinguish intra-racial offending among Blacks from intra-racial offending among Whites. In our effort to trace the origin of the term "Black-on-Black crime" back to its roots, we found that starting in the 1970s, prominent Black media outlets, civil rights organizations and Black public figures identified intra-racial violent victimization within urban neighborhoods as a social crisis needing immediate attention. Those concerns were first voiced in print in the *Chicago Daily Defender*, a prominent Black newspaper of the day. In 1970, an article was published that conveyed the views of civil rights activist, Jesse Jackson, on the improper handling of crime in Black communities by politicians and the police (Guilmant, 1970). In the article, Jackson reprimanded politicians for "their silence and ineffectiveness in dealing with the present black-on-black crime crisis" (Guilmant, 1970, p. 4). Jackson admonished the media for not understanding or explaining the problem from the perspective of the Black community. The intention was to require equitable justice on par with that in White crime victim cases, and a valuing of Black lives the same as White lives. Consistent with contemporary calls for police reform and accountability, five decades ago Jackson also called for an increase in Black officers so that the police force would more closely reflect the community (Guilmant, 1970).

Later that same year, African American psychiatrist Alvin F. Pouissant went on to publish an article in *Ebony*—a prominent Black-owned magazine. The article was titled "Why Blacks Kill Blacks" (Poussaint, 1970). The article became the precursor to a book with the same title that he would publish in 1972. In the article, Pouissant reiterated Jackson's concerns by rebuking the policies and policing practices that showed evidence of a devaluing of Black lives. In addition to discussing the numerous structural causes of 'Black crime', Pouissant advocated for members of the Black community to have decision-making roles in all aspects of the justice system; and pressed for a system that would maintain a goal of rehabilitating offenders (Poussaint, 1970).

An immediate response to these calls to action came from Cook County court judge Saul A. Epton in 1971. To dispel the notion that inter- and intra-racial Black offending was treated differently, Epton sentenced two Black men to 100 to 150 years in prison after each was convicted of murder–one for the killing of a White victim; the other for killing a person who was Black (Mock, 2015). This harsh treatment of the Black offenders was likely not what Jackson or Pouissant had anticipated in response to their demands for Black protection against crime and equitable treatment from the justice system. Yet it would soon become evident that the response to similar requests for parity in the future would also be met with the same punitive approach (Balko, 2013; Donaldson, 2015; Duck, 2015; Rios, 2011).

In 1973, *Ebony* published another article discussing the cause of crime among Black people. Quoting the work of Poussaint, the article, which did not list an author, argued that Black men were impoverished and frustrated, which led to violence. But, in strongly worded language, the article declared that, "[T]he black criminal must be told in no uncertain terms that his assaults and his thievery and his dope-pushing and his murders will no longer be suffered in silence" (Black-on-Black Crime, 1973, p. 200). The article's recommendations for change included that "decent black people" be willing to work for increased protection and the eradication of the poor social conditions that influence criminality. In words akin to Yale Sociology professor Elijah Anderson's *Code of the Street* (1999), the article asserted that "[D]ecent, law-abiding black people" would take matters into their own hands and fight against crime in their communities alongside prominent Black community organizations (Black-on-Black Crime, 1973, p. 200). Little to no attention seemed to be paid to the fact that the term "Black-on-Black" would obscure any distinction between Blacks who were "decent" and those who were serious criminals.

Ebony addressed the topic of Black intra-racial offending again in 1979 by publishing a special issue titled: "Black-on-Black Crime – The Cause, The Consequences, The Cures." The articles in this special issue covered a range of perspectives on crime in Black neighborhoods. Financial and political divestment from Black communities, introduction of drugs to those communities, racism, mental health, the media, unemployment, the breakdown of the Black family, and the flawed justice system were all discussed as underlying causes of crime. In one article, Napper (1979) acknowledged the socio-structural contributions to crime rates in impoverished communities; and, proposed that political involvement and a renewed sense of community in Black neighborhoods was required in order to bring about sustainable change.

The following year, the National Association for the Advancement of Colored People (NAACP) published an official resolution on Black-on-Black crime (National Association for the Advancement of Colored People, 1980). In the resolution, the organization took the position that, as the result of numerous social and structural factors, "Black-on-Black crime" was increasing. The resolution restated the demand posed previously–that the criminal justice system treat offenders equally, whether their crimes are committed against Black or White victims. In that same decade, the Black Legislative Caucus approached the federal government for assistance with violence in poor minority communities due to crack addiction and related drug markets. The result was mass incarceration and community devastation as 88% of the mandatory federal crack prison sentences were given to Black people (Clear, 2007; Jones-Brown, 2000).

In search of "White crime": the not so hidden racism of crime research and public discourse

In their seminal chapter, "Toward a Theory of Race, Crime and Urban Inequality," sociologists Robert Sampson and William Julius Wilson (1995) identify both micro- and macro level forces that contribute to the crime statistics in urban low-income spaces. They also identify historical and contemporary structural forces that have disproportionately trapped Blacks within such spaces—among them, deindustrialization, housing discrimination, and overtly racists policy decisions. Sampson and Wilson (1995) contend that these policy decisions created neighborhoods with a high concentration of poor minorities, social isolation, weak organizations, and a lack of access to opportunities for social mobility. Building off prior work by Sampson, they attempted to make racial comparisons while researching violent crime in Chicago. Again, they found that the racial differences in concentrated urban poverty were so substantial that the most deprived urban contexts in which Whites resided were considerably better than the average context of Black communities (Sampson & Wilson, 1995).

Despite the stark difference in community context across race, Sampson and Wilson (1995) found that the sources of violent crime appear to be remarkably invariant. For example, they found that: the percentage of both White and Black families headed by a female was correlated with juvenile violence within each racial group; predictors for robbery were substantially the same for each; and family disruption had a similar effect on both Black and White crime. Their formulation of family disruption included male joblessness and female headed households. For structural reasons that they detail, urban Black families were found to have higher concentrations of both these correlates. They concluded that Black family disruption was not a unique contributor to violence, nor could Black violence be attributed to unique cultural factors within the Black community. Peterson and Krivo (2005) confirmed that structural disadvantage is a predictor of violent crime, generally, and that when controls for neighborhood disadvantage are introduced, the racial gap in offending is substantially diminished.

Despite this and similar social scientific research documenting the correlation between inequality and crime, the "Black crime" myth has flourished, essentially without a White counterpart, although crime occurs daily within each racial grouping. This latter fact alone means that something other than Black "criminal proclivity" is at work. We make note that crime committed by Whites is not regularly referred to as "White crime". In her chapter titled, "In Search of White Crime," Russell-Brown begins with a quote attributed to critical race theorist and legal scholar, Richard Delgado (1994): "No one focuses on White crime or sees it as a problem. In fact, the very category "White crime" sounds funny, like, some sort of debater's trick" (Russell, 1998, p. 110).

This brings us full circle to the question of why, as a nation of scholars, policy makers, activists, advocates, researchers and ordinary people, we have come to focus our attention on crime committed by people who fall within a socially constructed racial category we call "Black" without similarly assigning a racial label to crimes committed by persons within the socially constructed racial category we call "White". The default response is often, because of Black disproportionality in criminal offending as reflected in crime statistics. A response we recognize as RDA. Having researched the origins of the term "Black-on-Black crime," another explanation emerged. When Black communities, through their leaders, sought government assistance to address neighborhood crime, they unwittingly reinforced the racist tradition of criminalizing the Black body, by using the term "Black-on-Black crime" to describe their dilemma. We propose that the term gained traction, in part, because it was consistent with a larger narrative about "Black crime".

Stanford University social psychologist, Jennifer Eberhardt and her colleagues (Eberhardt et al., 2004; Goff et al., 2008, 2014) have conducted research with police officers and civilians with findings that confirm Black criminalization and its influence on everyday understandings of, and reactions to crime, even among those who are not overtly racist. The concept of implicit racial bias has been developed by these and other social psychologists, as a means to understand and explain public reactions to Black bodies and their association with thoughts about crime and violence. This social psychological evidence has existed for some time (see for example, Allport & Postman, 1947) but has only recently been acknowledged in the field of policing which spent years denying the empirical existence of the unconstitutional practice called "racial profiling".[13]

Though Whites and Blacks can be subject to race-based profiling, studies of both overt and implicit racial bias suggest that Black targeting is most prevalent.[14] In their groundbreaking article, "Seeing Black: Race, Crime and Visual Processing," Eberhardt et al. (2004) provide empirical confirmation that seeing a target of Black racial identity influences the speed at which both civilians and police make the decision to shoot. Their findings also revealed a tendency to mentally associate Black faces with crime objects and animal images, specifically apes. In other studies involving civilian and police participants, Goff and his colleagues (2014) found that images of Black children were likely to be seen as older, and more criminal and ape-like than the images of similarly situated White children. Such findings suggest that a population of roughly 47 million people is condemned to being seen as criminal, dangerous, and animalistic although crime statistics show that the number of arrests involving Blacks is less than 4 percent of the total Black population. For homicides, the most serious of the violent index crimes, the percentage is less than .009.[15]

And what of the fact that Whites are implicated in roughly 70% of arrests annually without being assigned a "White crime" label or that annually intra-racial homicides among them are more than 80%? The raw numbers for 2019 (see Table 1) implicate a White perpetrator in nearly 5 million arrests compared to less than 2 million arrests for perpetrators categorized as Black. RDA and comparisons involving racial offending rates tend to mask this more individualized view of crime. We contend that the individualized view represented by raw numbers is most appropriate since a specific crime is committed by a specific person or person(s) who happens to fall within a socially constructed race-coded category and not by entire racial groups. Aggregate analyses like RDA and racial offending rates contribute to the racialization of crime and a misrepresentation of the character of the majority of individuals within each group. It also masks the fact that criminal conduct within *both* populations is markedly low given the adverse economic and other negative social conditions to which the members of each group are exposed (Barak et al., 2018). Given the multitude of adverse structural forces to which Blacks are currently and have historically been exposed, at least one pair of researchers has investigated why Blacks do not offend more (Gaston & Doherty, 2018). The focus on racial identity and crime denies the relevance of individual agency, social networks, social capital, and centuries old impediments imposed against Blacks and benefits bestowed upon Whites by racist structures and normative practices (Browne-Marshall, 2013; Katznelson, 2005; Sampson & Wilson, 1995). It also obscures the reality that the overwhelming majority of individuals, regardless of race and social circumstance, do not engage in serious crime. In addition, the continuous use of RDA, in the modern day, fails to take account of the ethnic and other diversity within each racial category that this simplistically dubbed "Black" or "White" (Joseph, 2006).

Before turning to our final argument for why the term "Black-on-Black" and other racialized labels for crime should be abandoned, we present a summary of statistics drawn from Table 43 of the 2019 UCR, Arrests by Race and Ethnicity, and note that these statistics counter popular race and crime narratives–one being that Black youth, especially Black male youth, are responsible for most crime in America (see Russell, 1998). To challenge this view without using RDA or racial rates of offending, we draw attention to statistics provided in *Crime in the United States*, 2019 (United States Department of Justice, Federal Bureau of Investigation, 2020) that implicate White individuals in crime. According to the report:

- White individuals were arrested more often for violent crimes than individuals of any other race and accounted for 59.1 percent of those arrests.
- Of all juveniles (persons under the age of 18) arrested in 2019, 62.5 percent were White, 33.9 percent were Black or African American, and 3.6 percent were of other races.
- White juveniles comprised 50.3 percent of all juveniles arrested for violent crimes, and Black or African American juveniles accounted for

46.4 percent of juveniles arrested for violent crimes. White juveniles comprised 54.9 percent of all juveniles arrested for property crimes.
- Of juveniles arrested for drug abuse violations, 74.8 percent were White.
- White juveniles comprised 56.4 percent of juveniles arrested for aggravated assault and 55.4 percent of juveniles arrested for larceny-theft.

The facts that Whites were arrested for nearly 60% of all violent crimes; and, comprise the majority of all juvenile arrests, are not regularly cited statistics. Nor is it regularly publicized that White youth are arrested for more than half of all violent crimes, more than half of all property crimes, and three-quarters of all drug offenses. We note that while many foundational delinquency theories were derived from studies involving White samples (e.g., Chambliss, 1973; Hirschi, 1969), this fact is also not widely advertised. The cumulative effect of this silence is a one-sided public picture of crime that is racist, scientifically unsound, and is especially damaging to the health and well-being of individuals who, by the accident of birth, are situated within the socially constructed group we call "Black".

Muhammad (2010) exhaustively documents how racist assumptions and statistical manipulations were intentionally designed to underpin and uphold the racial social order at the time of the first national census—a social order built on nearly three centuries of Black oppression and perceived inferiority and White supremacy and domination (McIntyre, 1993). We contend that the FBI's adoption of racial categories within its crime statistics in 1933 (see Knepper, 2000), increased the ability of race-focused criminologists to use official statistics in the criminalization of Blackness, even in the face of substantial criminal offending among Whites.

To reiterate, RDA compares racial representation in the general population to racial representation in crime statistics such as arrests.[16] This minimizes the significance of "White crime" by noting that Whites make up roughly 80 percent of the general population, which then is read to mean, Whites are "less criminal" because they are under-represented in crime by roughly 10%. The individual criminal conduct of White perpetrators becomes subsumed within this "less criminal" group identity. By contrast, RDA inflates the significance of "Black crime" by emphasizing that Blacks make up 12 to 13% of the general population, but 30% of crime statistics. Consequently, the group identity of Blacks as "more criminal" is inaccurately understood as 3 to 4 times that of Whites (calculated by adding together Black over-representation in arrests by nearly two and a half times their proportion of the national population and the 10% under-representation of Whites in arrest statistics compared to their percentage of the general population).

In our view, RDA over complicates the straightforward picture of race and crime presented by raw numbers and inaccurately shifts the focus to crimes committed by those identified as Black, leaving crime committed by Whites to be examined as race-neutral.[17] Throughout this paper we have attempted to refrain from using the terms "White crime" and "Black crime" so as not to undercut our call for de-racialization. It has been extremely difficult because the tendency to identify crime by race, but most especially Blackness, is so deeply engrained. This indoctrination is currently being used to unabashedly excuse or legitimize police violence against Blacks and diminish concerns about those Blacks who become victims of state and vigilante violence.

Attempted use of a myth to derail a movement

Having established that intra-racial violent offending is not a unique harmful behavior embedded in Black conduct or culture, we turn to why it is imperative to discard the "Black-on-Black" crime label. Though initially used as a cry for help from the Black community to government authorities, it is now a messaging tool that media pundits, politicians, law enforcement officials, and others employ to draw attention away from the problem of police violence against Blacks. In contrast to the Black media's messaging about "Black-on-Black crime" in the 1970s, the current media messaging by proponents of the "Black-on-Black crime" narrative is not designed to garner help for Black victims, nor spark conversations about holistic crime reduction strategies. Instead, these commentators use the term as a way of refocusing the narrative about police victimization of Blacks to Blacks' victimization of each other.

As shown in Table 3, politically conservative commentators such as Rudolph Giuliani, Sean Hannity, Bill O'Reilly, and the late Rush Limbaugh, have routinely raised the rhetorical question, "What about Black-on-Black crime?" when there are organized protests seeking to bring attention to police killings. To assess how often the term "Black-on-Black-crime" is used as a trope to draw attention away from the problem of police violence against Blacks, we conducted an internet search of media sources.

The references to "Black-on-Black crime" listed in Table 3 were obtained through a search for articles containing the phrase "Black-on-Black crime" for each year between 2012 and 2020 using the Google News search engine. A list of media commentators, politicians, and law enforcement officials who posited focusing on "Black-on-Black crime" during those periods was compiled from the articles. Specific proponents of this narrative were included in Table 3 if they were cross-referenced in at least two articles. The table first lists the use of the term in reference to the

Table 3. Black-on-Black crime references in media during organized protests of police and vigilante violence directed at Blacks between 2013 and 2020.

Black-on-Black crime references following vigilante George Zimmerman's killing of Trayvon Martin on February 26, 2012:
1) Bill O'Reilly on Fox News's *The O'Reilly Factor* on July 9, 2013;
2) Crystal Wright in *The Guardian* on July 13, 2013;
3) Ben Shapiro on Twitter on July 14, 2013;
4) Newt Gingrich on CNN's *Crossfire* on July 14, 2013;
5) Rod Dreher of *The American Conservative* on July 15, 2013.

Black-on-Black crime references following police killings of Eric Garner, Michael Brown, and Tamir Rice in 2014:
1) Rush Limbaugh on *The Rush Limbaugh Show* on August 14, 2014;
2) Jason Riley on NBC's *Meet the Press* on August 17, 2014;
3) Martha MacCallum on Fox News's *America's Newsroom* on August 18, 2014;
4) Bernard Goldberg in *The National Review* on August 18, 2014;
5) Ruldoph Guiliani on NBC's *Meet the Press* on November 23, 2014
6) Rudolph Guiliani on Fox News's *Fox News Sunday* on December 1, 2014
7) Alfred S. Regnery on Breitbart.com on May 24, 2016 (referencing Brown protests)

Black-on-Black crime references following police killings of Freddie Gray, Laquan McDonald, and Walter Scott, and Sandra Bland death in police custody, in 2015:
1) Bill O'Reilly on Fox News's *The O'Reilly Factor* on June 16, 2015;
2) Kimberly Guilfoyle and Juan Williams on Fox New's *The Five* on August 25, 2015;
3) Sean Hannity and Deroy Murdock on Fox News's *Hannity* on August 27, 2015;
4) Doug McKelway on Fox News's *America's Newsroom* on September 1, 2015;
5) Larry Elder and Sean Hannity on Fox News's *Hannity* on September 1, 2015;
6) Geraldo Rivera and Sean Hannity on Fox News's *Hannity* on September 2, 2015;
7) Donald Trump on Twitter on November 22, 2015;
8) Bill O'Reilly on Fox News's *The O'Reilly Factor* on November 24, 2015;
9) Mike Tobin of Fox News questioning a protester on November 25, 2015;
10) Jerome Hudson on *Breitbart.com* on November 28, 2015

Black-on-Black crime references following police killings of Alton Sterling, Philando Castile, Keith Lamont Scott in 2016:
1) Sean Hannity on Fox News's *Hannity* on July 8, 2016;
2) Katie McHugh on *Breitbart.com* on July 11, 2016;
3) David French in *The National Review* on August 15, 2016;
4) Donald Trump at an Ohio church meeting on September 21, 2016;
5) David Clarke, Sheriff of Milwaukee County, Wisconsin, on Fox News's *America's Newsroom* on September 23, 2016.

Black-on-Black crime references following the police killings of George Floyd, Breonna Taylor, and Rayshard Brooks in 2020:
1) Andrew McCarthy in *The National Review* on June 3, 2020 and June 25, 2020;
2) Heather MacDonald in *The Wall Street Journal* on June 2, 2020;
3) Mark Steyn on *The Rush Limbaugh Show* on June 9, 2020;
4) Robert Cherry in *The National Review* on June, 12, 2020;
5) Gregg Re on FOXNews.com on June 12, 2020;
6) Ken Blackwell on Sirius XM's *Breitbart News Daily* on June 17, 2020;
7) Geraldo Rivera on Fox News's *Hannity* on June 22, 2020;
8) Juan Williams on Fox News's *The Five* on July 7, 2020;
9) New Orleans Police Superintendent Shaun Ferguson on July 14, 2020;
10) Catholic League President Bill Donohue on Breitbart.com on August 10, 2020;
11) Rob Smith on FOXNews.com on September 9, 2020.

Source: Citations omitted due to space constraints. They are available upon request to the authors.

Black Lives Matter (BLM) founding event, the killing of Trayvon Martin. Though George Zimmerman was not a police officer, he aspired to be and was reportedly the self-appointed captain of the neighborhood watch for the residential development where the killing occurred (Jonsson, 2012).

In total we found 38 references to "Black-on-Black-crime" associated with the deaths of 14 victims–the killing of Trayvon Martin, and 13 other highly publicized cases that occurred after the emergence of BLM. We found five such references related to the death of Trayvon Martin and the acquittal of George Zimmerman in 2013; seven related to the deaths of Eric Garner, Michael Brown and Tamir Rice in 2014; ten related to the deaths of Freddie Gray, Laquan McDonald, Walter Scott, and Sandra Bland in 2015; five associated with the deaths of Alton Sterling, Philando Castile, and Keith Lamont Scott in 2016; and, eleven in reference to the deaths of George Floyd, Breonna Taylor and Rayshard Brooks in 2020. In contrast, we found no commentator references to "White-on-White-crime" in the wake of police killings of White victims like Zachary Hammond in 2015, Daniel Harris in 2016, or Justine Damond in 2017.

We contend that these commentators' selective invocation of "Black-on-Black crime" implies that crime committed by Blacks, unlike that committed by persons in other racial categories, is of a peculiar *racial* nature, and is consistent with the aforementioned long history of attributing crime committed by Blacks to genetic and cultural propensities (Bouie, 2013a, 2013b; Massie, 2016; Shabazz, 2020). Under social identity theory, these commentators' frequent invocation of the "Black-on-Black crime" label, is likely to resonate with those who already subscribe to the notion that crime committed by Blacks is driven by a unique, inherent criminal pathology (Bouie, 2013a, 2013b; Headley, 1983, Shabazz, 2020). Such pathologizing reifies and perpetuates longstanding essentialist stereotypes of Black criminality in the media and the community at large, especially for Black men who have historically been cast as violent, wanton, and depraved (Fishman 2002). The Say Her Name Campaign launched by the African American Policy Forum in 2014 has highlighted the fact that Black women and girls are not immune from police violence and perceptions of them as dangerous and criminal too.[18]

Black women, feminists, and others have long affirmed that language is powerful[19]; and, that it is also political, especially when weaponized by outsiders to frame the Black American experience in negative terms. African American Studies Professor Nikki Jones (2009) argues that the term "Black-on-Black crime" distorts the suffering of Black Americans as a whole, and of Black women and girls in particular. The relationship between race and language has also been highlighted by the founders of BLM, Patrisse Cullors, Alicia Garza, and Opal Tometi (Finn, 2020). They have exposed the role of language in legitimating state sanctioned violence against Black bodies while at the same time skillfully harnessing it to combat such violence. Ironically, although the movement has been nominated for a Nobel Peace Prize, it has also been assigned a racialized criminal label. In a report compiled by the FBI Counterterrorism Division (2017), BLM is referred to as a 'likely' Black Identity Extremist group.

To an uninformed public steeped in years of racialized history and social mores, the silence around White intra-racial offending helps claims about "Black-on-Black crime" sound true. Claims that paint the movement for the safety and reaffirmed valuing of Black lives as illegitimate and disingenuous because more Blacks die at the hands of other Blacks than die from police and vigilante violence. However, the breadth and depth of the protests that followed the release of the video-recorded death of George Floyd on May 25, 2020 provide evidence that the media commentators listed in Table 3 were largely unsuccessful in thwarting the efforts of BLM to call attention to the acute problem of homicidal killing of Blacks by police and private citizens, who claim to be enforcing the law. Sources indicate that protest occurred in as many as 60 countries. In the U.S., Portland, Oregon, a city with one of the highest percentages of White residents, clocked the highest number of protest days. While it is encouraging that BLM has been nominated for a Nobel Prize and many White allies recognize the need to affirmatively protect the lives of Black people, by abandoning the "Black-on-Black crime" label, it may become easier to focus media and other attention on the structural forces that contribute to crime irrespective of one's racial or ethnic identity—forces that disproportionately affect Black people.

Discussion, conclusions and recommendations

The racist contours of everyday language have been illuminated by many authors working across multiple traditions (see, e.g., Bell, 1973; Crenshaw et al., 1995). Here we want to be clear that the "Black-on-Black crime" label is overtly and tacitly racist; reflects a one-sided view of intra-racial offending; over-emphasizes the amount of crime among Blacks vis-à-vis the criminal behavior engaged in by Whites; and unnecessarily exposes Black men, women and children to the risk of police contact—both deadly and non-deadly (Rios, 2011; Roper, 2020). By tracing the practice of publishing race-coded national crime statistics across several academic disciplines, we have come to an understanding of how the Black body has been officially criminalized–first through discriminatory legislation that supported nearly two and a half centuries of Black enslavement; then through another two centuries of legislation, police and academic practice that targeted crime among Blacks as *the* focal point for understanding and preventing crime.

Though Sociologists contend that race is not real, the social construction of race is real in its consequences (Thomas & Thomas, 1928). By using the term "Black-on-Black crime" in their quest for government protection from violent victimization, Black media, civil rights activists and thought leaders unwittingly reinforced a false narrative about Blackness that remains in place today and is being used by conservative power brokers to thwart the very protection the term was intended to attract. Geography professor David Wilson (2005) suggests that adding the term "Black-on-Black crime" to the crime fighting discourse of the 1970s and 1980s led to a calcifying of the term in the American consciousness. Accepting the idea of "Black-on-Black crime" as a unique social phenomenon has had dire social consequences. Namely, it has contributed to the mass incarceration of Blacks for both violent and nonviolent offenses (Alexander, 2010; Clear, 2007); and, to the over control of Blacks through aggressive policing tactics such as stop-and-frisk and 'broken windows' enforcement. By our calculations, there are at least four groups who must be involved in efforts to dislodge the term and eliminate its influence – media commentators, social justice activists, academic researchers and national policy makers. What follows are our recommendations for how each can contribute to the de-racialization of crime, the umbrella under which the "Black-on-Black-crime" label can be abandoned.

First, since it appears that the Black community and Black media gave the "Black-on-Black crime" label its power, they must be central to a movement designed to take it back. A first step would be to dismantle and resist all mechanisms that focus exclusively on Black racial identity and "Black crime" as the central source of U.S. crime. The second step is to dismantle and resist all mechanisms that render crimes committed by Whites invisible. We note that this invisibility is harmful to White victims by under-stating the potential for serious and violent harm within White racially segregated settings. It also makes Black people vulnerable to vigilante victimization by falsely believing that White spaces are crime free and safe.

Next, armed with the knowledge that conservative pundits and sometimes even Blacks and White allies confound the issue of police violence against Blacks and Black intra-racial offending, those who are on the frontlines of activism must develop a set of talking points that reaffirm the right of Blacks to live in communities where they are safe from police violence *and* civilian crime. They must be able to articulate that the reallocation of funds urged by the call to "defund the police" is a legitimate request to reduce over-policing and increase social support in communities desperately in need of that change. Finally, they must be able to clearly articulate the fact that the peaceful demand for this support and protection, expressed by BLM and other community-based groups, does not constitute Black identity extremism. It is a constitutionally protected right.

There is a substantial role for academics in this transformative process. Knepper (2000) notes that "race and crime research is founded on a paradox" (p. 15). That is, researchers study race and crime—primarily Blackness or other nonwhite racial identities and crime—"in search of social science knowledge about race and criminality and race discrimination," although, as he also points out, "… researchers who study race and crime have noted the lack of an *objective* definition of race." In the absence of the contextual information provided by historians, one might miss the point that an objective assessment of the connections between race and crime is impossible because race, crime statistics and criminal law are all socially constructed. In the United States, the construction of all three intentionally favors Whites, including White criminals. Muhammad's work lays out in extensive detail how social statistics were manipulated to emphasize racial differences and to point the finger of "criminality" at Blacks, even when they did not represent the numerical majority of criminal offenders.

In addition to refraining from the use of the term "Black-on-Black crime," socially conscious academics across multiple disciplines must engage in anti-racist research and develop more students who commit to doing the same. These scholars must also develop mechanisms for elevating anti-racists research across academic disciplines and in public discourse. For example, Wilson (2005) suggested that instead of using the term "Black-on-Black crime," taking into account economic and other socially driven factors—a more accurate label would be "oppressed youth-on-oppressed youth" crime or "the disenfranchised-on-disenfranchised" crime (Mock, 2015). Inequality theories attempt to make this shift but theorists often become bogged down in the unproductive discussion of whether race or class connotes the "master status" for explaining Black disproportionality in crime and crime statistics (see Barak et al. 2018, pp. 137–139). This thinking represents an empirical and conceptual trap that still couples Blackness with crime.

Similarly, we issue a cautionary warning to the scholars who endeavor to develop a "Black Criminology," (see, e.g., Russell, 1992). Though well-intended and focused on structural causes of crime and discriminatory treatment within the criminal legal system, the label "Black Criminology" like "Black-on-Black crime" runs the risk of being hijacked and used to reinforce the idea that Black criminal behavior is a unique innate quality of Black racial identity (see Tan, 2016). It may also be used by implicit or overtly racists scholars to legitimize their own work that over-emphasizes Black offending through use of the RDA lens, again detracting from the reality that, each year, the number of Black offenders is substantially less than that of White offenders.

Eliminating racialized terms like "Black-on-Black crime" from social science research, public policy, and public discourse is one step toward de-racializing crime. We also recommend a more responsible handling of race as a variable in criminological research; and where possible, its total elimination. The extent to which a term like "Black-on-Black crime" contributes to the fear of Blacks by non-Black civilians may not be measurable, but it is worth noting again that the BLM grew out of outrage over the unpunished death of Trayvon Martin at the hands of a civilian, George

Zimmerman, not at the hands of the police. Similarly, the deaths of Ahmad Aubery, Jordan Davis, Renisha McBride and other unarmed Blacks occurred at the hands of non-Black civilians who used perverse claims of self-defense or crime prevention to justify their actions. We take note that the names of Black victims killed by non-Black civilians are often co-mingled with those killed by the police. While likely intended to convey the point that Black lives are devalued by civilian vigilantes and the police, it exposes a broader problem—a generalized fear of the Black body—a fear that is significantly exacerbated by racially coded crime references.

This brings us to our final and perhaps most controversial recommendation—the eventual elimination of racial categories from officially reported crime statistics. In our view, the reporting of national crime statistics using racial categories and racial disproportionality analyses have only served to reinforce the racialization of crime and the criminalization of Black people. Instead of reporting crime statistics by race, they could be reported in reference to employment status or education level. Both of these are demographic characteristics that will include individuals across different racial categories. And, unlike racial identity, they are demographic characteristics that can legitimately[20] be changed.

We recognize that eliminating racial categories from the reporting of crime statistics may seem to be a radical recommendation[21] and the likely retort will be: If we do that, how will we combat racial inequity in the criminal justice system? Our response is that racial inequity can still be traced through data collected separately by each component of the criminal justice system—police, courts and corrections—but that those internal statistics should not be reported as an allegedly accurate portrayal of "Crime in the United States." It will be incumbent upon ethical policy makers, media commentators, social activists, legal advocates and academics to remain vigilant against such data being used as a state-sanctioned tool of racial stigmatization and oppression.

Disclosure statement

No potential conflict of interest was reported by the authors.

Notes

[1] Table 43 of the FBI's Uniform Crime Reports, *Crime in the United States,* can be accessed through https://ucr.fbi.gov/crime-in-the-us showing this pattern for years 1995–2019. See Russell, 1998, Table 7.1, p. 111 summarizing this pattern for 1991 to 1995.

[2] While the words "black" and "white" are not capitalized in Muhammad's book, they are capitalized throughout this paper to highlight their social fact status.

[3] See McIntyre (1993) documenting that the criminalization of free Blacks began during slavery and continued post emancipation.

[4] Muhammad and others point to RDA as an intentional racist maneuver to subordinate, demonize and control Blacks and support White Supremacy.

[5] See for example the work of Black crime scholars W.E.B. DuBois and Ida B. Wells.

[6] Muhammad specifically identifies former census superintendent Francis A. Walker and the work of Harvard University professor Nathaniel S. Shaler (1884) as committed to promoting a social agenda that emphasized Black proclivity toward crime.

[7] We use the term "politically-motivated" to convey the fact the racism that is at the core of social structure in the United States was intentional, hypocritical and designed to build and maintain a social order grounded in White supremacy as the glue that would hold the otherwise disparate European ethnic groups together.

[8] The UCR currently uses the following race categories to report arrests: White, Black or African American, American Indian or Alaska Native, Asian, and Native American or other Pacific Islander.

[9] We use the term "socially-biased" to cover race, class, and gender biases and their intersecting influences.

[10] See for example NCVS data.

[11] The general pattern of violent crime statistics has remained relatively consistent over time, except for in 2009 and 2010 when the raw number of White homicide arrests exceeded that of Blacks (Snyder, 2011; United States Department of Justice, Federal Bureau of Investigation, 2011). This change in pattern after decades of collecting racialized crime statistics appears to have gone unnoticed, perhaps because of the already invisible nature of "White crime."

[12] The data in Table 2 do not include all homicides, only homicides where the race of both the offender and victim are known. These data are limited to intra-racial killings and do not measure all violent crime, or all intra-racial crime.

[13] In numerous studies showing significant racial disparity in pedestrian or car stops the findings have been attributed to the perceptions of the person stopped rather than racial-based targeting.

[14] The studies commissioned by government officials and conducted by private consultants for legal advocacy groups that support this claim are too numerous to cite.

[15] A common response to the statistics reported in this paragraph would be a resort to RDA. See for example Unnever & Gabbidon (2011, p. 1)

noting that, "approximately 6 percent of the United States population-black men-account for 56 percent of the official arrests for robbery." This is an example of RDA that is particularly harmful to Blacks because the disproportionality is so stark.

[16] For a myriad of reasons, arrests statistics do not completely and accurately represent actual crime occurrence in the U.S., or elsewhere; but, arrest statistics, are often used as a proxy for crime commission in racial disproportionality analysis.

[17] Hate crimes would be an exception to the general rule of treating crimes committed by Whites as race-neutral.

[18] To learn more about the #Say Her Name movement go to: https://www.aapf.org/sayhername

[19] See Spillers (1987), noting that the dehumanizing language that was used to name and frame Black women during slavery persists to this day.

[20] The use of the word "legitimately" in this sentence takes into account the phenomenon of "passing" where an individual who is born into one racial category later identifies as belonging to one that is different from the one into which she or he was born, in the belief that "passing" will entitle him or her to a benefit not typically enjoyed by the group to which he or she was born.

[21] The U.S. might follow the example set by Canada, a democratic nation that does not use racial categories in reporting its crime statistics. This is not to suggest that anti-Black racial bias does not exist there. The work of criminologist Scot Wortley (2002) and Wortley and Tanner (2003) has documented that it does. Recognition of racial harm is the first step toward addressing it.

References

Alexander, M. (2010). *The new Jim Crow: Mass incarceration in the age of colorblindness*. New York, NY: The New Press.

Allport, G.W., & Postman, L. (1947). The psychology of rumor. *Journal of Clinical Psychology, 3*, 247.

Anderson, E. (1999). *Code of the street: Decency, violence, and the moral life of the inner city*. New York, NY: W.W. Norton and Company.

Balko, R. (2013). *Rise of the warrior cop: The militarization of America's police forces*. New York: Public Affairs.

Barak, G., Leighton, P., & Cotton, A. (2018). *Class, race, gender, and crime: The social realities of justice in America* (5th ed.). Lanham, MD: Rowman and Littlefield Publishers.

Bell, D. (1973). *Race, racism and American Law*. Boston, MA: Little, Brown & Co.

Black-on-Black Crime. (1973, November). *Ebony, 29*(1), 200–201.

Black-on-Black Crime – The cause, the consequences, the cures. (1979, August). *Ebony, 34*(10), 1–162.

Bouie, J. (2013a, July 15). The Trayvon Martin killing and the myth of black-on-black crime. The Daily Beast. Retrieved from https://www.thedailybeast.com/the-trayvon-martin-killing-and-the-myth-of-black-on-black-crime?ref=scroll

Bouie, J. (2013b, July 17). Why "black-on-black crime" is a dangerous idea. The American Prospect. Retrieved from https://prospect.org/power/black-on-black-crime-dangerous-idea/

Browne-Marshall, G. J. (2013). *Race, law, and American society: 1607 to present* (2nd ed.). New York, NY: Routledge.

Chambliss, W. (1973). The saints and the roughnecks. *Society*, *11*(1), 24–31. https://doi.org/10.1007/BF03181016

Clear, T. R. (2007). *Imprisoning communities: How mass incarceration makes disadvantaged neighborhoods worse*. New York, NY: Oxford University Press.

Crenshaw, K., Gotanda, N., Peller, G., & Thomas, K. (Eds.). (1995). *Critical race theory: The key writings that formed the movement*. New York: The New Press.

Cullen, F. T. (1994). Social support as an organizing concept for criminology: Presidential address to the Academy of Criminal Justice Sciences. *Justice Quarterly*, *11*(4), 527–558. https://doi.org/10.1080/07418829400092421

Delgado, R. (1994). Rodrigo's Eighth Chronicle: Black crime, White fears—On the social construction of threat. *Virginia Law Review*, *80*(2), 503–521. https://doi.org/10.2307/1073528

Donaldson, G. (2015). *The Ville: Cops and kids in urban America*. New York, NY: Fordham University Press.

Duck, W. (2015). *No way out: Precarious living in the shadow of poverty and drug dealing*. Chicago, IL: University of Chicago Press.

Eberhardt, J. L., Goff, P. A., Purdie, V. J., & Davies, P. G. (2004). Seeing Black: Race, crime, and visual processing. *Journal of Personality and Social Psychology*, *87*(6), 876–893.

FBI Counterterrorism Division. (2017). *Federal Bureau of Investigation intelligence assessment: Black identity extremists likely motivated to target law enforcement officers*. Federal Bureau of Investigation. Retrieved from https://assets.documentcloud.org/documents/4067711/BIE-Redacted.pdf

Feagin, J. (2009). *The White racial frame: Centuries of racial framing and counter framing*. New York, NY: Routledge.

Finn, N. (2020). *How Black lives matter began: Meet the women whose hashtag turned into a global movement*. Retrieved from https://www.eonline.com/uk/news/1159433/how-black-lives-matter-began-meet-the-women-whose-hashtag-turned-into-a-global-movement

Fishman, L. (2002). The black bogeyman and white self-righteousness. In C. R. Mann & M. S. Zatz (Eds.), *Images of color, images of crime* (pp. 177–191). Los Angeles, CA: Roxbury.

Gabbidon, S. L., Higgins, G. E., & Wilder-Bonner, K. M. (2013). Black supporters of racial profiling: A demographic profile. *Criminal Justice Policy Review*, *24*(4), 422–440. https://doi.org/10.1177/0887403412442890

Gabbidon, S. L., Taylor Greene, H., & Wilder, K. (2004). Still excluded? An update on the status of African American scholars in the discipline of criminology and criminal justice. *Journal of Research in Crime and Delinquency*, *41*(4), 384–406. https://doi.org/10.1177/0022427803260268

Gaston, S., & Doherty, E. E. (2018). Why don't more Black Americans offend? Testing a theory of African American offending's ethnic-racial socialization hypothesis. *Race and Justice*, *8*(4), 366–395. https://doi.org/10.1177/2153368716688740

Gibson, M., & Rafter, N. H. (2006). *Criminal man by Cesare Lombroso: Translated and with a new introduction by Mary Gibson and Nicole Hahn Rafter*. Durham, NC: Duke University Press.

Goff, P. A., Eberhardt, J. L., Williams, M. J., & Jackson, M. C. (2008). Not yet human: Implicit knowledge, historical dehumanization, and contemporary consequences. *Journal of Personality and Social Psychology*, *94*(2), 292–306. https://doi.org/10.1037/0022-3514.94.2.292

Goff, P. A., Jackson, M. C., Lewis Di Leone, B. A., Culotta, C. M., & DiTomasso, N. A. (2014). The essence of innocence: Consequences of dehumanizing Black children. *Journal of Personality and Social Psychology, 106*(4), 526–545.

Guilmant, P. (1970, August 19). Jesse, McNeil hit 'silence' (p. 4). Chicago Daily Defender.

Headley, B. D. (1983). "Black on Black" crime: The myth and the reality. *Crime and Social Justice, 20*, 50–62.

Hirschi, T. (1969). *Causes of delinquency*. Berkley, CA: University of California Press.

Hoffman, F. L. (1896). Race traits and tendencies of the American Negro. *Publications of the American Economic Association, 11*(1/3), 1–329.

Jones, N. (2009). *Between good and ghetto: African American girls and inner-city violence*. New Brunswick, NJ: Rutgers University Press.

Jones-Brown, D. (2000). *Race, crime and punishment*. Philadelphia, PA: Chelsea House.

Jonsson, P. (2012, March 24). Who is George Zimmerman, and why did he shoot Trayvon Martin? *The Christian Science Monitor*. Retrieved from https://news.yahoo.com/george-zimmerman-why-did-shoot-trayvon-martin-141231964.html

Joseph, J. (2006). Drug offenses, gender, ethnicity, and nationality: Women in prison in England and Wales. *The Prison Journal, 86*(1), 140–157. https://doi.org/10.1177/0032885505283926

Katznelson, I. (2005). *When affirmative action was white: An untold history of racial inequality in twentieth-century America*. New York, NY: W. W. Norton & Company.

Knepper, P. (2000). The alchemy of race and crime research. In M.W. Markowitz & D. D. Jones-Brown (Eds.), *The system in Black and White: Exploring the connections between race, crime, and justice* (pp. 15–30). Westport, CT: Praeger Publishers.

Massie, V. M. (2016, September 25). Why asking black people about "Black-on-Black crime" misses the point. *Vox*. Retrieved from https://www.vox.com/2016/4/28/11510274/black-on-black-crime-poverty

McIntyre, C. (1993). *Criminalizing a race: Free Blacks during slavery*. Queens, NY: Kayode.

Mock, B. (2015, June 11). The origins of the term "Black-on-black" Crime. *Bloomberg*. Retrieved from https://www.bloomberg.com/news/articles/2015-06-11/examining-the-origins-of-the-phrase-black-on-black-crime

Morgan, R. E. (2017). *Race and Hispanic origin of victims and offenders, 2012-15* (pp. 1–20). United States, U.S. Department of Justice, Office of Justice Programs), Bureau of Justice Statistics.

Morgan, R. E., & Oudekerk, B. A. (2019). *Criminal victimization, 2018 (NCJ 253043*, pp. 1–37). United States, U.S. Department of Justice, Office of Justice Programs), Bureau of Justice Statistics.

Morgan, R. E., & Truman, J. L. (2020). *Criminal victimization, 2019 (NCJ 255113*, pp. 1–53). United States, U.S. Department of Justice, Office of Justice Programs), Bureau of Justice Statistics.

Muhammad, K. G. (2010). *The condemnation of blackness: Race, crime, and the making of modern urban America*. Cambridge, MA: Harvard University Press.

National Association for the Advancement of Colored People. (1980, November). NAACP 71st Annual Convention Resolutions. The Crisis, 87(9), 439-449.

Napper, G. (1979, August). Citizens must fight Black on Black Crime. *Ebony, 34*(10), 113–117.

Peterson, R. D., & Krivo, L. (2005). Macrostructural analyses of race, ethnicity, and violent crime: Recent lessons and new directions for research. *Annual Review of Sociology, 31*(1), 331–356. https://doi.org/10.1146/annurev.soc.31.041304.122308

Poussaint, A. F. (1970, October). Why Blacks kill Blacks. *Ebony, 25*(12), 143–150.

Rios, V.M. (2011). *Punished: Policing the lives of Black and Latino boys.* New York, NY: NYU Press.

Robinson, M. (2000). The construction and reinforcement of myths of race and crime. *Journal of Contemporary Criminal Justice, 16*(2), 133–156. https://doi.org/10.1177/1043986200016002002

Roper, W. (2020, June 2). Black Americans 2.5X more likely than whites to be killed by police. *Statista.* Retrieved from https://www.statista.com/chart/21872/map-of-police-violence-against-black-americans/

Russell, K.K. (1992). Development of a black criminology and the role of the black criminologist. *Justice Quarterly, 9*(4), 667–683. https://doi.org/10.1080/07418829200091601

Russell, K. K. (1998). *The color of crime: Racial hoaxes, white fear, black protectionism, police harassment, and other macroaggressions.* New York, NY: New York University Press.

Sampson, R. J., & Wilson, W. J. (1995). Toward a theory of race, crime, and urban inequality. In J. Hagan & R. D. Peterson (Eds.), *Crime and inequality* (pp. 37–56). Stanford, CA: Stanford University Press.

Sellin, T. (1928). The Negro criminal: A statistical note. *The Annals of the American Academy of Political and Social Science, 140*(1), 52–64. https://doi.org/10.1177/000271622814000109

Shabazz, S. (2020, June 11). It's time to eviscerate the 'But…Black on Black crime' argument again. *Scary Mommy.* Retrieved from https://www.scarymommy.com/black-on-black-crime-myth-debunked/

Shaler, N. (1884). The Negro problem. *Atlantic Monthly, 54,* 696–709.

Snyder, H.N. (2011). *Arrest in the United States, 1980-2009* (pp. 1–24). United States, U.S. Department of Justice, Office of Justice Programs), Bureau of Justice Statistics.

Spillers, H. J. (1987). Mama's baby, Papa's maybe: An American grammar book. *Diacritics, 17*(2), 64–81. https://doi.org/10.2307/464747

Tan, Z. Y. (2016, September 22). What does 'black-on-black crime' actually mean? *The Christian Science Monitor.* Retrieved from https://www.csmonitor.com/USA/Justice/2016/0922/What-does-black-on-black-crime-actually-mean

Taylor Greene, H., Gabbidon, S., & Wilson, S. K. (2018). Included? The status of African-American scholars in the discipline of criminology and criminal justice since 2004. *Journal of Criminal Justice Education, 29*(1), 96–115. https://doi.org/10.1080/10511253.2017.1372497

Thomas, W. I., & Thomas, D. S. (1928). *The child in America: Behavior problems and programs.* New York, NY: Alfred A. Knopf, Inc.

United States Department of Justice, Federal Bureau of Investigation. (2011). *Crime in the United States, 2010.* Retrieved from https://ucr.fbi.gov/crime-in-the-u.s/2010/crime-in-the-u.s.-2010

United States Department of Justice, Federal Bureau of Investigation. (2020). *Crime in the United States, 2019.* Retrieved from https://ucr.fbi.gov/crime-in-the-u.s/2019/crime-in-the-u.s.-2019

Unnever, J. D., & Gabbidon, S. L. (2011). *A theory of African American Offending: Race, racism, and crime.* New York, NY: Routledge.

Webster, C. (2008). Marginalized white ethnicity, race and crime. *Theoretical Criminology, 12*(3), 293–312. https://doi.org/10.1177/1362480608093308

Wilson, D.W. (2005). *Inventing Black-on-Black violence: Discourse, space, and representation.* Syracuse, NY: Syracuse University Press.

Wortley, S., & Tanner, J. (2003, July). Data, denials, and confusion: The racial profiling debate in Toronto Canada. *Canadian Journal of Criminology and Criminal Justice, 45*(3), 367–389. https://doi.org/10.3138/cjccj.45.3.367

Wortley, S. (2002). Misrepresentation or reality? The depiction of race and crime in the Toronto print media. In B. Schissel & C. Brooks (Eds.), *Marginality and condemnation: An introduction to critical criminology* (pp. 55–82). Halifax, N.S.: Fernwood Publishing.

Young, V. & Sulton, A. T. (1991). Excluded: The current status of African-American scholars in the field of criminology and criminal justice. *Journal of Research in Crime and Delinquency, 28*(1), 101–116. https://doi.org/10.1177/0022427891028001006

Reform or revolution: 'Community Policing' is not a Quick-fix

Invisible No More Police Violence against Black Women and Women of Color, by Andrea J Ritchie, Boston: Beacon Press, 2017, 324 pp., $21.00 (paperback). ISBN 9780807088982.

The Limits of Community Policing: Civilian Power and Police Accountability in Black and Brown Los Angeles, by Luis Daniel Gascón and Aaron Roussell, New York: New York University Press, 2019, 285 pp., $30.00 (paperback), $89.00 (hardcover), or (eBook). ISBN: 9781479842254 (paperback), 9781479871209 (hardcover), and 9781479807567 (e-book).

You can't Stop the Revolution: Community Disorder and Social Ties in Post-Ferguson America, by Andrea D. Boyles, California: University of California Press, 2019, 216 pp., $29.95(paperback), $85.00 (hardcover), or $29.95 (e-book). ISBN: 9780520298330 (paperback), 9780520298323 (hardcover), and 9780520970502 (e-book).

One if not the most researched topic in criminal justice continues to be law enforcement and early criminal justice programs in the United States grew out of national cries demanding changes in law enforcement practices. The National Commission on Law Observance and Enforcement, better known as the Wickersham Commission (1931), first described widespread police brutality and the use and infliction of pain and suffering on suspects and citizens. This and many other subsequent reports initiated a reform movement that included, among other things, a national movement for the professionalization of law enforcement agencies. But these efforts we know have fallen short. Today, national cries and demands for change in police practices are louder and more critical than ever.

Together the above-listed books provide multiple examples of why police agencies must change, and that change is urgent. Much like a medical emergency, these three books are a descriptive triage. *Invisible No More* identifies and narrates the experiences of female victims of police brutality. Recent and historical examples of brutality are supported with research and explanations of its causes that the author traced back to colonialism, slavery, and institutional racism. The second part of the triage, a detailed narrative assessment, is presented in *The Limits of Community Policing* by Luis Daniel Gascón and Aaron Roussell. The book "outlines the social organization, key actors, routines, and challenges of community policing" (pg. xiii) in South Los Angeles (California). It details the everyday work of leaders in the police department and in South LA communities who use community policing to improve the neighborhoods they serve and live in. In the third part of the triage, *You can't Stop the Revolution*, Andrea S. Boyles clearly describes the emergency scene created by the cumulative effect of social, structural, and racial disadvantage that culminated in "civil unrest in Ferguson during and after the protests sparkled by the killing of Michael Brown Jr." (pg. 14).

These books capture and bring to life the daily struggles and resilience in the life and even in the death of many urban minority communities and their residents. The reader will feel the daily struggles and be compelled to declare that transformative action and change are needed. In *Invisible No More*, Andrea J. Ritchie chronicles the experiences of girls and young women of color for whom the streets, the school, and the home are sites of oppressive policing (xiv). Unlike other books, the author extends the non-invisibility of women of color to include Indigenous, Latinx, Asian, Arab, Middle Eastern, Muslim, and South Asian women" (pg. 2). In this book, individual female stories are contextualized by identifying commonalities and distinctions in their own experiences and those of males of color (pg. 2). It also "explores the ways in which women's experiences of policing take forms short of fatal force, and how they are uniquely informed by race, nation, gender, gender identity, and expression, sexual orientation, poverty, disability, and mental health" (pg. 2-3). The book presents women's stories in these categories, such as Sandra Bland, Joyce Curnell, Monica Jones, Kayla Moore, Mya Hall, Rekia Boyd, and Dajerria Becton. Their stories take us on a sad tour of nations over time. In the U.S. alone, these are the stories of women who experienced racial profiling, police brutality, and immigration enforcement. These stories make us question our sense of safety, security, and trust in the official authorities charged with our protection. All of these stories are difficult to read.

In *The Limits of Community Policing*, Gascón and Roussell successfully contextualized community policing and the limits of civilian power in communities of color. Their research centered on the racially heterogeneous community of Lakeside. Like so many others across the U.S., this urban neighborhood has always been populated by minority residents, whose racial and ethnic composition has changed over time. Lakeside residents are Black and Latinos. The authors describe the realities of community policing and the limits of partnerships in these communities.

The book, *You can't Stop the Revolution* clearly describes the conditions that led to Brown's murder. But like a phoenix, the work focused on the transformation of the community, where residents (leaders, protestors) became the post-Ferguson transformative agents and the reconceptualization of (dis)order. The study describes many examples of "protect and serve actions taken by black citizens despite widespread community disorder" (pg. 25). As stated by the author, "this study highlights (dis)order-disorder and order-as culturally relative and sequential across diverse populations" (pg. 48). The book offsets the negative images of protestors propagated by media outlets.

In ten chapters (there are two forewords, one written by Angela Y. Davis, and the second by Mariame Kaba; Charlene Carruthers wrote the afterword), Andrea J. Ritchie's *Invisible No More* expands the readers' "understanding of the forms and contexts of police violence experienced by women and gender-nonconforming people of color enabling us to better understand the full shape and reach of state violence in ways essential to countering it" (pg. 15). Chapter one used the history of slavery and colonization to contextualize state generated violence against women of color. Historical images that still persuade, justify and maintain racially gendered hierarchies (pg. 42) in police interactions. Indian reservations, slave plantations, and border crossing have been used by state representatives to control women's behavior, sexuality, and agency while at the same time developing the narratives that have been used to negatively voice and express their world.

Chapter two serves to contextualize the present and the multiple "wars being waged in the United States that serve as both backdrop and driving forces for present-day racial profiling, police violence, and mass incarceration." (pg. 43). The four topics in this chapter (the war on drugs, broken windows, immigration enforcement, and the war on terrorism) should be forced discussion topics in courses. Not only will students learn how these topics differentially affect women of color, but also how discretionary law enforcement practices are suspended for women of color with devastating effects. This chapter alone can have a transformative effect in the way students think about these topics and how we teach them research where too often we take for granted the strategies and practices used in policing.

Chapters three through nine present stories of aggression and violence suffered by young girls and women of color. Chapter three webs the stories of several young girls whose life and movements between school, streets, and home, become the environment where they experience repressive and violent forms of policing.

In policing (dis)ability, chapter four recounts stories of elderly and young females with mental and physical challenges. These are the stories of minority women whom officers targeted at the time they were suffering a health crisis. Instead of getting the needed services and assistance, they experienced violence, arrest, involuntary confinement, and even death.

Chapter five discusses cases of police sexual violence. This chapter describes the sexual victimization of minority women and presents the structural conditions of the problem (sites of the incidents such as border crossings, police stops, etc.). As the women's stories are recounted, we learn about the obstacles victims face when they come forward to report the abuse; the reader is left with the question of what justice would look like for the victims of police sexual violence.

Many forms of gender bias are addressed in this book, but chapter six focuses on policing issues when the gender binary assumptions are questioned. Much of the chapter discusses the historical impact of the enforcement of sumptuary laws (pg. 128). The interpretation and enforcement of these and other laws (bathroom, clothing, and searches) have been used to justify harassment, profiling, and criminalization of gender nonconformity despite legal changes. This chapter underlines how the normalization and understanding of gender have been developed around "idealized notions of white womanhood developed in service of white supremacy, which implicitly excludes and punish nonwhite women" (pg. 127). These notions set assumptions and standards of behavior to the detriment of all others.

The enforcement of prostitution laws is covered in chapter seven, where the image, both legal and sociocultural, that have been created overtime survived across time and space. Words (Jezebel, hot-blooded) recreate images, and these images reproduce systems of punishment disguised as morality. This chapter's stories and images depict the selective and discretionary enforcement of prostitution where loitering, disorderly conduct, buy-bust, and other operations become evidence for prostitution.

In policing motherhood, chapter eight poignantly recounts how from the enforcement of minor offenses to fighting drugs, women of color have been devalued and victimized. The stories of minor legal violations that escalated and led to the use of a Taser and force make one question law enforcement's oath to serve and protect. The officers in these stories devalued the females and dismissed their pregnancies. The war on drugs has been described as a war on females. This chapter's stories evidenced that the war on drugs led to the criminalization of black mothers and mothers of color. Delivery rooms became arrest sites, women were charged with delivering drugs to a minor, delivery room specimens were preserved without consent, and newborns were separated from their mothers. The author links these scenes to slavery, immigration enforcement, and indigenous women. The last section of this chapter describes how the enforcement of child-welfare laws has been used against mothers whose only crime is that they are poor. In too many instances being poor equates with failure to be a good mother and charges of child abuse and neglect, even when there is no evidence of abuse and neglect. In the enforcement of these laws, officers commit acts of violence with impunity.

What happens to women of color when they are victimized and seek police protection is addressed in chapter nine. According to the author, "police violence against women of color takes place disproportionately, and with alarming frequency, in the context of responses to domestic and sexual violence." (pg. 185). Like so many instances in this book, official violence takes many forms from verbal abuse, to physical violence and even refusal to respond to calls for service. The chapter present cases where police officers victimize domestic violence victims; they do not file complaints out of fear of retaliation. The author states that "racial profiling and police brutality in the context of responses to violence remains, quite literally, invisible." (pg. 187).

The stories in these nine chapters are poignant and difficult to read, but each chapter ends with a resistance section. In these sections, the book's title becomes more than just a description of the many instances of official violence perpetrated against women of color. These sections on resistance are about moving forward, about grassroots organizations, about community support, and it is also about support strategies. This is the theme of chapter 10. This chapter does for the reader what the murder of George Floyd did to the nation. Readers and all Americans must self-examine our long-held assumptions about justice and fairness, and we must become part of the efforts not just to mitigate but to eliminate police violence against Black women and women of color. We must do our part to erase invisibility.

In *The Limits of Community Policing: Civilian Power and Police Accountability in Black and Brown Los Angeles*, Luis Daniel Gascón and Aaron Roussell review the origins and transformation of the South Los Angeles Lakeside community and the history of racial conflict and police reforms of the LAPD. Using this racially heterogeneous community as their background, the authors describe police-community events, protests, and violence as evens used to develop police reforms that were superficial and failed to address the root causes of police-community conflict. The authors identify these causes as minority citizen's oppression and brutality at the hands of the same police department trying to resolve the problems. The authors successfully contextualize community policing (they describe the origins of community policing) and offer vivid details of its limits. They also describe the reality of community policing as a partnership in a Black and Latino community as they describe the evolution of the community and the racial/ethnic competition in south Los Angeles over time. Like other urban communities across the U.S., Black and Latino Lakeside residents face economic challenges (job prospects are not equally distrusted among residents), internal friction (job competition), and stratification. These are problems that LAPD community policing efforts cannot resolve, although police leaders reassure residents that they can collaborate to solve these community problems. The authors use community policing examples, such as the Community-Police Advisory Board (CPAB), to show that community problems are not solved and how the efforts actually increase police power and control over the residents' ability to respond to internal issues.

The authors make three conclusions about community policing. First, and contrary to its intended purpose, community policing is used to expand police power, and it promotes crime control as a remedy for community discord (pg. 5). Second, community policing allows law enforcement to limit civilian power through negotiated partnerships driven by police motivations (pg. 6). Finally, they state that community members' inability to share community goals inhibits successful collaborations needed to make real changes within the community (pg. 6).

The introduction and chapter one begin to contextualize the above conclusions. The authors recount the origins of community policing within the academic discipline and look back at Los Angeles's history as one of change, conflict, and police intervention (pg. 29). The reader learns that police relations with the Black and Latino communities have been conflictive from the start. While the conflicts described (Zoot Suit riot, Rodney King, and others) are local, the sequence of events are national. From the structural preconditions of each disturbance to the reports and reform agendas described, the reader becomes aware of the historically negative relationship between the LAPD and the communities of color.

Chapter two focuses on the impact of social, economic, and demographic changes from the community's perspective, specifically through the experiences of long term residents represented by Mrs. Mayfield. In this chapter, we quickly learn that Lakeside, like other cities in the U.S., had its share of residential mobility where one ethnic group (Latino) encroached in the space of long time Black residents. A recurring theme in the chapter is the lack of understanding and trust among residents and the perception that new residents do not recognize the neighborhood's history as a community. This chapter highlights the importance of the term "community" vis-á-vis the transformation of the physical community. The authors' field notes clarify the residents' sentiments and conflicts over community transformation and multicultural coalition-building efforts.

Chapter three details the structure and dynamics of community meetings. It is focused on the LAPD captains and their leadership styles. While differences in leadership styles are expected, the authors' description point out the impact these differences had on community organization efforts. Not only do we learn about community conflicts from a different perspective, but we also begin to understand the reasons for the three conclusions drawn by the authors about community policing (pgs. 5-6). For example, community meeting discussions urge residents to take ownership of the community's safety and security. However, the authors explain that crime control efforts follow the LAPD's crime control agenda where residents become the department's eyes and ears. That is, during the meetings, residents provide more information to the officers than what the officers offer residents. The chapter also discusses the language barrier between both community members and the officers. The language barrier widens the conflicts and divisions between the Black and Latino community representatives and police leaders become the voice and articulate neighborhood collective needs but in so doing the police expand their interests and powers.

The theme of community meetings continues in chapter four, where the emphasis is on the official handling of citizens' complaints using three examples. With these examples, the readers learn about police discretion and how officers direct their considerable latitude. The authors use three examples of complainants as "archetypes of policeability or the likelihood that a complaint will result in police action on behalf of the civilian" (pg. 122). Accordingly, complaints are met with one of three discretionary responses: cooperation between officers and residents to correct the identified problem; denying services identified as outside the police functions' scope (described as control), and conflict or resistance between police and community residents disagreement with discretionary police decisions.

Community policing efforts also include the business community. These efforts are described in chapter five as part of a larger urban renewal plan, which characteristically tends to follow urban unrest and displace long-standing local business. In this chapter, we see how the police have access to the business community (especially corporations) and articulate and become the community's voice. The authors conclude that police and business "push for a controlled, predictable marketplace and the installation of a security network schema promulgated and anchored by police" (pg. 171). This becomes another opportunity for the police to regulate the community spaces and the residents while expanding their security and surveillance goals.

Chapter six describes the power struggles between the police, its community policing goals, and the antagonism between Black and Latino residents. As first described in chapter two, the Black and Latino communities view each other as separate groups within the community. The separation and division defeat the residents' ability to influence and shape community policing goals to their benefit. This lack of collaboration benefits police and community leaders who play symbolic roles with limited capacity to produce neighborhood or police change (pg. 205). According to the authors, community needs translate into more police authority and crime control strategies independent of community needs. The authors conclude that community policing efforts have remained unchanged because the residents can not advocate for themselves and their community.

In the concluding chapter, the authors illustrate the title of the book. Accordingly, community policing is limited and is not an adequate forum to hold police departments accountable for their actions. Community-based initiatives respond to the state's needs, support police brutality and successfully silence minority power and community interest. The authors support their conclusions by referring to previous chapters.

Gascón and Roussell contribute to the community policing literature using an ethnographic methodology. In so doing, they painfully describe the limited effect of this strategy to bring about change and collaboration in the Lakeside community. The book's strength is that the authors successfully overcame their outsider persona to bring a fair and detailed description of the events they observed and participated in. While the book present racial, social, and economic differences among the Black and Latino residents, the book also makes a case for coalition building in communities of color.

The last book in the triage, *You Can't Stop the Revolution* by Andrea Boyles, is a three-year ethnographic field study after Michael Brown's murder. As a criminal justice professor at Lindenwood University, she was intimately familiar with Ferguson's history of poor socio-structural conditions and racially motivated mistreatment of residents. Although Brown's murder is the book's framework, Ferguson's preexisting historical conditions ignited what happened afterward. These conditions are exposed in the introductory chapter. In the tradition of social disorganization theory, the book examines community, neighborhood, and individual experiences. But unlike that tradition, the book theoretically re-conceptualizes disorder as rooted in pervasive discrimination to include social and physical disorder, as well as the community. The author exposes the readers to a "post-Ferguson framework for understanding the often unanticipated alignments of mostly black citizens as they organized to protect black lives from both police brutality and interpersonal neighborhood violence" (pg. 17). This introduction includes a detailed description of Brown's murder and incidents, including the author's arrival at the murder scene and her subsequent community involvement to write this book.

In chapter one, the author opens up about her childhood experiences, the formal and informal rules of socialization and adaptation under seemingly disorganized conditions, where she describes examples of solidarity and residents "looking out for one another (pg. 25)." The chapter also looks into the history of negative black stereotypes and fears and their impact on post-Ferguson black consciousness. She ends the chapter the way it started, by placing herself as an adult and a researcher at the center, juxtaposing her roles as an activist and a scholar, making sense of the intersectionality of these two and her identity and experiences.

In chapter two, Boyles expands her reconceptualization of disorder in post-Ferguson. She first argues that the original definition reflects the dominant class (White) definition and offers one based on the culture and perspective of the place and its people—disadvantaged black citizens (pg. 48). In offering a Black cultural perspective on the disorder, this chapter contributes to the literature by clarifying the relationships on order and disorder where racial discrimination is, in fact, a form of disorder. The chapter highlights how citizens serve and protect one another despite lack of resources, poor police-community relations, and discrimination.

Chapter three examines discrimination, police brutality, black violence, and its effects (citizen fear and mistrust) across the community. The chapter is about those fighting in the trenches. It describes how they learn to navigate disorder, engage in informal community integration, and create alliances with neighbors to safeguard themselves and others during protests.

Chapter four chronicles the denigrating effects of systemic deprivation through the life stories of three Black males. Despite the deprivation and adversity, they become an integral part of the community and become productive community members. Their lives are also the stories of the legitimate and illegitimate opportunities in the community. The chapter also highlights three black women-centered roles in the community. In these roles, women provide buffers to disorder and its effects and leverage cultural influence (pg. 126). They provide care, support, and carry out Black cultural traditions.

Chapter five centers on neighborhood groups and nonprofit organizations (churches, community groups). Community members either belong to these organizations and actively worked to further their agendas, benefit by receiving assistance from these organizations, or volunteer their services. Of all the community organizations, those engaged in interpersonal violence efforts received more support and exposure.

The last chapter summarizes key findings and discusses how black citizens combat discrimination and find ways to navigate dilemmas and advance the race. It also discusses suggestions for improving disorder in Black communities while advancing broader political, economic agendas.

Together these three books offer context to police-community relations in communities of color. All three are provocative and make valuable contributions to the criminal justice literature in general and police-community relations in particular. These are also three books for readers who are interested in minority women's experiences with law enforcement, urban social movements, survival adaptation strategies in communities of color, minority community victimization and responses to official control and violence, and the criminalization of those nonconforming or not fitting within the official gender expectations. The books also contribute to research methodology, and all took multiple years of topic exploration, collection, and analysis, as is the case with historical and fieldwork analysis. The authors successfully navigated their researcher roles, and the people, events, and places studied were given the respect and credit they deserved. The data is translated into words that move the reader; these are provocative books, and class discussions will be transformative.

Reference

Wickersham Commission (1931). *National Commission on Law Observance and Enforcement.* Report on the Enforcement of the Prohibition Laws of the United States, January 7, 1931. Retrieved from https://www.ojp.gov/pdffiles1/Digitization/44540NCJRS.pdf.

Myrna Cintron

Index

Note: **Bold** page numbers refer to tables and page numbers followed by "n" denote endnotes.

African Americans 66; mobility of 107n1; prolonged maltreatment and subjugation of 107n1; radical reconstruction 102
Alpert, G.P. 46
Anderson, E. 106, 140; *Code of the Street* 140
anti-Black narratives 102
anti-Black racism 134
anti-Black violence 102
Arrested Justice (Richie) 67
Aubery, Ahmad 151

Balbus, I.D. 91
Baltimore city: demographic and socioeconomic indicators 70; residents and protesters 65, 68; socioeconomic indicators 70; younger activists 68
Baumgartner, F.R. 46
Becton, Dajerria 160
Bell, M.P. 115
Bell, Sean 31
Black civilians: historical structural arrangement 27; modern policing 24–26; police against 23
Black Cops Against Police Brutality (B-CAP): community activism 30–33; community policing 33–34; crisis action plan 37–38; education and training 24; formal and informal policing 23; mission 39n4; proactive policing strategies 32; support system 32; workshops 40n5
Black crime 138, 139, 141, 142, 144, 145, 149
Black criminality 134, 147
Black Criminology 150
Black Lives Matter (BLM) 4, 91; Black-on-Black crime 146; COVID-19 guidelines 118; literature review 113–115; media's illustration 112; media's representation 114; proliferation 112; protest paradigm 112; protests/demonstrations 119–124; public perception 114; qualitative analyses 112; racial-conflict interpretations 117; theoretical framework 116–118
Black Lives Matter (BLM), protests/demonstrations: events framing 119–120; official responses framing 120–122

Black men: killed by police 8–16; law enforcement 67; negative police interactions 67; police/civilian interactions 67; qualitative differences 81
black narratives: the children 103–104; social control 90–93; theoretical framework 89–90
Black newspaper 139
Black officers: crisis action plan 24; defying police culture 26–28; double marginality 29, 31; hiring produces 23; impact 23; integrity and activism 28–30; police-civilian encounters 23; police violence and misconduct 22; recruitment and hiring 22; *vs.* White officers 23
Black-on-Black crime 4, 5; anti-racist research 150; Black Lives Matter 146; internet media sources 133; myth to derail a movement 145–148, **146**; origins of 138–140; recommendations 148–151; unique social phenomenon 149
Black people: law enforcement 68; police-civilian relations 65; prevention and reduction 83–84
Black perpetrators 132, 137, 138
Black Police Associations 25
Black police officers 100–101
Black political mobilization 111
Black protesters: demographics characteristics 71, **71**; interviews 68; local newspaper 68; local public library and an advertisement 68; neighborhood characteristics **69**, 70; police force and broader justice system 111; on social media 68; study setting **69**, 70
Black protest events 115
Black racial identity and crime 133
Black social advancement 114
Black social movements 117
Black wall of unity 29
Black women: criminal legal system 67; killed by police 16–19; law enforcement 67; police sexual violence 67; police violence with 67; qualitative differences 81
Blake, Jacob 34
Blalock, H.M. 115, 116
Bland, Sandra 91, 147, 160

Blauner, R.: *Internal Colonialism and Ghetto Revolt* 90
Blue wall of silence 29
Bonilla-Silva, E. 116
Boyd, Rekia 160
Boyles, Andrea S.: *You Can't Stop the Revolution* 6, 159, 160, 164–165
Boyles, A.S. 6, 92, 159, 164, 165
Brooks, Rayshard 118, 147
Brown, Michael 3, 68, 69, 75, 89–91, 94–96, 147, 164
Brown, Michael, Jr. 159
Brunson, R.K. 67, 92, 93
Bureau of Justice Statistics (BJS) 138

Carnegie, Joyce 30
carnival frame 112
Carroll, L. 47
Castile, Philando 147
Chan, J.M. 114
child welfare systems 33
Christopher Commission Report (1991) 22
Cobbina, J.E. 3, 67, 93
Cobbina reports 3
Code of the Street (Anderson) 140
colonial model: Black police officers 100–101; Black residents' narratives 90; critical race theory 89; police 97–100; policing's ecological theories 97; tolerating community violence 101–103
colonial social system 90
community-centered policing 34–35
community crisis action plans 37–38
Community-Police Advisory Board (CPAB) 162
community-police relationship 36
Cooperrider, D.L. 36
Costello, S.K. 66
COVID-19 pandemic: protests 4; related protesters 125; restrictions 4
Craig, M.O. 4
crime: Black-on-Black (*see* Black-on-Black crime); Black racial identity and 133; myth of **136**, 136–138, **137**; and race assumptions 133–135; White 140–145; White-on-White-crime 147
crime fighter 45, 47
crime-fighting strategy 45
criminal justice system 39, 125; Black racial identity and crime 133–134; Bureau of Justice Statistics (BJS) analysis 138; myth of crime **136**, 136–138, **137**; National Crime Victimization Survey (NCVS) data 138; race and crime assumptions 133–135; White crime 140–145
criminal legal system 5, 33, 67, 91, 150
critical ethnographic research: data analysis 97; participants 95; procedures 95–97; research question 94; study setting 94–95
Cruse, H.: *Revolutionary Nationalism and the Afro-American* 90

Cullors, Patrisse 147
Curnell, Joyce 160

Davenport, C. 111, 112
Davis 2
Davis, Jordan 151
Delgado, R. 141
Drenth, A.R. 56
"driving while Black" (DWB) 43
Du Bois, W.E.B 29

Eberhardt, J.L. 142
Epp, C.R. 46
Epton, Saul A. 139
ethnic threat 127n3

Faison, Earl 30, 39n2; civil rights 31
Fanon, F.: *The Wretched of the Earth* 90
fatal police attack 2
Feagin, J.R. 126
Federal Bureau of Investigation (FBI): adoption of racial categories 144; Counterterrorism Division 147; national homicide data 132; Uniform Crime Reports 151n1
Ferguson city: demographic and socioeconomic indicators 70; residents and protesters 65, 68; socioeconomic indicators 70; younger activists 68
Floyd, George 1, 22, 34, 88, 117, 118, 120, 122, 127, 147, 162
Freedom Movement era 90

Garner, Eric 91, 147
Garza, Alicia 147
Gascón, L. D: *The Limits of Community Policing* (Gascón and Roussell) 6, 159, 160, 162–164
Gascón, Luis Daniel 6, 159, 160, 162, 164
Gau, J.M. 44
gender: normalization and understanding of 161; perceptions of police 65–68; police-civilian encounters 65
Giugni, M. 114
Giuliani, Rudolph 145
Goff, P.A. 45, 57, 142
Gonzalez, M.L. 47
Gray, Freddie 3, 31, 68, 75, 78, 147

Hall, Mya 160
Hammond, Zachary 147
Hannity, Sean 145
Hawkins, D.F. 66
Hoffman, F.L. 134, 135
Holliday, George 91

immigrant threat 127n3
Internal Colonialism and Ghetto Revolt (Blauner) 90
interviews: black protesters 68; direct and indirect experiences 69; locations 69; open-ended

questions 69; positive and negative interactions 69; semi-structured interviewing process 94
Invisible No More (Ritchie) 5, 67, 159–162

Jackson, Jesse 139
Jim Crow laws 25
Jones-Brown, D. 4
Jones, Emma 38
Jones, Monica 160
Jones, N. 147

Kerner Commission Report (1968) 22
Kilgo, D. 115
Klahm, C.F. 47
Knapp Commission Report (1972) 22
Knepper, P. 149
Kochel, T.R. 29, 31
Koeppel, Ted 36
Krivo, L. 141

law enforcement: adverse effects 87; bifurcation 88; Black men's and women's emotional reactions 68; hyper-aware 81
Lawlessness in Law Enforcement (1929) 22
Lawrence-McIntyre, C.C. 90, 93
Lee, C.C. 114
Leopold, J. 115
Levit, J.K. 55
Limbaugh, Rush 145
The Limits of Community Policing (Gascón and Roussell) 6, 159, 160, 162–164
Livoti, Francis 31

Martin, T. 91, 113, 146, 147, 150
mask mandate/stay at home order (MSH) protests/demonstrations: events framing 122–123; official responses framing 123; protesters framing 123–124
McBride, Renisha 151
McDade, Toni 88
McDonald, Laquan 147
Miller, J. 67, 92, 93
Million Man March 115
minority group threat 116
Mollen Commission Report (1994) 22
Moore, Kayla 160
Muhammad, K.G. 131, 134, 144

Napper, G. 140
National Association for the Advancement of Colored People (NAACP) 140
National Crime Victimization Survey (NCVS) 138
neighborhood violence: inductive analytic techniques 69; positive and negative interactions 69; primary contextual and perceptual information 68–69; primary data 69; qualitative in-depth interviews 68–69

news coverage and social protest 116–118
newspapers 68, 118, 126
non-negative interactions 56
Nowacki, J.S. 44

Oliver, P. 114, 117
O'Reilly, Bill 145

Peel, Robert 24
people of color (POC) 27
Peterson, R.D. 141
Pittman, J.P. 29
police: aggressive order maintenance 66; black LGBTQ community 19–20; civilians' perceptions 65–68; direct personal encounters 66–67; extra-legal harassment 99; gender intersects 65–68; harsh enforcement styles 66; inductive analytic techniques 69; negative police encounters 65; neighborhood context 65–68; positive and negative interactions 69; primary contextual and perceptual information 68–69; primary data 69; proactive policing 66; qualitative in-depth interviews 68–69; and race 65–68; sexual violence 67
police, afraid of: indirect experiences 72–74; mistreatment from police 74–75; negative direct 72–74; police intimidation 71–72
police-civilian encounters 23
police decision-making 56
police, not afraid of: act when confronted by police 77–79; "human just like me" 75–76; hyper-aware of police 79–80; job to protect and serve 79; obey the law 76–77
police officers: current study 48–49; dichotomous dependent measure 49; pretextual stops 45–46; social conditioning model 46–48; traffic stop data 49
Police-Public Contact Survey (PPCS) 44
police reforms: appreciative inquiry 35–36; community-centered policing 34–35; crisis action plan 24; defying police culture 26–27; implementation 24; integrity and activism 28–30; policing while black 24–26; recommendations 24, 34–38; trauma-informed policing 37; true community policing 36–37
police violence: against Black victims 133, 145, 149; fatal 2; and misconduct 73; protest marches and demonstrations 39n4; strategy for reducing 23; used against protestors 4; victims 6
policing: Black civilians, modern 24–26; community 33–34; community-centered 34–35; ecological model 105; ecological theories 97; formal and informal 23; proactive 32, 66; proactive policing strategies 32; trauma-informed 37; true community 3, 36–37; women's experiences 160
Pouissant, Alvin F. 139